Jonathan Kuttab's fascinating n
Free, was published after Israelis and Palestinians reverted to major political turmoil and violence, making renewed negotiations and peace even more distant. The catalysts for recent grave eruptions were Prime Prime Minister Benjamin Netanyahu's reelection and his choices of nationalist/settler extremists for security and finance ministries. These radical rightist politicians have introduced draft laws that, if passed, would cripple Israel's Supreme Court , the last redoubt of democracy and the rule of law in Israel.

The Truth Shall Set You Free bookends and provides vivid context for his 2021 book, *Beyond the Two State Solution*. The latter is a taut, lawyerly prescription for a one-state model that is flatly rejected by Israel and suspected by many others, including the U.S., as radical and naive. Nevertheless, the one state formula is, gaining new attention by scholars, especially for its requirement for democracy, if not by politicians."

This new book ends with a declaration of faith and hope:

"The truth is finally out and the path to freedom may well be paved now. Freedom to both Palestinian Arabs and Israeli Jews requires them to live together in a unified state serving both on the basis of equality, dignity, and human rights. The utopian ideas I explored in *Beyond the Two State Solution* may now be seriously considered, and form a vision we can all strive toward fulfilling. As a Christian Palestinian, I can say only that the path is now clear. I can pursue it in good conscience for the benefit of all God's children in the Holy Land."

—PHILIP C. WILCOX, AMBASSADOR,

retired, U.S. Consul-General Jerusalem 1987-1991

This is the long awaited autobiography of a Christian Palestinian who has spent many years of his life in the service of Justice and human rights fearlessly confronting the distortion of biblical teaching by powerful groups in their blind support of Israel.

Through a number of lively vignettes in this excellent book Jonathan Kuttab illustrates his struggle to reconcile his Christian faith with the daily challenges that life under the harsh Israeli occupation presents.

—RAJA SHEHADEH,
Author and Human Rights Activist

Jesus says the peacemakers will be called the children of God, not just the many peace lovers--which is easy. But to fight for peace the way soldiers fight for war is much harder. Jonathan Kuttab is genuinely and courageously a warrior for peace in one of the most complicated and seemingly impossible conflicts on our planet. The biblical call to bring darkness into light entails telling the truth that Jesus says can only set us free. That is what Jonathan does--and this is his marvelous story.

—JIM WALLIS, Archbishop Desmond Tutu Chair
in Faith and Justice and Director of the Center on Faith
and Justice at Georgetown University

JONATHAN KUTTAB

THE
TRUTH SHALL
SET YOU FREE

THE STORY *of a* PALESTINIAN HUMAN RIGHTS LAWYER
WORKING FOR PEACE & JUSTICE *in* PALESTINE / ISRAEL

PROLOGUE

—————

I STARED BLANKLY at the stack of letters and Notes on my desk, hardly able to deal with the turmoil arising in my gut.

A moment before, the phone in my law office in Jerusalem rang and a friend had delivered terrible news. Israeli settlers had shot a Palestinian shepherd and left him to bleed to death while they stole all his sheep, taking them to the settlement of Fasayel in the Jordan Valley.

Not that this kind of "news" was new in any sense, I mused, staring out at the sky over the so-called holy city of Jerusalem. We hear rumors and stories like this all the time, and they were sometimes reported in the Palestinian papers, as well. The accounts, however, never had any impact other than to inflame the Palestinian population. Nobody in Israel or the outside world knew or believed these reports.

Why? I shouted inside my mind. Why doesn't anyone believe us?!

I needed to go out to the scene and find out for myself whether there was any truth to this report. It seemed impossible in a democratic and law-abiding society such as Israel, in a nation of people who had themselves suffered terrible oppression for many centuries.

As a human rights lawyer my colleagues and I knew that most of the evil in the world occurs in the dark: Oppressive regimes always pretend in public to be good and upright regimes. They label reports of their wrongdoings as false: lies promulgated by their political opponents. Just so, Israel enjoyed a wonderful reputation abroad as a "democratic country" and "the only democracy in the Middle East." Yet judging by the facts that I and so many others witnessed, Israeli officials constantly deceived not only the outside world, but themselves and their own population as well. This was possible because many Israelis never went into the occupied territories to witness the reality of what was happening there. Many found it hard to believe that a civilized people—their own—could possibly be committing the atrocities which Palestinians attributed to them. The head of Amnesty International once told me that one of his donors, a Jewish philanthropist, on his deathbed, asked him, "tell me the truth. Is it possible that Jews, who had weathered the Holocaust, could possibly be guilty of torture, as your organization's reports suggest?"

And yet right in front me was a stack of letters and notes I'd been painfully wading through just before my phone rang with news of the latest atrocity. People begging for my help. They wanted justice, or if that was not available at the moment, at least some kind of assistance.

"My son was arrested by Israeli soldiers right off the street—and he is only fifteen and has disappeared. Please help us find him."

"My husband has been held without charges in a prison in Jerusalem for sixteen months and he is suffering without the medications he needs."

"The army came and gave us one hour to leave our home, on land my family has farmed for over two hundred years. Then they came back with bulldozers."

Flipping through these notes and letters again, my frustration rose. Since I returned home, I have been gripped with the imperative that I needed to document these events. To record them for history, and maybe for some future time when justice can be obtained.

It was imperative that such events be documented rigorously and accurately. Every detail reported must be verified with proof. Documentation had to consist of "courtroom quality" evidence, which is unassailable, otherwise it would be dismissed as "unsubstantiated". Even if eyewitnesses testified, I knew by hard experience, that the opposition would find others to dismiss their testimonies by giving an alternative account. The Palestinian version was always discounted as biased and unreliable. We could not afford to be caught in lies, exaggerations, or even true statements that we cannot support and document to the satisfaction of a neutral, outside observer.

As I stood from my desk, I thought of my task and that of all human rights workers in biblical terms. If wicked deeds were done in the dark, and hidden where no one could see them, our task was to shine light into that darkness, so that those deeds would be exposed—as it says in John 3:19: "Yet, people loved the dark rather than the light, because their actions were evil."

Locking the door to my office, I decided to go investigate the story of the murdered shepherd, question any witnesses, and look at the evidence myself. There was no report of the incident in the papers and, I myself—even knowing of so many other abuses and atrocities—found it hard to believe that the settlers actually left the man to bleed while they stole his entire flock and led it with them from the outskirts of Bethlehem to the settlement of Fasayel, in the Jordan valley, over thirty miles away across rough terrain in the wilderness.

It was already getting dark as I arrived in the village of Ubay-diyyeh southeast of Bethlehem and drove out to the house of the martyred villager. After paying my condolences, and sipping the obligatory unsweetened coffee, I asked if there were any eyewitnesses who saw what happened. Different people offered to tell me what happened, all speaking loudly and with agitation, but I insisted upon hearing the story only from actual eyewitnesses.

Finally, they quieted down and one of the man's relatives stepped up and told the story in detail.

"The settlers said the sheep had grazed on their land and demanded a ransom of several thousand shekels to return the flock. I refused, at first, and they told me it would cost an additional fifteen shekels a day per sheep for feed, until I paid the ransom."

Pulling out a wrinkled paper, he showed me a receipt written in Hebrew for the money he actually paid.

"He was standing on ground that was not theirs, demanding they stop coming to demand their ransom money. And then . . . ." His voice broke.

I sat in sympathetic silence, averting my eyes, while he took a few deep breaths and wiped his eyes. After he recovered, he agreed to take me to the location where the tragic events happened.

We walked in the dark for over twenty minutes in the rough terrain until we got to the hillside. A gully lay between the hill we were climbing and the next hill. I could not help wondering if this is what my law school education was about, and what my Wall Street colleagues would think if they saw me trudging in the wilderness in my leather -soled, professional shoes in the dark, trying to get to the bottom of this story.

When we reached a certain point on the hillside, my guide stopped and pointed to a spot on the ground.

"He was standing right there—and that's where I found his body. The settlers shouted at him across this gully, then they shot him, and let him bleed out. . . right here."

"And you witnessed this yourself?"

"I heard the shouting and the shot, rushed here to find him bleeding on the ground with the settlers rounding up the sheep and taking them. I carried him on my back to the village, but he was dead by the time we arrived at the house."

"Did you see the actual shooting."

"No."

My heart sank. He had not himself seen the actual shooting, though he heard the shot, and so he could not give me firsthand evidence of what actually took place. Nor could he give me the exact time—hour and minute—when the settlers had shot the shepherd, as he had no watch. How could I explain to him that such details were vital?

But his story about finding the shepherd wounded and bleeding did add up. By the light of my flashlight, I saw traces of blood on several rocks at the location. As we walked back to the village, I saw other drops of dried blood on the ground which I photographed thankful that I had brought my camera with me. When we got back to the house, I took a detailed statement from him, under oath. I also obtained a photocopy of the receipt that was written in Hebrew. All this was useful initial evidence, but I needed more. It was more than enough if I were a journalist writing for a newspaper, but I held myself to much higher standards.

Later, I found that there was an Israeli veterinary station located inside the settlement of Fasayel, and that "inspectors" from the station had in fact confiscated a herd of sheep. The family was charged a fee equivalent to $10 per sheep for inoculation of the flock, and it was their practice not to release the sheep till the bill was paid. They would, indeed charge a daily fee for feed till the owner paid the bill and collected his sheep. So that must have been the "ransom" the villagers claimed was demanded of them: the bill for the inoculations. There was no mention of anyone being shot or left to bleed when the flock was rounded up and taken for inoculation and quarantine. The Israeli police did not investigate, and the family did not see any point in filing a complaint against the settlers.

"Why?" I wanted to know.

As far as they were concerned, they had no faith that the Israeli police would seriously investigate the settlers or that they would receive any measure of justice. They knew what they experienced. They had their narrative, and the Israelis had theirs.

It came down to this: What the Palestinians saw as naked oppression by a powerful enemy, Israelis saw as a perfectly functioning system run by proper laws and regulations of an enlightened occupation. I knew that the shepherd's family was right. I could already imagine how the story, if it went public, would be explained by Israelis—both to themselves and to the world. In their narrative, the "settlers" were actually government inspectors from the veterinary station, doing their official duty to protect the livestock of the country from diseases in the interest of everyone, including Palestinians. And if there was ever an investigation into the shooting, it would be shown to be justifiable self-defense against a shepherd who did not follow their instructions and who was throwing stones at them and resisting them in carrying out their official tasks.

For weeks afterward, I could not get this account out of my head. A man was dead. A flock—the livelihood of a family—had been taken away from them. Without an eyewitness or other proof of the event claimed—murder—there was nowhere to go with this in the Israeli justice system.

And yet this incident was only one of thousands of stories of injustice and oppression. There were murders and beatings, torture, imprisonments without cause, deportation and house arrests, severe restrictions on movement, and curfews. There was destruction of property and home demolitions, confiscation of lands for the building of Jewish settlements. There was collective punishment, and prohibition of all social, political, or cultural activities without a permit—and an ever-lengthening list of activities that required permits which were often arbitrarily denied or used to pressure people to become collaborators. Others would be reduced to begging and humiliation as they groveled for permits to carry out the most mundane and necessary of activities.

And I knew that all these injustices were carried out under the guise of law and with various justifications and excuses that sounded reasonable to those who did not see the effects on the ground. Israel had invested great effort into creating a "legal" system that allowed them to commit such acts, all while maintaining a facade of decency or at least legality.

How could I use my legal training and skills to reveal and explain this system? As I read through letter after letter from the stack on my desk, I found myself needing to bridge the gap between the two narratives, or at least the gap between Israeli claims and the reality on the ground. I didn't doubt that the Palestinian people writing to me were telling the truth as they experienced it. But so much was hearsay, and I knew that in the eyes of many it could be dismissed or explained away.

"My son was coming home from school. He was doing nothing wrong, yet he was arrested by the Israeli soldiers, as so many young men are."

But no one had actually witnessed the event. He must have done something wrong, an Israeli judge could say.

"Our house and most of our belongings were destroyed by the settlers."

But no one had taken pictures to prove it beyond the shadow of a doubt—and the settlers could claim the house was sold to them or on a right-of-way granted by the government.

Facts were facts, though. Perhaps by carefully avoiding bias and emotions, perhaps, I could document and show where the truth actually lies, and by discovering and revealing the truth, maybe some relief can be obtained.

In the weeks, months, and years following the story of the shepherd's death, I thought long and hard about what I should do in response to accounts like this.

I remembered what my colleague Raja Shehadeh had communicated in 1979 through the International Commission of Jurists, in Geneva, to Justice Haim Cohen, the Israeli Chief Justice, who was a member of the prestigious Commission. Raja informed Justice Cohen that Palestinians did not have access to the military orders under which they were governed. Justice Cohen was visibly astonished. He himself was on the High Court when the first military order was issued by the commander of the West Bank in 1967. He wrote an angry letter to the Defense Ministry which ensured that all Israeli military orders issued in the Occupied Territories were published in Hebrew and Arabic and were made available to us and other lawyers in the West Bank.

To many that may seem like a small victory, but it showed that many Israelis were not knowledgeable of the facts on the ground. I was hopeful that we might be able to get somewhere if we approached them intelligently and exposed to them and to the outside world the true nature of the injustices, and the system we were living under.

It occurred to me, as clearly as a light dawning, that this was my mission. I would verify and document the objective facts to any neutral observer. Perhaps, I even believed, there could be redemption and reconciliation: that Israelis might alter their behavior when confronted with the embarrassing truth. But redemption and forgiveness first required repentance and admission as to the injustices that were perpetuated. At the very least, I would strip the mask and deprive them of the ability to claim that they were all that democratic, enlightened, and liberal, when their behavior towards us was so oppressive and unjust. The first step was to establish the truth and then publicize the facts and force the issue.

Was I naive to expect that anything would come of my efforts, though? The work of bringing justice for Palestinians in Israel was certainly frustrating and the chances of actually helping anyone through this legal approach were slim. Where did I get this heightened sense of morality and the need for justice and the rule of law to govern even a hostile occupation?

Sitting at my desk staring out the window, scenes came back to me from my boyhood in Bethlehem, where roots of justice, morality and the belief that there is a way to live together in peace had begun to grow in me.

CHAPTER 1

IT WAS A SUFFOCATINGLY HOT, dry day in Bethlehem, and I was a tired little nine-year-old boy, trudging home from school, lugging my heavy backpack full of books. I was done with lessons for the day, at least the kind you get in school. Up ahead was the beginning of a very important life lesson, that was about to be delivered by someone wearing beat-up tennis shoes.

From a street corner up ahead, near one of the shops selling olive wood carvings and religious pictures and souvenirs, a slightly older boy was shouting, "*Eskimo fanneh!*" He was selling popsicles called Eskimos, and apparently not going to school at all. Maybe he was working to help his family, or maybe he was a refugee kid from the nearby camp of Dheisheh. Whatever the case, he was a practiced salesman, waving his product around for us all to see—and want.

When I got close, I watched him as he took a *piastre* from a client, who had already bought one popsicle, and flipped the small coin in the air. He caught it and slapped it down on his forearm, careful to keep it covered.

"If you guess correctly—heads or tails—you get the Eskimo for free or you get two popsicles for the price of one."

"What if I lose?" said the other boy, though he looked eager, like he really hoped he was going to win.

The older boy shrugged. "If you lose, you take the one you just paid for and keep walking."

"Tails!" the younger boy guessed, sounding excited.

The older boy peeked under his hand. "Oh, too bad. Heads." And he showed the coin.

When the young boy turned to leave, his face slightly sad, I stepped up quickly. I really wanted to try this game, even though I felt a bit uneasy. On the one hand, it felt vaguely like gambling, which I knew to be a sin—after all, I was the preacher's son, and deeply felt the need to act in a proper way, because God is always watching and sees everything we do. On the other hand, it was hot, I had a *piastre*, and I really wanted to play this game and test my luck. It was as if those cold, sweet popsicles were winking at me, daring me.

I mustered up my courage, paid the piaster, and watched the young salesman flip the coin. As it flew up, I shouted "Heads!"

When he took his hand off the coin laying on his forearm, I'd won!

I stuck out my hand to retrieve my winnings.

"Hold on," he said, "you have to play again."

JONATHAN KUTTAB

"What? No. I won and I want my popsicle."

He shook his head, refusing. "You need to win twice, to get the prize."

I felt cheated, but—well, he was bigger than me, and even though I objected he remained firm.

The second time he flipped the coin, I shouted "Tails!"

I won again!

The older boy shook his head and pocketed my piaster. "You can take your popsicle and go on your way, or you get nothing at all. It's your choice." He turned, and started shouting *"Eskimo fanneh!"* as if he had not taken my money and cheated me.

I was so mad, and kept staring at the other popsicles in his little ice cooler. "Give me what I won. It's mine."

"Just get out of here," he said, doubling his fists and looking angry now.

He was bigger and obviously much stronger than me. And anyway, it was wrong to fight and I knew I should not quarrel with other children. It was clear I was not going to win the argument, and there was no one to complain to who would intervene. I took the popsicle I had bought, and shuffled away down the street, feeling the sting of this highway robbery.

For years after, I would feel the shame, anger, and helplessness of being cheated.

In my home and in school, I knew there were grown-ups who maintained order and taught us right from wrong. While they were strict, my parents were also fair and would always listen to a good argument or appeal from a little boy. Because of that, my moral compass told me that what the older boy had done was wrong. Beside the first problem of having my money taken, the other thing was I'd had no recourse. He had pocketed my coin and was gone, and there was nothing I could do about it.

Over time, too, I would wonder if that boy thought it was fine to cheat because he was bigger, stronger, and could take advantage of me. At some level, maybe, I also felt I was perhaps wrong to play his gambling game, and that moral twinge further undermined my ability to protest too much against him.

Another time I realized that unfairness exists in the world I was in fifth grade, at St. George's School in Jerusalem.

St. George's was a very good private school, with a mix of rich kids whose parents wanted them to have a good education and who were usually boarded at the school, and kids like me from lower middle class who were there on part scholarship, and whose families sacrificed to give them a good education. In addition to prepping us for a good higher education, there was an emphasis on good behavior and ethics, as well. Here, there were rules and teachers to maintain law and order, even on the playgrounds. Sometimes, however, justice was blind in a bad way.

The system of education was such that we students remained in our designated classrooms for each period until the bell rang and then whatever instructor was teaching—say, history or math— would leave. In a few minutes, the next instructor would arrive and teach his subject for a whole period. Between classes, it often happened that some students, left alone and unsupervised, would get rowdy, jump on desks, throw paper planes around, and generally have a grand old time. I, however, raised to be a "good boy," would sit at my desk wishing very much to join the illegitimate fun but staying proper and well-behaved.

During one such rowdy fun time, the classroom door flew open, and the vice principal stepped in. The laughter and joking quieted down instantly and students shuffled quickly back to their desks. It was too late, though. The disobedience had been witnessed.

The vice principal glared at us. "You're all going to be punished. Each one of you will write one hundred times, 'I will behave properly between classes.'"

One hundred times? I could almost feel my hand cramping.

I felt as if I'd been scalded. Why should I be punished and have to suffer? Was it not enough that I was a good boy, and had foregone the pleasure of misbehaving? Now I had to be punished with the others, as well? That feeling I'd sensed years before having my prize denied to me was back with a vengeance.

With the vice principal standing over us, glaring and tapping his foot, I refused to pick up my pen and write. That did not sit well with him, the conflict escalated, and off I was sent to the principal's office.

In tears, I told him, "I will not write the lines or accept the punishment."

The wise principal, Mr. Issa Boullata, folded his hands on the desk and fixed his gaze on me. "You are a member of a group. Just as in society at large where you are a member of a tribe or a group, you must take responsibility for what the group does.

"You, personally, may not be guilty," he emphasized, "but part of the price of belonging to a community is that you must take the consequences, good or bad, for what others in your group do."

I was unconvinced. "Why should I be punished for what others do," I continued to argue, "especially when I deliberately refused to go along with what they were doing wrong?"

He cleared his throat and looked around the room, as if searching for words. I could tell he was not going to let me win the argument. He had all the power and had to keep it that way. In a moment, he let out a long sigh—and what he said next would stick with me forever after.

"The world is sometimes unfair and unjust, and you have to learn to deal with it."

Once again, my sense of what was right, and fair suffered a blow. "The world is unjust. . . deal with it."

Eventually, I had to deal with that outside world. The real confrontation took place in 1967. I was still living in my sheltered cocoon. So, when my schoolmates, the radio—which I rarely listened to—and the whole society was abuzz with anticipation of a coming war between Israel and the Arab countries in 1967, I was not much concerned. I was almost fifteen years old by then. Even so, I wondered if Israeli forces might in fact win the war and capture Jerusalem and Bethlehem where I lived. My doubts were greatly relieved when an American missionary who was working with my father, Sister Margaret Gaines, assured me that Israel would not be able to capture East Jerusalem at this time, because it clearly said in the Bible that "Jerusalem shall be trodden by the Gentiles until the times of the Gentiles shall be fulfilled" (Luke 21:24).

"So, you see, Jonathan, Jerusalem has been ruled—trodden—by Gentiles since the time of Christ and will continue to be so until the End Days, when Jesus shall come again. Only then shall the time of the Gentiles be fulfilled."

Since we considered the Bible to be the Word of God, and took its words literally, this made perfect sense to me. At my young age, it never occurred to me that there might be another way to interpret that text. I was so excited about this prophetic insight that I even shared it at school with my Moslem and "nominally Christian" friends.

Then came the war of 1967, and with it, the shattering impact it had on the entire Arab world. In a few short days, the Israeli air force destroyed the Arab planes—mostly on the ground—and proceeded to rout their armies. All of this was happening while Arab radios blared out martial music and made glowing, false reports of victory after victory.

During the fighting, I was in Bethlehem with my family. Other than some bombardment by Israeli planes and artillery, we saw little actual fighting. We just followed the events by listening to the radio nonstop. In fact, the Jordanian soldiers in and around Bethlehem just laid down their arms and fled. One Jordanian soldier came to our house, having discarded his uniform and boots. He begged us for shoes and civilian clothes so he could make his escape across the river to the East Bank of Jordan.

By the third day, there were no Jordanian soldiers left in Bethlehem, and a long line of refugees snaked their way east across the wilderness towards the Jordan River. Our family, however, was determined not to leave. The lesson of the Nakba—Arabic word for Catastrophe—of 1948 when so many Palestinians fled or were driven away, only to remain refugees and never be allowed to return was fresh in our memory. We were determined to stay in Bethlehem even if we were killed there.

Luckily for those fleeing from Bethlehem to Jordan, the town of Jericho (on the Jordan River) fell to the Israeli forces before Bethlehem did. From the roof of our house, I was able to observe the long line of refugees turn around and return to their homes that same afternoon since they were too frightened of the Israeli forces to continue towards Jericho, which lay between them and the Jordan River. Soon Israeli soldiers appeared in Bethlehem and imposed a curfew on the town which prevented anyone else from fleeing.

Most people in other parts of the West Bank and Gaza were also stunned by the rapid Israeli victory and had no time to flee. Despite this, about three hundred thousand people did in fact manage to flee to what they thought would be temporary safety in Jordan. As happened in 1948, Israel did not allow them to return, and they all ended up becoming refugees, some of them for the second time.

As a 15-year-old boy, the effects of the 1967 war in Palestine-Israel were devastating. It awakened my political instincts precisely at a time when any faith in Arab society and its political system was thoroughly shattered. I felt the defeat and humiliation of the entire Arab nation upon my shoulders personally. The crowds of jubilant, Jewish Israelis who triumphantly flooded Bethlehem to visit Rachel's Tomb, which was just up the street from my home, only deepened this humiliation. They joked and yelled obscenities about the Arab world and its leaders. While I basically shared their assessment and had no faith in the Arab political leaders whatsoever, their insults landed on me personally.

"Dirty, stupid Arab!" bit hard.

If I had felt cheated by minor incidents in my earlier life, those blows were nothing compared to what I experienced in the wake of the Six-Day War.

Daily, we Palestinians suffered humiliation after loss after betrayal. The State of Israel had defeated the surrounding Arab countries in six short days, and was gloating with its power over us, as we felt both betrayed by the Arab world, and subject to humiliation and defeat.

The enemy, which had caused our Nakba in 1948 and stolen our homes and lands and driven most of us into exile, had not been punished but had defeated us again and expanded its rule over what remained of Palestine. Instead of avenging our losses in 1948, and returning to our homes in triumph, now we had to deal with additional losses, foreign rule, and a brutal military occupation.

The military imposed a curfew on us, and all services were suspended as we tried to figure out what our future would hold. There was no contact with the outside world, and my father could not collect his meager salary as pastor. In fact, he was trapped outside the country, and we had no idea how or if he would be able to return home. Everything about our lives was up in the air, as our whole world turned upside-down and there was nowhere to appeal our losses. Now we were utterly powerless.

And not only powerless, but nearly destitute, as well, since most means of making a livelihood were now denied us. The reason for this, it was clear to me, was to pressure and drive us out of our own homeland.

With my family desperate for money, I decided to try and sell off some of the knickknacks we had at home to the crowds of Jewish-Israeli visitors who came to visit Rachel's tomb, which lay at the entrance of Bethlehem. Fashioning a makeshift display tray out of a drawer, I hung it around my neck using a belt and went among the crowds to sell my wares.

Out in the streets, with people going by eyeing my offerings, I felt ashamed. I'd never had to do that kind of work before—but I also felt it was my duty, as the eldest son, to earn some money till my father could return and once again get his salary.

An older man picked up a small, wooden statue of Joseph leading a camel. Then he smirked at it, and at me, and dropped it back on the tray.

From down the street, I saw a young Israeli soldier, barely older than me, fix his attention on me. Without hesitation, he came toward me, carrying a big gun and shouting at me in Hebrew. I didn't understand him, but his angry tone and violent expression said everything. I couldn't even sell my own possessions to make a living.

Without warning, he drew back one foot and, with his boot, kicked the tray holding my possessions, sending knickknacks flying. Some broke as they hit the street.

I stooped to gather what had not broken or chipped, but—still shouting and waving his gun—he chased me away.

Why is he doing this? I shouted inside myself. I'd done nothing wrong.

My face was hot with anger and my hands shook with my frustration. Within me, something surged that had only one term for it.

Hate.

I hated that young soldier and wanted very badly to hurt him. This was such a difficult thing for me to acknowledge. I hated all those Israeli Jews walking down the streets of Bethlehem, my town, as triumphant conquerors while I was being kicked around and abused. This one teenage soldier represented all the humiliation, frustration, and rage I felt. He represented Israel and Israelis. They now had all the power on their side, and I and my people had none.

Eventually, my father, who happened to be away at a conference in Germany when the war began somehow managed to return to Bethlehem, as a clergyman, through the intervention of the International Red Cross. We were overjoyed to see him. The curfews were beginning to be relaxed a bit, but my mother really wanted to go see her family in Amman and reassure them as to our safety. There was no phone, or mail service between the occupied territories and Jordan, but a radio announcement from Israeli Radio in Arabic announced that the bridge would be open for two weeks. Those who wanted to travel to Amman could safely do so and would be allowed to return if they returned within 14 days. My Mom took my baby sister Grace (who was still nursing) and decided to go with a neighbor, Um Ziyad, who also wanted to visit her family, to Jordan. Sister Margaret Gains, the American missionary, offered to take them to the bridge in her car, but my mother asked her if she would first go with her to the Police Station in Bethlehem (where

Israeli Commanders were located) to verify that she would indeed be allowed back. The fear that she would be separated from us and become a refugee and never again be allowed to return to her family was very real.

She was reassured by the Israeli soldiers at the police station, and by all the Israelis at the checkpoints and at the bridge that if she came back within 14 days she would be allowed to return. So, she went to Amman. She only intended to stay for 2 or 3 days. However, when she tried to return, the bridge was closed. No one was allowed to return, although those leaving were still allowed to leave!

My mother asked her brother, Jacob, to find out what the story was. He went to the offices of the International Red Cross in Amman and found crowds of Palestinians all in the same dilemma, trying to get permission to return to their homes and families having been out of the West Bank when the war started, or having left during or shortly after the war, or like my mother, having been tricked into leaving. They were all clamoring to return but were told the Israelis were not allowing anyone back except in very very limited cases.

My uncle (who was very savvy) said he knew some people who could help her across at the Northern portion of the Jordan River, where the water was shallow, and people could get across. My mother tried that route, but Israeli soldiers from the other side yelled that they would shoot any "infiltrators" who tried to come and fired in the air to frighten people away.

Not to be deterred, my mother, with the help of her brother kept trying. Eventually, my mother, carrying my baby sister, with um Ziyad, found another group. This group enlisted the help of a tractor driver, who for a fee of 5JD (around $15) a person, would take passengers across the river in a tractor at another shallow spot further north. The river Jordan, in fact, is neither deep nor wide.

Having taken them across, my uncle, and his nephew Kassab, turned back to Jordan, while Um Ziyad and my mother, burdened with my baby sister climbed up a steep hill to where a bus was waiting at the top of a hill overlooking the river, to take the "infiltrators" to town.

By the time they reached the top of the hill, however, the bus had already left, and they were stranded in the wilderness. They noticed an Israeli helicopter flying overhead and tried to hide in a deserted hut (sort of like a guard's cottage). The hut was empty and totally deserted, so they tried to look busy, as my mother changed for the baby, while Um Ziyad put together some dried sticks and formed them into a broom and pretended to be sweeping the dirt floor of the hut. Soon, they heard an Israeli army jeep screech up and three young soldiers trooped in.

"Who are you? Where did you come from?" They asked in broken Arabic.

My mother, who would not lie, answered evasively, "We are from The Land" (in Hebrew, *Ha Aretz*). Then she tried to distract the soldiers—really just boys, she thought—by asking them for water, pointing to the baby.

One of the soldiers shared his canteen bottle, as she fussed over the baby. then he told her, "Look, stick to the road, and do not walk into the fields at all, or you will be shot as an infiltrator." He pointed out over the hills. "See that helicopter!"

And sure enough, an Israeli army helicopter was still hovering above. The helicopter had spotted the bus my mother had missed and was directing it back to the border to have all the passengers sent back to Amman.

Emboldened by the generosity of the soldiers, and knowing she was in an area that was part of Israel proper, and not in the newly occupied West Bank, the three of them stepped right onto the asphalt road and waved to a passing truck to stop. They asked the Arab truck driver to be taken to Nablus. She assured the driver that he could safely do so, since the soldiers had already seen them and told them they were allowed to go to town as long as they kept to the road. For a small fee, the driver of the truck took them to Nablus. Um Ziyad sat next to the driver with the baby, while my mother climbed on the top of the truck for the bumpy ride till they got into town. From there, it was easy to find busses to Jerusalem and Bethlehem.

The lesson, however, was learned: Israel would not hesitate to lie and deceive to keep Palestinians out of the Land. We were always told that the aim of Zionism is to take the land and spit out the people. That was the only way to create a Jewish state. From then on, the central struggle for each of us was to remain steadfast. Whether we chose to be politically involved or not, our very presence in the land and our very identity was antithetical to Zionism, and by maintaining any connection to the land, much less claiming it as our own, we were denying Israel its legitimacy and its very rationale for existence as a Jewish state. To assert that we, Christian or Moslem, were indeed a people and had an organic relationship to the land is the most subversive thing we could do when Zionism is busy stating that this is a Jewish land just for the Jews, and that there was no such thing as Palestinians, and that the Arabs who happened to be there were recent comers who needed to return to the surrounding Arab countries they came from. But my political education was only justbeginning.

More and much worse incidents piled up. People were arrested and held for months without charges. Olive and fruit orchards were confiscated. Homes bulldozed or dynamited after their owners were given only an hour's notice to clear out. We had no guns, as the Jordanian army was careful over the years to keep us unarmed and to confiscate any weapons, so now that they left, we were alone and defenseless.

My rage and frustration sometimes made my head ache and my hands shake and consumed all my waking hours. But it went further than rage at the Israeli Jews. I had no faith in Arab leaders, either. We could count on nobody but ourselves. In time, I came to feel personally responsible to do my part regarding Israel and its occupation and the injustices I was experiencing together with all my people. It became a personal obsession.

The desire to strike back became so strong I didn't care if I lived or died. I had to do something about it no matter what others did or did not do. I realized that most if not all Palestinian youth of my age felt the same passion and need to fight for our country and were equally disenchanted with Arab leaders. But for me, it was intensely personal. It was my nationalist duty, and it was fueled by a passionate determination. I had moved from someone who did not care about politics, and considered it a worldly matter, to someone totally obsessed with the political situation. The emotion behind it was fierce, and there was only one word to describe how I felt, and it was a revelation for me to admit it. It was Hate, pure and simple.

But I had a huge problem.

I was a believing, born-again Christian. Hatred, war, and violence were not things that I could accept, justify, or tolerate. Hate, especially, was as sinful as sin can be. Jesus teaches that hate is closely akin to murder. And so, this nationalist impulse I felt created a real dilemma for me. Christ taught us to love our enemies, not to hate them.

How can you love your enemy and stick a knife in his back at the same time?

It was clear to me that my national duty was to fight and kill as many of my oppressors as possible; as a Christian, however, I was supposed to love them.

Unlike the situation in the United States and many other countries throughout history, where most Christians find all sorts of excuses to fight and kill, in Palestine, Christians of all denominations understood Jesus' teachings to clearly forbid violence and killing. We are supposed to turn the other cheek, to love our enemies, and to return good for evil. Violence was not really an option for a true follower of Christ. Even Moslems, who revere Jesus as a prophet, understood this fundamental teaching of his. They were always amazed how violent and militant followers of Christ down throughout history turned out to be.

As a Christian who took his faith seriously, and who believed that Christ needs to be Lord of all aspects of my life—including my politics—the dilemma of violence and war was very real.

What was I supposed to do with all this hate? All of my early life training shaped my mind and soul with Christian beliefs and Christian ways to live and act.

I had been baptized in the River Jordan when I was ten. This was quite an event since the church I grew up in was aggressively against the child baptism prevalent among Christians in the Holy Land. How could one make a decision for Christ when one was just a baby?

To justify my baptism at such a young age, I had to give my public testimony. On the appointed date, several busloads of true believers came from Bethlehem, Ramallah, and Jerusalem for the baptismal service, which was to be followed by a wonderful picnic in the luscious surroundings of the River Jordan, where we could pick *Aqqoob, Khubeizeh, Za'tar, Meramiyyeh*, and many other wild herbs, which grew around the banks of the river. I was the center of attention. I was required to recite scriptures I had memorized, several psalms and excerpts from the Sermon on the Mount and was questioned by church elders about my personal faith and commitment to Christ, as well as my knowledge of scripture.

My father and another minister had ropes tied around their waists to avoid being dragged away by the current, and after my examination, they led me into the muddy river and baptized me by full immersion. I emerged from the water to the sound of more hymns and singing.

Leading up to this public declaration of my faith in Christ, though, the ground of my soul had been well cultivated. And this experience was much more than a stage on which to recite things by rote. I really, truly, deeply believed. How could I not, given the atmosphere in which I was raised?

My father was a minister in the Church of God, a Pentecostal denomination with roots in the American South. From the beginning, my life was full of church services and Sunday school, Wednesday prayer meetings and Thursday Bible studies, and a consecrated life in between. I was raised to be obsessively concerned with finding God's will for my life, sharing the gospel, and saving souls.

I started teaching Sunday school even as a young boy. I viewed my obligation to witness to others and bring them to Christ as my most important duty and burden. What else could I possibly do, when I believed that those around me were sinners doomed to eternal damnation? Whether they were Moslem or what we called "nominal Christians" did not matter: they all needed to be saved. Every aspect of my life had to be lived in a manner that would help lead them to Christ. If any area of my life or behavior was not exemplary, there was the frightening possibility that I could become a stumbling block to someone else's salvation. And the Bible taught that it was better to have a millstone hung around my neck and be thrown in the sea than to be a stumbling block to one of these weaker brethren.

For this very serious reason, even marginal things that were not necessarily sins but merely questionable, and which might be perfectly acceptable for others, I would have to forgo. Clear visible sins included smoking, drinking alcohol, dancing, "worldly" music, and cinemas. For my sisters, the list of forbidden things was even longer. They were also required to forego lipstick, nail polish, earrings, sleeveless tops, short skirts, and immodest clothing. Those who exhibited any of these actions were "clearly" sinners in need of repentance and salvation.

Looking back later, I would see that at some level, the structures of a patriarchal, conservative Arab society, which separated boys from girls, also became part of the requirements to live a righteous life before God. As I grew older, I would begin to chafe against the many boundaries set by society and my Christian faith, but I would keep my doubts mostly to myself.

Suffice it to say, as a boy I experienced a strict upbringing, very focused on pleasing God in every way.

This meant that, while my Palestinian society was very concerned with reputation and outward appearances, I was also concerned with a God who could not only see and hear everything I did, but to whom my innermost thoughts were also known and revealed.

"The LORD does not look at the things people look at. People look at the outward appearance, but the Lord looks at the heart," I Samuel 1:16, was a verse from the Bible that ground itself into my awareness. The condition of my heart and my inmost thoughts were wide open to God, and even my moods and attitudes mattered to him, and I would have to give an accounting for them before Him some day.

This belief system set me up for a deep-level conflict when matters in Israel-Palestine shifted dramatically. Until then, as a young boy, everything was settled. I was a Christian who had to obey God and my Lord Jesus Christ, who was called The Prince of Peace, and what went on in terms of "worldly matters" were no concern of mine.

This meant that politics, which permeated all aspects of society in Palestine, were an evil, worldly matter as far as I was concerned. I grew up knowing, of course, that Israel had been created on the lands of Palestinians, after sending hundreds of thousands of us into exile in 1948. I sort of believed the Arab propaganda that promised to defeat Israel some day and return Palestinians to their homes. Even so, righting these injustices was a matter of politics, and in our way of thinking, born-again Christians had nothing to do with politics. I loved to chant the Egyptian chorus that said in colloquial Arabic:

> But I am not from here.
> I have another homeland.
> Neither money, fame nor wealth are of any concern.
> My Beloved Lord awaits me.

Yet here I was now, living under occupation, and feeling a passionate need to do something about it. Everything around me screamed at me, "It is your duty to fight for your homeland?" Those words ground against the very loud, inner voice that said, "Aren't you a Christian, Should you not, rather, lay down your life and your rights to show that you are a true follower of Jesus Christ?"

To say these two forces began to war within me would be an understatement. In short order, I became tormented.

CHAPTER 2

IT WAS PROBABLY A BLESSING that I was yanked out of that atmosphere in Palestine. I am sure I would have ended up killed or in prison had I remained there during those youthful years. I was getting increasingly obsessed with the need to do something about the humiliation, defeat, and oppression of our nation.

One day I caught myself taking the steps of the long stairs leading to the public market in Bethlehem, two or three at a time and feeling guilty about it. How could I possibly allow myself to be so carefree? We were under occupation, and that meant grief and gloom and serious determination, and not a happy-go-lucky spirit that would jump and skip and take steps with such happy abandon. Such was the level of my anger, frustration, and obsession that it bled into every aspect of my life—including "free" moments, which, in reality, no longer existed.

Even in America, I did not escape the overwhelming, passionate desire to fight the injustice and humiliation that was imposed on my people through the occupation. I found myself again daydreaming of fighting Israelis, and marveling at how vulnerable the United States itself would be if it were faced with an armed insurrection by violent terrorists, who did not care for the value of human lives or felt justified to attack civilian targets. I could not help noticing fuel depots sitting next to major highways, where a passing vehicle could easily lob bombs at them and create huge explosions and fires and simply drive away undetected; mass meetings at stadiums could also be vulnerable to scenes of mass carnage. If I were in Palestine, such thoughts would have been always on my mind.

Instead, I was entering a new phase in my life as a young Palestinian student at a small Christian liberal arts college near Harrisburg, Pennsylvania. A Mennonite missionary at Hope Secondary School in Beit Jala, near Bethlehem had recommended Messiah College to my parents as a good place to start my education in the United States. I had applied and was accepted on a part-scholarship. It was strange to move from Bethlehem and Palestine to cold snowy Pennsylvania. The weather was only one aspect of it though. It was a location a world away from my usual surroundings in every possible way.

On top of all the changes that I had to go through, I was now among other college students who were wrestling with their faith and holding late night and early morning discussions about philosophy, religion, the existence of God, and true Christianity.

To begin with, I was quite surprised at the conservatism of most of my fellow students on the political issues of the day: racism, poverty, colonialism, and the Vietnam War which was raging on year after year. To be sure, Messiah College belonged to the Brethren in Christ denomination, one of the historic peace churches, and so I expected the students to be strongly anti-Vietnam War and to be part of the movement in many colleges and universities across America that were protesting the war. Instead, most of the students appeared to be hawkish in their politics, and supportive of the U.S. engagement in the war, even though many of them were exempt from the draft on religious grounds as conscientious objectors. Most of the professors, however, were genuinely opposed to all forms of violence and there was a clear divide between most of the faculty and most of the students.

A typical discussion in the dining room would begin by some student overhearing me discussing Vietnam with my roommate Frank Demmy. One day, someone shouted, "You are totally unpatriotic and a Communist sympathizer."

I said, "The U.S. used to be known as a friend of democracy, and unlike the European colonialists, the U.S. favors democracy and self-determination for people throughout the world. President Wilson's Fourteen Point are well known throughout the emerging nations."

"But we need to fight godless Communism everywhere. Otherwise, we'll need to fight them here in our own country."

I was confused. "This has nothing to do with Communism, but with the Vietnamese people's desire to be free from colonial rule."

"But then why is Viet Nam supporting Communism?"

Did these people not know the truth about current events? "The Vietnamese were fighting to get rid of French colonialism. And when they defeated the French, the U.S. stepped in to support a murderous and corrupt regime, while Communist China and

Russia supplied weapons to Ho Chi Minh and his freedom fighters. Did you know that Ho Chi Minh came to Washington to beg for America's help with shaking off colonial rule and Truman would not even see him? How ironic is it that the U.S. ignored a chance to support democracy—causing the Vietnamese to accept help where they could find it?"

"See?" the guy insisted, ignoring my points. "It is Communism fighting against the U.S."

Frank would get angry at the utter lack of understanding and raise his voice. "But we have no business being in Southeast Asia. The Vietnamese do not care about us or about Russia or China. They just want to be free. Vietnam is halfway around the world, and we have no business to be there. No one there is threatening us."

As tempers rose, someone threw a sugar container, which crashed on our table. At that moment, we realized that the entire dining hall was listening to us and that we were creating a scene, so we quieted down.

I found that I was more often than not labeled "liberal" because of my political and social views. My opposition to the Vietnam war, however, was based on my anti-colonial and anti-imperialist position and not on Christian pacifism.

I also found myself at odds with many of my American Christian brothers and sisters on other important issues. Whereas I was concerned about racism, about world hunger, and social justice, most of the students in this largely White, conservative campus did not think that there was a problem with racism and world hunger only appeared on their radar screen, briefly, when there was a famine somewhere. As for racism, they certainly did not "hate" Black people, but if pushed they would admit they hardly met any. In discussions, they were only marginally aware of the situation in urban centers or that racism can be an institutional evil embedded in culture and in social structures.

I was astounded at how limited the vision and concern of my fellow Christian students was.

For many, religious issues and controversies had more to do with the divide between those who emphasized conservative Christian piety and saving souls and those who favored issues of peace and justice, and who were concerned with poverty, inequality and racism. The latter were often disparagingly labelled "Social Gospel" proponents. I clearly was slotted in this second category. If they knew so little about their own country, how could I possibly expect them to know or care about Palestinians, the Occupation, or what was going on in my own homeland?

For me, there were also other, far more serious discussions to be had. I was beginning to question my own faith and to debate the existence of God himself and wondering whether I was a Christian at all just by reason of my upbringing. Being in a Christian college was a fortunate experience that provided a safe space allowing me, for the first time, to question my own faith and beliefs in a serious way. I was no longer identified as the eldest son of a preacher, who was a lone "true" Christian believer, defending my faith among Moslems and nominal Christians. I was surrounded night and day by fellow believers. Strangely, that allowed me to feel free to question my own beliefs and to relish being exposed to new philosophies in a safe atmosphere. I dived right into the exercise, not only or primarily in classrooms, but more often in dorm discussions that continued till all hours of the night and into the early morning. The few "rebellious" students who were "liberal" and with whom I hung around were much more open to such discussions. My roommate, Frank Demmy, was like myself, a rebel, and an articulate critic of much of American society.

I felt it was important to question everything, as I knew there was no virtue in following a set of beliefs that are false or wrong. God gave each of us a brain and we had to use it to think rationally and examine every side of each argument. I found great comfort in the story of the Prophet Elijah and the prophets of Baal. He actually conducted what we would today call a scientific experiment, with a "protocol" and "control". He suggested a test that made sense to me: He would build an altar to God, Yahweh, and the idol worshippers would build an altar to their God, Baal. Each would place a sacrifice upon the altar but not place any fire and each side would pray to their God and the God who answered with fire is the true God. This appealed to my rational brain. I was willing to subject all my beliefs to rational examination and if they survived, they would be that much purer and if they did not, who needed them? And if certain elements (impurities) were burnt off, that would be painful, but the result would be so much purer. I had no use for a false religion, and no interest in deceiving myself.

The shift in my views was starting to become very far reaching.

I was also very suspicious of the insistence on "faith", which I had grown up with. To my mind, requiring faith at all could lead to "auto suggestion"—a new term I had just learnt. I felt that each person was fully capable of self-deception, and if you require that

I believe, without proof or a rational means of persuasion, then I could easily be deceiving myself and "manufacturing" the experiences touted by believers as "proofs" of God's existence and activity in the world. For me, something had to be based in rationality and logic or I would not accept it.

By now, the emotional altar calls at church and during chapel, and the insistence on "feeling" the presence of God, prompted by plaintive organ music playing "Just as I am" and threats of eternal damnation, I viewed with great suspicion and skepticism.

The strange thing is that my questioning of my Christian faith did not translate into strengthening my inclination towards armed struggle and wanting to wreak violence on Israeli Jews. Even though I was still following up on the news from Palestine, and saw increasing evidence that Israel was not interested in peace but in capturing and keeping the occupied territories and taking more and more land and setting up exclusive Jewish settlements, yet I also was becoming more aware of the futility of armed resistance and the need for new strategies in fighting the oppression of the occupation. Through my professors and the readings, they assigned, I became increasingly aware not only that nonviolence and pacifism were integral to the message of Christ, but also that active even militant nonviolent strategies can be just as successful, and often more successful in fighting injustice as resort to violence.

The example set by Martin Luther King, Jr., and Mahatma Ghandi was very appealing. I wondered—can we translate those examples to Palestine? Can the Palestinian people resist the occupation and achieve their rights through nonviolent resistance rather than armed struggle? In some ways, it seemed as if these methods were tailor-made to fit our situation and would enable us to find a common language with Israeli Jews who also opposed settlements and oppression of Palestinians. After all, many Israelis joined the Peace Now movement and were willing to demonstrate against settlements—not to mention that the religious orthodox Jews, many of them original inhabitants of the land, did not easily accept Zionism or believe the secularist State of Israel was the only true "Messiah", considering that belief to be a sacrilege. Why did we not make a joint cause with them against the secular Zionist movement that seemed more interested in colonialism and control than in any religious attachment to the land?

Still, with all these other questions, the religious/intellectual issue remained a big focal point for me. What was the truth about God, and was he just a figment of human imagination? For me, that question lay at the root of everything and would determine the approach to every issue.

At this juncture, I was fortunate to come across the writings of C. S. Lewis, which I devoured avidly. I also discovered Francis Schaeffer, and the writings of other Christian apologists. I was intrigued and persuaded by some of C.S. Lewis' writings, and soon became convinced by his arguments that atheism was a much harder sell intellectually than belief in God. I therefore started labeling myself an agnostic. I never was a true atheist; that was too difficult and extreme a position, to intellectually assert a denial of the existence of God.

In his book Miracles, as well as in Mere Christianity, C.S. Lewis made very strong points in favor of the existence of God. I was particularly impressed with the argument from morality and ethics. Since I thought what had happened to my homeland was immoral, where was my basis for insisting upon morality? If the only ethic in the world is based on "might is right", then the fact that a stronger military force had conquered us Palestinians was the way it should be and we should just accept the reality and the "facts of the ground" and go along with having our homes and lands taken from us. And if I believed that was wrong—well, again, on what basis could I say that?

Even if the Faith and spiritual tradition in which I was raised could not be proven rationally to be "the one true Faith" and even if our set of behaviors could be proven to be the only kind "pleasing to God"—well, what did God want? What was his character like? What was his will for the world? What did he want of me?

These questions were more than academic. My people were living under occupation, and for me that was a totally consuming matter. I still felt the burden of needing to do something about that injustice, as a personal duty. With each news item about the failure of the Arab world and the international community to do something about our suffering, I felt a greater need to act. The Palestinian movement, under the leadership of the Palestinian Liberation Organization, was succeeding in bringing attention to our cause—but it was the wrong kind of attention. We were being portrayed as terrorists, hijackers of civilian airplanes, and perpetrators of violence against the innocent. We, the primary victims, were branded the evil aggressors, while the true aggressors were supported and coddled as "the only democracy in the middle east" and the valiant seekers of peace facing a hostile evil world that would not accept them just because they were Jews.

Huge as this issue was, I kept asking myself, what is my role in addressing this situation? And my college years were providing me with space to consider these questions in depth outside the pressure cooker atmosphere of living under occupation in Palestine.

As I read the Christian apologists, however, I felt a distinct urgency—as if the wellbeing of my soul depended on it. And as if something of great importance needed to be resolved. And so, I followed Lewis and others down to the roots of morality and ethics.

Here is where I found solid footing again:

If we deny the existence of God, they said, there was no logically consistent basis for justifying morality or ethics. I have no legitimacy for doing the right thing myself or demanding or expecting it from others, especially when it runs against my personal (or tribal, or national) interest if I did not believe in God. Likewise, I have no basis for saying that someone else is doing the wrong thing: Whatever is, is; and whoever wins, no matter how they won, decides the reality of any given situation. What makes the Palestinian cause more just and righteous, especially if they did not have the physical power to win and impose it on others?

Without God as the basis for morality, I realized, no one can explain why anyone should act "morally," especially where such morality would not be in his own selfish, tribal or national interest. Without morality, the world should just be a "dog eat dog" place.

But there was another dilemma. To believe there is a God is one thing. To assert the truth of Christianity was something else entirely.

My mind and soul had found a bit of bedrock on which to stand. Even from that position, however, belief in Christianity was still a huge leap. At this point, Professor Ron Sider and his teachings about the historicity of the Resurrection became pivotal for me.

I continued my spiritual questioning, reading many books about the story of the Resurrection as well as the history of recording the stories of the disciples, looking for internal and external inconsistencies as well as examples of corroboration. F.F. Bruce's book on the authenticity and reliability of the New Testament documents fed into my attempts to study the issue of the Resurrection with objectivity. For as St. Paul said, "If Christ had not risen, our faith is in vain" (1 Corinthians 15:14). I was determined to view the biblical stories and records of the Resurrection, not through the lens of "faith" but with objective neutrality and skepticism so that I would not submit to a faith that was, on the face of it, vain.

In the end, the evidence was quite persuasive to me. Unless one dismissed the concept of God and resurrection, *apriori*, there was no better explanation for the events surrounding the death and disappearance of the body of Jesus Christ or the dramatic change in his disciples after the purported miracle of the Resurrection. Internal and external indicators pointed in that direction. The fact that later, these same men were willing to die to assert the truth of that which they at first denied—well, that to me was a very persuasive argument in favor of the Resurrection hypothesis. Unless one ruled out God and miracles outright, no other hypothesis explained the facts, as well.

What this might mean to my overriding desire to return home and my mission to "liberate Palestine"—almost single-handedly—remained to be seen. I was still angry, and still felt the obsession and duty to return and work/fight for the liberation of my homeland. But I was slowly becoming more nuanced about what that meant, and how specifically I would conduct the struggle. To be a Christian *and* a pacifist did not mean that I would abandon my nationalism or my desire to fight for Palestinian liberation, but now the term justice was paramount, and new terms such as "reconciliation" and "coexistence" were creeping into my vocabulary.

CHAPTER 3

MY FAITH MANAGED TO SURVIVE, but not so my church affiliation. I still felt that most Christian churches strayed very far from the teachings of Jesus. I felt much more comfortable with groups like The Sojourner community in Washington, DC, and their brand of committed, radical, social justice minded Christianity.

The Christianity I was comfortable with was, at least in theory, communal, committed to issues of justice, radical, insistent on the sovereignty of God over all aspects of one's life, and definitely pacifist. To be a Christian, I felt, was to be radically committed to the teachings and lifestyle of Christ. Yet, I did not find a church or group of believers that I felt comfortable enough to join as a member. I still felt comfortable with the basic tenets of orthodox Christianity and saw no need to question the concept of virgin birth,

THE TRUTH SHALL SET YOU FREE

repentance, forgiveness of sins, Jesus' dying for our sins, and his
resurrection from the dead.

What I could not accept was comfortable, consumerist Christianity, the highest aim of which is to be comfortable, turning a blind
eye to the world's suffering and need. I also could not accept any
form of Christian Zionism which justified what was happening to
my people—not only because it was unjust, but also because I felt
it was biblically incorrect. A form of heresy used to justify colonialism and ethnic cleansing, as was the "Discovery Doctrine' and
other forms of pseudo religious doctrines used in the past to justify
slavery, colonialism, racism, apartheid, and discrimination. I knew
enough history to see how the powers that be can use religion to
oppress others and justify their own privilege and power.

Meanwhile, as I pondered what I could do about these atrocities, I had become a history major. Under professor E. M. Sider, I
learned the tools of critical analysis. I became familiar with the
concepts of bias and perspective, objectivity, and skeptical neutrality. I learned the tools for searching for and approaching truth as
much as possible in historical documents. This form of intellectual
discipline I brought to bear, not only on questions of faith, but also
on my politics.

Something else was becoming clear. Israel was winning at the
communication—not to say propaganda—game.

I was amazed and dismayed at the level of ignorance that most
Americans had about Israel and Palestine. I was convinced that
Americans were basically good people and stood with an under-
dog in a fight. But it was clear to me that the media was totally

biased and presented them only the Israeli point of view. Palestinians were nothing but terrorists and Arabs generally were hostile and a backward people. Jews, on the other hand, were persecuted people, who had returned home after millennia of persecution. Israelis, especially, were idealists who "made the desert bloom", and were the only democracy in the Middle East. They were civilized, Western, almost White. They desperately wanted peace, but were only met with hatred, hostility and anti-Semitism. These stereotypes were very real and deeply rooted in the minds of Americans and extremely difficult to dislodge, since they were embedded in literature, movies, and the common culture. I felt that if only Americans knew the truth and reality of the situation in Palestine, there would be no question that they would support the legitimate rights of Palestinians.

With such lopsided communication going on, I became obsessed with the need to explain the true facts to ordinary Americans. That process was not easy because of the vast lack of knowledge about world affairs in general and the Palestinian-Israeli conflict in particular.

On the other hand, it was more possible and meaningful to get into discussion/arguments with American Jews, who at least knew the basic historical outline, and with whom I could talk about Anti-Semitism, the holocaust and how the Zionist program, however much they felt it was necessary, was creating a solution at the expense of another people: the Palestinians.

True, open, communication was almost impossible with many American Christians, whose knowledge of Middle East "history" began with Abraham coming from the land of Canaan, Joshua and his conquest of the land, and ended with bits of the New Testament—particularly the book of Revelation and a presumed Armageddon, and the rebuilding of the Temple in anticipation of the Second Coming of Christ.

How was this narrow interpretation of the Middle East and even biblical history so entrenched in Western Christian minds—so much that it blocked all other incoming messages that went contrary to their meta-narrative?

"You are ignoring the entire message of Jesus and the New Testament," I would tell them.

"Well, Jesus said, 'I did not come to deny the Law but to fulfill it'," was often the reply.

"God's promises are eternal and do not change with time," was another.

"But look at what the Israelis are doing to people—including your Christian brothers and sisters, who are Palestinians," I would insist.

"Israel's unfaithfulness does not negate God's faithfulness. They will eventually come around and recognize Jesus as their Messiah when he comes to rule and reign from Jerusalem."

"Wait—Jesus made it clear that his kingdom is not of this world. He did not come to establish an earthly kingdom."

"This restoration of Israel is an important first step before the Second Coming of Jesus, when he will establish his kingdom over everyone."

The conversations were infuriating. Not only did they skip over almost the entire New Testament but also over 2000 years of history. They seemed to have been indoctrinated in one interpretation of scripture, and thus they were living in a Never-Never Land of total fantasy that had no relation to this world. Terrifyingly, they were using that fantasy to create real changes in this world, supporting a nuclear-armed, hostile presence in the midst of the Arab world.

When I pointed this out to them, they seemed almost happy. Yes!—the end of the world was near! And they were doing their part to bring it about by supporting the state of Israel! Not even the most fanatical Israelis I knew had such inhuman notions or such arrogant certainty about their positions.

When I made a last-ditch effort to quote scriptures to them, they would simply shrug their shoulders, repeat a few stock phrases they heard from televangelists, and say, "We really don't know all the facts or interpretations, but we stand with the State of Israel because this is what God wants us to do. Because God said, 'I will bless those who bless thee and curse those who curse thee.' Those who do not support the state of Israel will incur God's wrath. That is all."

Yes, Israel was winning at the game of communicating a certain spin on its existence and total rights over the land and anything they wanted to do with it. And there was another big card in play.

Living in the U.S., I had become aware of how much the story of the Holocaust had permeated and impacted American society and everything related to Israel and Palestine.

There was no question in my mind that anti-Semitism and hatred of Jews continued to exist in American society, but it was clear that it was not tolerated or accepted at all in the public discourse. To the contrary, the literature, movies and the media were full of the story of the Holocaust, the persecution of the Jews, and the absolute need for support of the State of Israel as a counter to millennia of Christian anti-Semitism. In parallel with this, to speak for the rights of the Palestinians was a precarious matter, as it could almost automatically trigger accusations of anti-Semitism.

This was a problem, since Zionism made clear that it wanted to create a Jewish state in my land, and the struggle in Palestine was clearly between Jews and Arabs. How could I explain to Americans that our struggle had nothing to do with anti-Semitism and hatred of Jews, but simply a desire to be free and independent? We would feel the same about British or French colonialism and any other attempt to displace us with foreigners, no matter who they were.

When I spoke up, I was very clear about the distinction between Zionism and Judaism. Judaism is a religion, like Islam and Christianity, and in fact, it was the basis for Christianity in the first place. On the other hand, Zionism is a modern, secular, political movement that wants to secure a Jewish state for Jews in Palestine, sometimes using religious terminology to advance its political interests. Many religious Jews were vehemently anti-Zionist, and others found it a convenient political ideology. I felt no animosity towards Jewish Americans or towards Judaism at all. To the contrary, I felt more comfortable with Jewish Americans who had some knowledge of the conflict, than I did with most American Christians who could not find Palestine or Israel on a map.

With such super-saturation of a slanted message about Israel—what was I supposed to do?

During my first year at Messiah College, the college celebrated "Israel week" and invited representatives from the Israeli Embassy who spoke smoothly and convincingly of Israel's historic rights in Palestine. Before the week's events took place, I was invited for a "talk" by Professor E. M. Sider, who was also the advisor to international students.

"You know, Jonathan, Messiah College tries to expand the horizon of its students, and every year we have a program highlighting one country, with a number of events, speeches, films, food, and the like. This year, we will be highlighting Israel.

"Now I know this might make you uncomfortable," Dr. Sider continued, "and things will be said that you will find objectionable, but we expect you to show proper respect. You know you are here as a foreign student on scholarship, and it would not be proper for you to bring up your controversies here to the college.

"We expect you to act in a proper way and to observe the events in a proper fashion, even if it makes you uncomfortable."

I was floored. It was clear he was telling me not to raise a fuss or create a scene.

Of course, I had no plans to create a scene, but it was a painful reminder that the bias in the United States against my people and my cause was being supported by the subtle pressure of people like this soft-spoken professor, whom I greatly admired.

I assured him, "Do not worry. I will behave properly"—and left his office, feeling miserable.

The next week was pure hell for me. The college conducted many events, all of which I attended while fuming inside. They showed the movie "Exodus", and speakers quoted biblical references of God's promises to Abraham and his children. They even planted a tree in honor of Israel, saying this represented the mission of the young State: to make the desert bloom!

I was outraged but could not respond to this onslaught. What about my people? What about our land, cutting down our olive groves and fruit orchards, destroying our fields, our homes and our businesses? What about the many, many injustices? I felt angry and frustrated and hated the fact that I could only think in negative terms of wanting to cut down the tree they planted, though I could clearly see how such an action would only reinforce the stereotypes of Arabs being hateful and violent.

At the end of the week, I could not contain myself any longer and I met with the dean of the college.

"I demand that you show the other side of this conflict. Why not invite a representative from the Palestinian Liberation Organization to come a speak to the students and faculty?"

To my great surprise, he obliged. Messiah College invited someone from the unofficial PLO office in Washington to address the student body at chapel.

The person who showed up, however, was an utter disappointment to me. His English was poor and heavily accented. He smoked incessantly at this Christian campus where nobody smoked, which further identified him as a "sinner" and "evil" person. He had little knowledge of Christianity or of American culture and society and made a very poor impression even upon me. I was crushed. His presence and his speech had nothing of the impact I had hoped for. He rattled off UN resolutions, and nationalistic slogans which may have served at an Arab rally, but which rang very hollow to a US audience. If anything, it reinforced negative attitudes towards Palestine and Palestinians.

Several very important things occurred to me at that time.

I realized that we Palestinians were a part of the problem and that we could not simply complain about bias against us in the media or lack of understanding of our plight if we did not know how to articulate our position in terms that could be understood by an American Christian audience.

It also became clear to me that for many students, the word Israel, in the Bible, was automatically equated with the modern-day state of Israel, and the Philistines, who were the enemies of the Hebrew tribe in the Bible, translated in their minds to the Palestinians of today who are in conflict with the state of Israel. That being the case, how could they not be biased in favor Israel, if God himself was on their side, and against Palestinians, the supposed "enemies" of "God's people"?

Being a conservative Christian myself who also took the Bible literally as the Word of God, I was forced to look at the question again. I already recalled the incident with Margaret Gaines, which showed how biblical texts can be taken out of context, so I decided that I was going to do a thorough search of the Bible. I actually read the whole Bible again, from cover to cover using a yellow highlighter (this magic tool I had just discovered) and highlighted all verses that I felt had any relevance: to Israel, promises pertaining to the land, God's chosen people, prophecies, and the end times. The process was very instructive to me.

I could see that in the Old Testament, God's promise of the land was always conditional on proper behavior by the people of Israel. God demanded that his people be faithful to him by not worshipping other gods. He also demanded that they do justice to the poor, the widows and the orphans. Failure to obey God either on the religious or the social justice front would result in their being banished from the land and would result in defeat before their enemies. There was no sense of entitlement in the promises of land or chosenness. God had no problem even in reversing himself based on how people acted with respect to his commandments. Moses intervened several times to prevent God from punishing the Hebrew people, and the prophet Jonah was certain that God would mercifully forgive the people of Nineveh, the enemies of the Jews, and reverse his judgement that he would destroy Nineveh for its sins (Jonah, Chapter 4). Jonah was so certain of this, that when God ordered him to prophecy and tell the people of Nineveh that God will destroy them in forty days, he tried to run away, until he was swallowed by a whale and brought back to fulfill his mission. He had been afraid that God would reverse himself, spare the city, and leave him looking like a fool. Which is exactly what happened: the people of Nineveh repented, and God reversed himself and forgave them, much to his chagrin.

The New Testament was much clearer on that issue. Jesus rejected any claims for privilege, superiority, or God's favor that were based on being children of Abraham. God "can make out these stones children for Abraham" (Matthew 3: 9). The New Testament was clear that God's salvation was open to everyone, Jew and Gentile alike. We were now the inheritors of the promises (Galatians 5: 21). We, Jews and Gentiles alike, who have accepted Jesus Christ, are now the people of God.

In later years, I was to learn how this teaching was turned by anti-Semites into a displacement theology that justified anti-Semitism and hatred of the Jews, blaming them for having refused to accept Jesus as the Messiah, and vilifying them as guilty for the killing of Jesus Christ. I did not see it that way at all. For me, it was clear from the New Testament that God still loved the Jewish people and wanted them to be saved. He just expanded the concept of "God's people" to include all those who believed in him and not only the blood descendants of Abraham. He rejected their sense of superiority and entitlement based on blood lineage. Jesus also rejected the territoriality of the Old Testament in favor of the universality of God, who saved all nations and who loves the whole world and not just the Jewish people and the land of Palestine.

Furthermore, Jesus refused to accept political and earthly power. He resisted those who wanted to make him king. He made it clear that his Kingdom is not of this world and that his followers were not called upon to carry the sword to defend his power. He preached a new message that was universal and open to all; this was in clear contrast to the territorial and tribal themes of the Old Testament.

On the issue of Prophecy, it was also clear to me that the passages that seem to predict the End Times had been systematically and consistently misunderstood by Christians throughout their history as to when the end times are and when Jesus will come again. Jesus himself said that no man knows the hour and time, not even the angels in Heaven (Matthew 24:36). We are called to live in constant expectation of his Second Coming, but it is definitely impossible to predict the time when this will happen. Much of the prophecy industry in the United States was built on sensationalism and was taking verses out of context to fit into modern political events. It seemed that televangelists were not open to the real spiritual message of the prophets, who called people to repentance and obedience, but were rather more enamored with the sensational business of horoscopes and predicting events.

I spent many hours debating and discussing these things with other students and was surprised to find that I knew my Bible far better than most of them. They could "proof text" any proposition they liked, but they were ultimately more interested in justifying their particular biases than in learning what God and scripture really taught. They had little or no problem with a clearly materialistic lifestyle but were very strict and sanctimonious about things like drinking, smoking, and dancing. The consumerism and individualism that permeated their churches was far from the communal model that was described in the New Testament. The "pietism" that was central to their teaching to me smacked of Pharisaical legalism. So, while I had rediscovered and affirmed my Christian faith on rational grounds, I could not feel comfortable joining or declaring membership in any particular church in theUnited States.

Many years later, I would again meet Professor E.M. Sider: at Messiah Lifeways, an assisted living facility where my own mother-in-law was residing. He had recently taken up residence there, and I was excited to meet him. While visiting her, I called his room and asked if I could arrange to see him for a few minutes, and he said he would love that.

When I entered Professor Sider's room and warmly greeted him, he surprised me by saying that he had been wanting to see me for many years. He felt that he owed me an apology. He still remembered that incident forty-five years earlier, when he effectively silenced me during the Israel Week events.

"We did not know anything at the time about Palestine or Palestinians and were all caught up in the 'miracle' of Israel's founding and creation." It had been weighing on his mind.

"Jonathan, I want to apologize and ask your forgiveness."

I was floored. He had been a hero and a mentor to me during my years at Messiah, and from him I learned much of the techniques of historiography, and the importance and methodology of documentation, and analysis of historical records. (These were the very skills I would be using years later in setting up Al Haq.) I had all but forgotten that it was he who deftly warned me not to make a scene during "Israel Week". The fact that it had weighed on his mind all these years and that he felt he needed to apologize for it decades later was truly a testament to the integrity of this great man.

✧ ✧ ✧ ✧ ✧

While there were no Jewish students at Messiah College when I was there, there were many at Temple University, in Philadelphia, where Messiah College had a satellite campus and where I spent two semesters. I started conversations with some of those Jewish students.

Unlike the few Israeli Jews I knew at the time, these people were friendly, liberal, and did not exhibit any of the arrogance or racism towards me that was part of my daily life in Palestine. They were clearly good, civil people, and I could not understand how they could possibly support the oppression of my people. I also met a few Israelis traveling or living abroad; they also tended to be liberal and open minded. They supported Peace Now and seemed willing enough to make peace with Palestinians if only Palestinians agreed to it. They still repeated, however, the same Israeli arguments that they wanted peace, and that Palestinian resistance was illegitimate, and that the PLO was nothing but terrorism and anti-Semitism. I was convinced that Zionism was different from the Jewish religion—which I thought I understood by reading the Old Testament—or Jewish people throughout the world. Yet so many of them were supportive of Israel, and I needed to engage with them directly and understand what I was missing. I had a notion that if all the facts are known, people of goodwill should reach pretty similar conclusions. And so, I was determined to listen to them with an open mind and try to understand how they could possibly arrive at their positions, once they were confronted with the true facts.

From my new-found Jewish friends, I learned in great detail the story of historic Christian anti-Semitism against the Jews. I learned of pogroms in Russia and the Inquisition in Spain; these revelations made clear to me how resistant Jews were to any attempt to evangelize them. It seems that throughout history, Christians have had an obsession with converting Jews and found it almost a personal insult that Jews did not accept Jesus as their Messiah.

Given the persecution and pressure placed on Jews to convert to Christianity for millennia, I could understand their resentment of any missionary or evangelizing efforts. Past attempts to forcibly convert them seem to have left very deep historic marks. This was a difficult lesson for me to learn, though, since I grew up believing that Jews who failed to recognize Jesus did so purely out of stiff-necked, stubborn prejudice, and had deliberately forfeited their chance at salvation and were doomed to hell as much as Moslems or any other non-believers.

Politically, I learned from these friends mostly about the Holocaust. How this horrible evil pushed most Jews towards Zionism, since they felt they could not trust anyone with their security. Even in the heart of progressive, civilized, Westernized Europe, they had met the most evil form of anti-Semitism: genocide on a massive scale. Now I could understand why, after the Holocaust, many Jews were desperate to find a homeland, particularly since the United States and Canada closed their doors to Jews seeking to escape from Hitler. I could even understand how such a trauma would drive even decent Jews to positions which in any other context would be considered clearly fascist and obsessively militaristic.

Yet this did not justify in my mind what they did to the Palestinians. The crux of their argument with me was that the creation of a Jewish State was an absolute necessity. They were unsafe anywhere in the world and so needed a state of their own as an absolute existential necessity. They faulted Arabs and the Palestinians for not accepting the UN Partition Resolution of 1949 and for their resistance to Jewish immigration into Palestine and to the Zionist movement.

I argued that Palestinians and Arabs generally were not at fault for Western Christian anti-Semitism and even with all the sympathy in the world, the Zionists were not simply seeking refuge in Palestine, but were seeking to conquer the land in a classic settler-colonialist fashion and had actively sought to forcibly displace its Arab population. They denied this vehemently. They said that they would have gladly lived side by side with Arabs, and only Arab resistance led to their expulsion and dispersion. I pointed out that they did in fact forcibly expel the Arabs, and while some of them, like my family, fled from the danger, Israel had then sealed its borders and prevented Palestinians from returning to their homes—despite repeated yearly resolutions by the United Nations demanding such right of return.

They countered that if they allowed Palestinians to return, their numbers would overwhelm Israel. Arabs would become the majority again and Israel would cease to be the Jewish state it wanted to be. I thought this only proved my point that all along they wanted to displace the Palestinian Arabs. Since the land was already fully populated, there was no way the Zionist project could succeed without necessarily ethnically cleansing the land from its rightful inhabitants. I remembered what had happened with my mother and the attempts to trick her into leaving, and it made perfect sense to me. This was not just a question of desperately seeking refuge for an embattled Jewish people fearing genocide, but a deliberate attempt to displace me and my people, in the plan to create a new state where Jews were dominant.

My liberal Jewish friends also argued that the 1967 war was not the war of aggression I had experienced.

"It was merely a defensive war that occurred because Israel expected the Arabs to attack them and therefore struck first. Israel has no territorial ambitions and would be very glad to return the land they captured in 1967 in exchange for peace," they insisted.

They actually believed that Israel was committed to peace, and it was only Arab rejection and intransigence that prevented it.

When I pointed out that Israelis were busy creating facts on the ground and setting up Jewish settlements throughout the occupied territories, they downplayed the settlements and said they were few and far between, and in fact they were merely "bargaining chips" to persuade the Arabs to recognize Israel and accept it, and that the majority of Israelis would gladly remove these settlements in return for peace and acceptance.

This was actually true enough—at that point. It was the early 1970s, and the Arabs had not yet agreed to negotiate with Israel, because they still considered it their duty to liberate all of Palestine. So there seemed to be some power behind my Jewish friends' argument.

Israelis and their friends also insisted that they could not negotiate with the PLO, which was a terrorist organization committed to their destruction. While they viewed the use of force by Israel and the Zionist movement to be an existential necessity and a supreme value, they were not willing to accept that Palestinians also had an existential right and need to resort to the gun in their own fight for freedom and liberation.

Still, it became clear to me that it was not only necessary for the Arabs to agree to negotiate with Israel. It was also necessary for Israel to be willing to accept and negotiate with Palestinians and their leadership, the Palestine Liberation Organization. Once the Arab world agreed to negotiate with Israel, as Egypt did, and as Jordan did later, we found out that Israel was still having a hard time agreeing to talk to Palestinians or their leadership. They preferred to talk to the Arab leaders rather than to the Palestinians. In a way, that was understandable, but only if you negated the Palestinians as a people. How could you negotiate with a people you wished to eliminate and replace politically and culturally, if not physically? Easier to negotiate with Arab "neighbors".

From my perspective as a young Palestinian who arrived in the U.S. at 16, it was clear that my friends were as ignorant of my reality. Just as I and most Palestinians were ignorant of the historic realities of Jews in Europe that had led the majority of them to believe in Zionism and seek a Jewish state. As a person who strongly believed in justice and peace, and who believed as a Christian I should not support war, I saw it was important to seek reconciliation first and foremost by seeking mutual knowledge, understanding, and respect between opposing sides. We could then work for compromise and reconciliation instead of violently fighting for our own viewpoint while being totally oblivious to the viewpoint of the other side.

Living in the United States, where the entire culture had accepted the Zionist narrative and did not know the Palestinian side of the story at all, I felt the need to educate and inform others of the Palestinian point of view. I also felt it was important to seek solutions and programs that promoted peace and justice, rather than violence and war.

One day I woke up to the fact that the fiery young man who had wanted to fight and kill as many Israelis as he could, had matured into a man who saw that peace is necessary—and that we need to fight for justice nonviolently and with an understanding even of our enemies.

I still sorely resented, however, the way the Zionist narrative, which was widely accepted in the United States, painted Israelis as peace-loving and labeled Palestinian positions towards Israel as violent, aggressive, and terrorist. The fact that the PLO was officially labeled a terrorist organization in the United States only contributed to this atmosphere.

I personally had never engaged in armed struggle, and indeed was by this time becoming a confirmed pacifist again—but this did not change the fact that I felt it was unfair to label Palestinians who resorted to armed struggle as immoral and terrorists, while Israel's military obsessions and their violent actions towards our people were viewed as legitimate self-defense.

I was in an awkward position at this point, often defending the PLO and the right to engage in armed struggle, even though as a follower to Jesus Christ, the Prince of Peace, I did not believe in war or violence.

How was I going to resolve this position?

CHAPTER 4

GIVEN MY INTENSE CONCERNS about the people of Palestine, it was quite natural that I gravitated towards the study of law. There was something very satisfying about the sense of justice inherent in the concept of law. I particularly admired how a nation's constitution embodies principles of justice and rights and provides an overarching mechanism against which government actions, even legislation passed by a democratic society, needs to be measured.

I was particularly proud, as a newly naturalized American, when the U.S. Supreme Court, in a unanimous decision written by the conservative Chief Justice William Rehnquist, struck down state laws that criminalized the burning of the American flag. The principle of freedom of speech protected symbolic speech like burning the flag, even though such a desecration of the cherished national symbol was extremely unpopular.

But Justice Rehnquist stated, "This flag protects the freedom even of those who disrespect it."

I was never so proud to be American. I knew that Israel did not have a constitution, yet I hoped that in a society that claimed to be democratic there would be opportunities for me to use the law to achieve some measure of justice for my people. I did not think the Israeli courts would overturn military orders, yet I knew how much effort Israelis were then placing into painting a good picture of the occupation, and I thought that might give me an opening.

Along with the motivation I felt from my personal goals to study law, I loved the rigorous exercise of rationality involved in that discipline. Everything was subject to discussion and rational argument, on both sides of any issue. The Socratic method used in teaching law at American law schools encouraged questioning and challenging all assumptions. I loved engaging in debates on many topics and fully enjoyed my time in law school.

Unlike many of my classmates, I had no ambition to work on Wall Street and make tons of money. I knew that I wanted to go back home to Palestine when I finished my studies. I saw no value in seeking high grades, though I got them anyway. I chose subjects I liked, not necessarily those that would be valued by the corporate world. Instead, I took courses in international law, human rights, and such other subjects as law of the sea.

During those years, I continued to follow from afar what was happening in Palestine. I also had a number of liberal Jewish friends and acquaintances with whom I discussed these things. Many were supporters of Peace Now, and they wanted to see a peaceful solution. I knew there were religious Jews who were anti-Zionist and did not support the state of Israel, but most of my contacts were with secular, liberal Jews, who nonetheless were supporting the state of Israel, sometimes apologetically.

These friends kept telling me, "Israel has no interest in ruling over another people," and that Israel's was a "liberal occupation that is trying to improve the lot of ordinary Palestinians." They would bring up the undemocratic nature and practices of the Arab regimes, and I would heartily agree. Yet I told them, "This is not a reason to accept the Israeli oppression."

They thought that the majority of Israelis would gladly give up the occupied territories in return for peace; they viewed the situation as a tragic conflict between two peoples who had been victimized by history and thrown against each other.

As we discussed these matters further, they would always refer to the Israeli High Court being "a restraining influence." Yet I could not see any evidence of that. It was true Palestinians had a right to go to the High Court, but did they ever prevail there?

I would later study the decisions of the High Court carefully and learn that the truth of the matter was that the Court only provided legal excuses and arguments to permit the occupation to continue. For one thing, it always deferred to the judgement of the "security experts" and where army officials presented a security claim, almost any practice was considered legal.

"But the actions of the Israeli military are brutal and constitute collective punishment," I would complain. "They place whole towns and villages under severe restrictions, they demolish homes, and deport whole families for the alleged actions of resistance by one individual."

"Ah yes," they would concede, "but that is based on the existing British Emergency Regulations, not on Israeli laws. And in fact," they argued, "such practices create a deterrent, preventing further acts of terrorism and violence." In the end, they insisted, "Jonathan, everything is done legally in Israel. It's a democratic country, a nation that abides by the rule of law."

I would have very interesting and heated arguments with my Jewish liberal friends, but almost none with Christian Zionists. With them, discussion of any kind was impossible. For them, Israel could do no wrong. The Jews were the "Chosen People of God," fulfilling His purposes in the universe. International law and universal values were meaningless to them. Their utter ignorance of the reality on the ground was only matched by the stubbornness of their firm beliefs.

"God is behind all these events, and they portend the end times," they insisted. End of discussion. But if God permitted and ordained such unjust activities, of what value was international law and the UN or anyone else, I wondered?

It was beyond frustrating to see what I was up against—the belief that Israel was only performing legal actions against my people, and that God had ordained our suffering. These atrocious beliefs, combined with ignorance, blinded people to the reality of facts on the ground.

Meanwhile, as my law education continued, I wondered how I would do when it came to defending a real person in a real case?

My first chance to find out came while I was still in law school. The University of Virginia had an honor system, and a student accused of an honor offense would be tried, prosecuted, and defended by law students, and if found guilty would be summarily dismissed from the university.

One student, a Puerto Rican, came to my residence one night and asked if I and my roommate, Michael Kushner, would defend him. He was distressed and almost crying.

It seemed that one of his professors had accused him of plagiarism. Jose* [*Not his real name.] was an older student from a poor neighborhood in New York and was the first of his family to even attend college. He had made it into law school on an affirmative action program, but his professor, a known racist, thought he had no business at all being at a prestigious school like UVA. He accused him of failing to properly attribute materials in a research paper he had written, which constituted plagiarism. The professor had asked two students from the JAG School (Judge Advocate General) to be the prosecutors and bring Jose up on honors charges.

Michael and I had already established our reputation as liberals since we had taken on the conservative students in a debate about establishing a Virginia Public Interest Research Group (PIRG), to be funded by a positive checkup, allowing one dollar from the tuition of each willing student to go to funding that consumer agency. We favored the initiative, and the conservative students opposed it. We did such a good job challenging them in their own club (the Jeffersonian Society) that they even invited us to join, though we both declined. I believe I would have been the first Palestinian and Mike would have been one of the first Jews to be admitted to that club. They had only recently allowed women into that highly exclusive group.

73

So, there we were: a Palestinian and a Jew, charged with defending a Puerto Rican student who was about to be kicked out of UVA in disgrace for plagiarism, when he was probably only guilty of not having learned the proper methods of footnoting and attribution in the miserable public school he attended in New York.

Jose was a very devout Catholic. In fact, he was very pious and puritanical, and I learned that he had dated his wife for seven years without having sex with her until they finally got married. In modern American society and in a party school like UVA, that was incredible and phenomenal. It gave me an idea for a novel defense in his case. I would argue that a person with such high moral standards was morally incapable of committing an honor offense. He simply lacked the technical understanding and skills to properly footnote and could not possibly have the dishonorable intent—*mens rea*, or "guilty mind"—required to commit an honor offense.

Michael and I worked hard. We retraced Jose's research work step by step and showed how his paper was actually constructed. It was clear to us that he had actually done the laborious research needed to produce the paper and did not intend to deceive anyone by stealing the work of others.

Then I had another idea. If our theory was correct, and our argument solid, we could try to argue it directly with our opponents and not have to go before an honor committee at all. My thinking was that the two accusers, though very conservative, were themselves honorable people, and would be open to a rational argument. If our argument was good enough to convince an honors committee, then maybe it was also good enough to convince our opponents, who would listen to it in a comfortable, non-adversarial context and might be persuaded to drop the charges altogether.

It was certainly a new approach—and a long shot.

When we mentioned our plan to Jose, he looked anxious. He needed this degree and most definitely did not need to go home in disgrace.

The week before the hearing date, we tried my plan—amazingly, it worked.

The two law students from JAG were especially impressed with the argument that Jose was an honest, highly ethical person motivated by strict religious and moral values. Surely, he would not stoop to cheating on a research paper. The JAGs reported back to the committee that they were convinced that Jose was innocent, and according to proper protocol they burned all the so-called "evidence" and arguments they had prepared.

Their professor was furious, but he could do nothing about it.

This showed me that there could be ways to work around unjust, prejudiced systems and to discuss the issues calmly and peacefully with adversaries.

Given my true, heartfelt motivations for studying law and my desire to help innocent individuals, it was therefore a surprise to me when I ended up being recruited by a Wall Street law firm. Like everyone else looking for a job after law school, I had applied to law firms all over the country. Of the three Wall Street firms that invited me for a further interview at their New York offices, one failed to ask me the crucial question of where I saw myself in five or ten years. Had they asked, I would have told them the truth and

I would not have been hired. They assumed that I would be desperately trying to make partner and so willing to work unholy hours to achieve that pinnacle of success. After all, this was a venerable firm that once had Richard Nixon and John Mitchell as partners.

In the end, I decided to take the job for a limited period. As it turned out, the life of a "Yuppie" (Young Urban Professional) in New York City was certainly interesting and a new experience for me. For a time. The law firm had 160 lawyers and its offices occupied eight floors in the same building as the New York Stock Exchange. The hours were long and the standards rigorous, but it was also boring and not very fulfilling.

Once I had earned enough money to cover my student loans, though, I decided to go where my heart really was. I accepted a job as a volunteer with the Mennonite Central Committee, to work in Palestine on issues of law and justice. That was my dream job.

For two years, I would use my time to learn Hebrew, study Israeli laws and military orders, and encounter many ways to use law to work for justice and human rights. My room and board were paid for and I would have a stipend of $25 a month on top of it.

What more could I possibly want?

CHAPTER 5

MY HOMECOMING as an MCC volunteer was indeed as wonderful and glorious as I had pictured it.

The job description (which I had helped write) was to study Hebrew, Israeli laws and military orders, join the Palestinian Bar association, and seek ways to use law for justice and human rights. Basically, I was being sustained ("paid") to do precisely what I had wanted to be doing all along. It was a very open-ended assignment. I determined that I was there to learn, and that for the first six months at least, I would not take any positions, make any political statements, urge others in any way or direction, or participate in activism, but just observe and learn.

I saw that the occupation, which everyone was treating as a temporary state of affairs, was getting more and more entrenched. More Israeli settlements were being set up and more and more land was being taken under a variety of convoluted legal pretenses.

Military orders, which initially just froze Jordanian laws in place and substituted Israeli officers for the different government ministries, were changing the laws constantly in all areas. The direction of the changes was clear: either to enable more settlements and land grabs, and slowly annex more and more of the West Bank into Israel and its systems, or to create and enable a matrix of control whereby all aspects of life were subject to permits and licenses which would be issued or not at the discretion of Israeli officers. In fact, it was an elaborate scheme for population control through fiat and administrative decisions. Attempts were made to create a system of Arab collaborators through the "village leagues", but that was failing. The population was solidly nationalistic and standing behind the PLO, even though the leadership of the PLO was in exile and the PLO itself was illegal.

There was some effort at armed resistance by PLO factions, but it was miniscule and laughable. The local population firmly supported armed struggle in slogans, words, poetry and rhetoric, but very few actually participated in armed resistance. Weapons were not available, nor training, nor supply lines, and Israeli intelligence was quite effective in infiltrating the different groups and intercepting and aborting most armed actions even before they were carried out.

As a confirmed pacifist, I was no longer tempted towards violent actions, but I could also see that apart from my beliefs there was no realistic option for achieving freedom by defeating and "out violencing" the Israelis. My years abroad allowed me to assess the situation objectively and rationally: Palestinians, alone or with the support of the surrounding Arab countries, were in no position to fight Israel or to defeat it militarily. Likewise, the PLO forces were being driven farther and farther away, after they were defeated in Jordan and later in Lebanon, and now sought to "liberate" Palestine from their basis in Tunisia, thousands of miles away.

Despite these realities, most Palestinians still talked of armed resistance! In large part, this was the result of the heavy oppression they were feeling, and the strong desire to do *something* rather than submit and accept defeat. Israel harshly and collectively punished entire towns, villages or categories of Palestinians for any act of resistance. They controlled all aspects of life through permits and licenses. It was worse than classic colonialism, because these settlers sought to displace, not just rule the locals.

Meanwhile, during that time of the early 1980s, it became clear to me that it was necessary to articulate and explain a whole strategy of nonviolent resistance and not just to call for abandoning armed struggle. Most factions (all of which were illegal), were concentrating on competing with each other for control of civil society institutions, trade unions, and charitable societies and the like. Student elections at universities were major political events, yet little was done to effectively challenge the occupation itself.

One day, when I went to Bir Zeit University with a friend, he took me to the cafeteria. "There you see at that table are the Fatah people," he said, "and over there are the PFLP guys, in deep discussions, and over there the Communists."

"What do you mean?" I replied. "These are illegal organizations, and you can get six months for mere membership in any of them."

He shrugged. "Everyone knows which faction everyone belongs to."

"But that means the Israelis also know. If I belonged to an illegal secret organization, I would not allow even my mother to know."

Again, he merely shrugged.

I decided at once that I would never join any of these groups but would work independently. The facts of the oppression and the human rights violations were not a surprise to me or to any Palestinian. What we expected and experienced were closures, curfews, collective punishments, and deprivations—all common practices and they did not surprise me. Because of them, I was more and more confirmed in my nationalism and desire to fight these abuses. I was totally disenchanted, however, with the political factions and I was somehow pleased that the PLO leadership was away in Tunisia. I did not mind their taking the credit for leading the struggle, but I was not going to take orders or direction from them or anybody else.

Yet what amazed me most was the contrast between the reality on the ground and the images and stereotypes that were prevalent in the West about our situation.

One painful reality involved tour buses full of American and other foreign tourists which roamed the country freely. Yet their tours were carefully orchestrated and controlled to promote Israeli propaganda. They were warned not to stay in the Arab areas "for their own safety", and tour guides were almost always Israeli Jews. Moshe Dayan once famously said that he would rather allow the training for an Arab fighter jet pilot, who could be shot down over the desert, than to license Arabs to be tour guides, who would expose the truth about Israel to Westerners. They did not see the refugee camps and almost never Gaza and were driven by and through Arab towns and villages. Yet every single Israeli "Holy Land" tour would include Masada, the site of the last stand of the Maccabean Revolt against the Romans where the defenders ended their lives by mass suicide rather than surrender. The place has no religious significance for Christians or Jews for that matter. In fact, the famous Jewish historian, Josephus, refused to even mention the incident in his history, believing suicide to be antithetical to Jewish values. Yet for modern Zionism, Masada is an important part of the mythology of a small, spartan country fighting overwhelming odds and preferring suicide to defeat and surrender. Many Israeli military units held their ceremonies of induction at that site.

Of course, the small futile acts of armed resistance by Palestinians were widely reported to visitors and labeled as acts of terrorism and hatred, rather than legitimate resistance to occupation and oppression. It was no wonder that those who took the "Holy Land Tour" returned home even more entrenched in their End Times theologies and totally oblivious to the true realities on the ground. They were elated to walk where Jesus had walked and to fantasize that they were seeing fulfillment of prophecy and the nearness of the Second Coming. Jews, for whom such an End Times scenario meant either annihilation or forced conversion to Christianity, were quite willing to humor these Christians for the sake of gaining their support—while laughing at their theology behind their backs.

It was clear that I had my work cut out for me. I had returned to support my homeland and its cause, but my efforts were going to take a totally different form than what others were pursuing. And the first step was, of course, to learn as much as I could and to try to understand Israel and the system of oppression it had created. Then to figure out how in God's name it could be so oppressive to Palestinians while appearing so wonderful to outsiders.

Two other major questions stared me in the face.

As a pacifist, how was I to combat nonviolently what Israel was doing violently to my people?

Also, because I maintained contacts in America—how was it possible that Americans bought into the lie that Israel was the oppressed and not the oppressor?

I had already begun to work on answering the first question.

A year after arriving home in 1979, and while still working with MCC, I had begun my apprenticeship with one of the best Palestinian legal firms in Ramallah. Aziz Shehadah, the founder, was a native of Jaffa who had begun practicing law under the British Mandate. His family fled Jaffa in 1948 and ended up in Ramallah where he continued to practice law. Aziz was a well-known lawyer in Palestine and Israel and one of the first to suggest a two-state solution based on the 1967 lines.

During that time, Aziz's son Raja and I, who were about the same age, began a great friendship. Like me, Raja Shehadeh had just finished his legal training overseas and had now returned home to Ramallah to practice law with his father. He was intelligent, intense, passionate, and often far too serious.

Knowing a little bit about him but having never met in person, I had written to Raja before I returned home, asking for his ideas about using law to work for justice and human rights in Palestine. Not long after I arrived in Jerusalem we met together, and he suggested we start a new organization to promote human rights and the rule of law. Raja had been a member of Justice (the Amnesty International branch in England, where he was studying law) and had many ideas for starting a human rights organization in the West Bank. He also introduced me to his friend Charles Shammas, a Lebanese American who had recently come to the West Bank, married a Palestinian, and was also interested in the same ideas.

In many ways, the three of us were similar. We all wanted to introduce new ideas to Palestinian society but were ourselves still learning how to best employ them, given our unique situation under occupation. We were fully part of Palestinian society, yet in many ways we were totally different. For one thing, we were all Christians in a largely Moslem society. All three of us were Western-educated, and very committed to public service. We were skeptical about the local politics and the different political factions (all of which were illegal under Israeli law). Most of all, we were interested in understanding how Israel used law and military orders to control all aspects of our life.

We also had our differences.

While Raja and Charles were clearly secular, my core motivations had to do with my faith. I did not usually discuss religion with them, but I felt that the acknowledgement of human rights was a natural extension of the belief that all people were made in the image of God. For this reason alone, all humans are worthy of respect, dignity, and rights. I felt that the values of international law were merely an extension of the ethical teachings of all religions. Therefore, my activism for Palestinian human rights was part of doing what I believed pleased God.

Raja knew the Executive Director of the International Commission of Jurists, Mr. Niall McDermott, who encouraged him to set up a branch for the ICJ in the West Bank. Not long after our initial meeting, Raja, Charles, and I decided to create a new organization that would carefully and thoroughly document human rights abuses in the Occupied Territories and try to bring them to the attention of the international community. We named our organization, "Law in the Service of Man." Later, we changed the name to Al Haq, meaning Truth, or Rights. It was the first human rights advocacy organization in Palestine and one of the first in the Arab world.

Even with international support, however, we were very aware of the minefield we were stepping into. There was every danger that Israel and its military government would quickly crush our efforts, and even land us in jail, since all political activities were illegal under Military Order No. 101.

At the same time, all community organizations, charitable societies, unions, and the like were a fertile battlefield for competing Palestinian factions. Unable to practice politics openly or hold elections, many of these groups tried to take control of civil organizations on behalf of their respective political factions, all of which belonged to the Palestine Liberation Organization (the PLO). Anyone who was involved in any kind of public activity was likely to belong to one, or another of the political parties, which included Fateh—by far the most popular faction, as well as the Communist Party, the Popular Front for the Liberation of Palestine (PFLP) and the Democratic Front for the Liberation of Palestine (DFLP). Hamas, the Islamic group, was barely starting at that time and never joined the PLO.

By contrast, the three of us did not belong to any of these factions. In fact, we felt there was great value in being politically independent. We were determined to keep our new organization from being dominated by any of the political parties. This was partly a measure of self-protection, as each of these factions was defined as a "terrorist group" by Israel. It did not matter if the activities of a particular organization were strictly charitable and nonviolent—any affiliation with an illegal organization made it illegal as well. Mere membership in or even contact with an illegal organization was a sufficient basis for imprisonment. The factions were infiltrated by Israeli agents or collaborators anyway, and we could not afford to be associated with any of them.

This stance fit well with my own regular distrust of politics and my Christian belief that I should never allow any ideology or political party to have dominion in my life. Besides, I valued my independence.

Because of this, however, Palestinian society at large was very suspicious of the three of us. The fact that none of us had a large tribe behind him or belonged to a political party that could vouch for him made us more of a target for suspicion and even slander. People did not understand who we really were and why we were doing what we were doing.

"Why is Charles in Palestine at all?" they wondered. "Although he married a Palestinian, he is Lebanese, and his Arabic is atrocious."

They distrusted Raja because his father, Aziz Shehadah, was considered too liberal and too willing to reach a peaceful solution with the Israelis.

They also did not understand why I had left most of my family and a good Wall Street job in the United States to return to Palestine as a volunteer. They wondered whether I was really an agent for the CIA.

Our methodology also increased people's suspicions. We were talking in a different language: human rights, international conventions, and the rule of law. We were using law to fight the occupation, but we were not willing to engage in blatant political activities. When Israel committed some outrage, we avoided bombastic rhetoric. We refused to write political polemics denouncing the occupation and its practices in local papers.

For example, Palestinians might attack or throw stones at the car of a Jewish settler whose settlement was just established over the land of that particular village, causing injury to the armed settlers. The Israelis, in retaliation, would surround the village, cut off its electricity, keep it under 24-hour curfew for weeks, and cancel all permits to the inhabitants—meanwhile allowing Jewish settlers and soldiers to enter houses at will, destroying furniture and beating people up. All factions would publish denunciations in the local papers and use bombastic language vowing "revenge upon the barbarous occupiers". We, on the other hand, would not publish any such fiery denunciations. Instead, we would meticulously document these events without exaggeration, and publish a carefully balanced report months later, pointing out the illegality of collective punishment and the prohibition under the Geneva Conventions of mistreatment of noncombatants. We would even include in our report the Israeli narrative and its public justification for such actions.

While others were perfectly happy to use international law and human rights conventions as political tools to bad-mouth Israel and its occupation, we actually believed in these principles and held them to be universal. We felt that they should be applied to friend and foe alike. We critiqued Israel under universally recognized standards of human rights, including international law and Israel's own military orders and legal decisions—all concepts of human rights that Israel loudly claimed to be following.

We were also more attuned to Israeli society and the international community than the average Palestinian. We understood how the Western world viewed both Israel and the Palestinians, and we felt that we could best serve our country and our cause by operating within that world and addressing it on its own terms.

After setting up Law in the Service of Man, we tried to include the different political factions, as well as both working and striking lawyers. Shortly after the occupation began in 1967, lawyers went on an open-ended strike, which had continued sustained by monthly stipends from Jordan. Eventually other lawyers began to practice and serve the population, particularly in military courts, so now there were both striking and practicing lawyers. We held lengthy meetings to convince the striking lawyers of the importance of the work we were embarking upon. The striking lawyers felt that any recognition given to Israel and its courts and military orders lent legitimacy to Israel and its bogus claims and narrative. The factions repeated to us that the PLO Charter clearly states that armed struggle is the way to liberate Palestine or would badger us with the futility of applying international law, which they said had no teeth.

In the end, our attempts to create this group failed, because it became just as political and factionalized as Palestinian society at large. In one stormy meeting, several of the group's members openly hinted at some of the accusations against the three of us and stated that they were paying a high political price just to associate with us. We later found out that some of them were spreading rumors against us—even as they were in discussion with us to be part of our group!

We decided on the spot to dissolve the group and refund the seed money of $1000 we had received from the ICJ.

The very next day, Raja, Charles, and I secretly set up a new organization under that same name and registered it as a not-for-profit company. Nonprofit corporations are well-known in the United States but were totally novel in the West Bank at that time. Local laws only acknowledged charitable societies and regular business corporations. So, I came up with the idea of setting up what was basically a charitable society, but calling it a company, with the members labeled "shareholders." The company would not materially benefit its shareholders, however. The charter of the "company" would allow it to have general powers that enabled us to carry out legal and human rights work, documentation, research, publication, and the like.

This gave us the chance to stay under the government's radar for a while. The military government, which closely monitored charitable societies, was not too interested in the activities of a corporation. We later learned that the Registrar of Companies in the West Bank (an Israeli military officer) misread the name of our company and thought it was called "Law in the Service of Teeth" (the word *asnan*—"teeth" in Arabic—sounds like *insan*—"mankind"). Apparently, he thought we were some kind of dental corporation and registered us without much scrutiny. If he had realized that we were a human rights organization he would have refused to register us at all, or would have insisted on his right to approve our Board of Trustees and to monitor and control our bank accounts and other assets and to review and approve—or not—any of our activities. The military government was already doing those things to other charitable organizations.

So, we were now approved and fully legal, and we proceeded to work in silence, knowing full well that the less attention we drew the better.

Our first project was to collect the existing Israeli military orders, analyze them, and determine their purpose.

When Israel began to occupy the West Bank in 1967, it had announced that the occupation would be a temporary situation. The first military order stated that all existing Jordanian laws and regulations would continue in effect, until changed by the Commander of the Area. The second military order announced that the Commander would exercise all legislative, judicial, and administrative functions of the Jordanian government. This was followed by hundreds of new military orders amending existing laws in all areas of life. These orders were initially difficult to get a hold of and many of them had not been published. We could occasionally find some of the military orders at the courthouse or be given a particular military order when we asked for it, but they were not readily available, even to lawyers.

Israel claimed that it was abiding by international law, which limited its ability as an occupying power to change a local situation, except as "necessary for security purposes." In reality, however, the ongoing onslaught of new military orders superseded existing laws and were held to be superior even to any constitutional provisions in Jordanian law that contradicted them.

Raja went secretly to the United Nations and testified as "Expert M" about how the military orders were impacting Palestinian society. By this time, there were almost a thousand military orders. Niall McDermott of the ICJ encouraged Raja and I to write up our findings and promised to have the ICJ jointly publish with us the book we were working on describing the legal situation.

Titled *The West Bank and the Rule of Law* and published in 1981, the book was a careful analysis of the Israeli military orders which altered existing Jordanian law in radical ways. Raja and I described how these military orders affected all areas of Palestinian life, from the legal courts to the economy. We showed how they were facilitating the absorption of the Occupied Territories into the Israeli sphere but keeping the non-Jews who lived in the territories in a subservient position. Finally, we showed how the Orders facilitated the process of land acquisition for the creation of Jewish settlements throughout the territories. The book was first published in English and later translated into Arabic.

As we started publishing our findings in both English and Arabic, we slowly began to be known and accepted within Palestinian society. We also made a big splash abroad. Israeli apologists were finding it hard to answer our charges, particularly since we kept our words measured and our conclusions understated and judicious.

Analyzing, writing, and publicizing the legal issues was only part of our work. Equally important was our effort at careful documentation of the violations of human rights practiced by the Israeli authorities.

For this purpose, we started a research program and trained a cadre of field researchers to collect and document stories of incidents throughout the West Bank that showed violations of human rights. These researchers became the backbone of our organization.

One of the most important truths we learned is that most of the evil in this world takes place under cover of darkness. Oppressive regimes pretend to be good and upright, and label reports of their wrongdoings as lies promulgated by their political opponents.

This brought me at last to the answer to my second big question: How did Israel get away with looking like the victim rather than what they were—the oppressor?

Israel enjoyed a wonderful reputation abroad as "the only democracy in the Middle East." In that regard, Israeli officials not only deceived the outside world, but their own population as well. Many good people around the world could not psychologically believe that a people who had suffered the horrors of the Holocaust could possibly themselves commit the atrocities which Palestinians attributed to them.

Therefore, it was vital that we make it a priority to rigorously, accurately, and carefully document all that happened. Our documentation had to consist of courtroom-quality evidence and thus unassailable by our critics. We could not afford to be caught in a single lie, exaggeration, or even a truth that appeared evident but could not be thoroughly documented to the satisfaction of a neutral outside observer.

Holding to these principles was sometimes tricky.

On the one hand, we were sometimes asked to report events and work on cases in which there had been no actual eyewitness like the terrible incident I mentioned in the Preface of the Palestinian shepherd who was killed by Israeli settlers and who had his sheep stolen.

The guide who led me to the spot where the shooting had taken place was, in fact, the victim's cousin. But although he had discovered his cousin's body, he had not actually seen the shooting. What he did see were the Israeli settlers rounding up the scattered sheep. The family of the dead man claimed the settlers were demanding they pay a ransom to buy their own sheep back—while the settlers could insist that they were health department employees, and that since they'd had the sheep inoculated, they should be reimbursed for the substantial veterinary bill before returning the flock. The family, of course, only knew that the settlers had taken their sheep to their settlement and would not return them until the ransom was paid. In the end the family did pay the bill and got their sheep back.

The shepherd, however, was still dead.

The Israeli police did not investigate, and the family did not see any point in filing a complaint against the settlers. They had no faith that the Israeli courts would give them any measure of justice.

This event, among others, showed me how important it was to have exact and accurate evidence, and in signed statements and affidavits, to document what actually happens. It also showed me the importance of following even the faulty procedures that existed to try to establish the truth. To get anyone to believe the Palestinian story and to demand that Israelis follow their own procedures and properly investigate the killing, it was necessary to collect iron-clad documentation of the facts. Otherwise, we were left with mere allegations that would be dismissed as politically motivated.

As it turned out, other than the data that we collected and filed in our office, nothing more was ever done about this particular case. It was just one more incident among many in the West Bank.

The murdered shepherd was forgotten to all except those who knew and loved him best. His name would just be one more added to the long list of the thousands of Palestinians who would be killed in the coming years of the Intifada.

CHAPTER 6

WHEN I RETURNED TO PALESTINE in 1979, many
Palestinian lawyers were still honoring the general strike, which
had begun in 1967. The civilian courts in the West Bank, which had
been set up under Jordanian law, were now administered by the
Israeli Officer in Charge of the Judiciary. These local Palestinian
courts handled most disputes between Palestinians. They were not
held in the highest regard by the locals, however, partly because
they lacked robust enforcement mechanisms and partly because
they were under the authority of the Israeli Officer in Charge of
the Palestinian judiciary.

More important were the Israeli military courts that had been
established by Israel at the beginning of the occupation in 1967.
They functioned as a direct arm of the Israeli army and meted out
severe punishments on the Palestinian population. They also handled any matters that were of interest to Israelis, including land

cases. Palestinians were subject to both systems of courts, and Israelis alone decided which courts would end up handling a particular matter. Since military courts were conducted in Hebrew, many West Bank lawyers did not do well in those courts, and Palestinian defendants often relied on Jewish or Israeli-Arab lawyers.

Many West Bank lawyers did not see the need to learn Hebrew or to appear before military courts. They still felt that Israeli rule would be temporary and that participating in the Israeli courts was a despicable concession to the ongoing occupation: a form of legitimizing its policies. I was of a different mindset. I believed that it was imperative to learn and understand the Israeli legal system from the inside, and I was particularly interested in practicing in their military courts.

One of the first tasks I had given myself upon returning home, therefore, was to learn Hebrew. While Palestinians who grow up in Israel learn Hebrew in school, few in the West Bank were willing or eager to do so. Those who knew any Hebrew usually learned it while in prison or by working menial jobs in Israel. Unlike West Bank residents, however, I was able to travel freely in Israel due to my East Jerusalem residency. I decided that a proper full-time *ulpan* would be the best way to study Hebrew and learn about Israel from a Jewish perspective.

The *ulpan* is a unique Israeli institution that was created by the Zionist movement as part of their plan to revive the Hebrew language and to create a common destiny among the new Jewish immigrants. Since they were coming to Israel from so many different countries, the Ulpan provided a necessary linguistic and cultural immersion into the new nation.

I chose the famous Ulpan Akiva, a residential ulpan in a lovely, resort-like kibbutz setting on the shores of the Mediterranean. Set near the town of Netanya, the immersion program would last for one month, and I was determined to get the most out of it. I wanted to feel what a new immigrant would feel and understand the way that Israelis looked at things.

The experience would be eye-opening.

At Ulpan Akiva, Hebrew was the only language used in the classroom or anywhere else. Unlike other language classes, we were not first taught the letters of the alphabet or any grammar. Instead, we were thrown directly into the sea of the Hebrew language. It was sink or swim.

On the first day of class, the teacher stood in front of a class of fifteen or so students from different countries and began to point to herself and then to students, saying, *Ani morah; ata talmeed; at talmidah.* "I am a teacher (female); you are a student (male); you are a student (female)."

Then she would gesture and add: "Hu Talmeed. He Talmidah." (He is a male student. She is a female student). And "Shmi Sarah. Mah Shimkha? Mah Shmo? Mah Shimha?" (My name is Sarah. What is your name? What is his name? What is her name?) and so on.

In a mere five minutes, each student had learned a few nouns and pronouns, the male and female formulation of the word, singular and plural, and a few practical phrases. The ulpan is an amazing system and reminded me of Paulo Friera's successful teaching of literacy to Latin American peasants, described in his book *Pedagogy of the Oppressed.*

Students enrolled at the ulpan had five hours of classroom language training in the morning, then a number of field trips, sports, and other activities in the afternoon and evening, all of which were conducted in Hebrew. The ulpan not only taught Hebrew, but provided indoctrination in Zionism, an introduction to *Ha-Aretz*, "The Land", its geography, food and plants, as well as an introduction to Israeli society and the problems faced by new immigrants living in Israel. I was the only Palestinian at the ulpan, apart from Moreh Ali, a legendary teacher of the Arabic Language who taught a separate program for those already proficient in Hebrew.

It was surreal to be the sole Palestinian Arab in a full-time study intended primarily for new Jewish immigrants.

We were taught to sing a number of patriotic Zionist songs. One of them was "Eretz, Eretz, Eretz."

A rough English translation goes like this:

> *The Land, the Land, the Land,*
> *The Land of milk and honey.*
> *The Land where we will live, come what may.*
> *This is the Land of the people, the eternal land,*
> *Like a mother and father to us.*
> *The Land where we were born,*
> *The Land where we will stay.*
> *And we will continue to live here,*
> *Come what may, come what may, come what may."*

I sang it lustily, knowing that I was the only one there who was actually born and grew up in the Land. I deeply felt the emotions that they were trying to artificially manufacture within the newcomers. As the song declared, I loved The Land, I belonged to it, and I considered it my Land. I was equally determined to live here come what may. Every time the program called for us to sing, I would request that particular song and the teacher would glare at me.

On my first evening there, I took a long walk along the beach in my shorts and T-shirt, enjoying the Mediterranean breeze. I was thinking about how I felt, a world away from the West Bank and the occupation, and how even though it was only an hour's drive to the beach, most Palestinians could not enjoy it.

Suddenly, there was a powerful searchlight from the hill behind me, sweeping the deserted beach. I suspected they were guarding against any possible infiltration from the sea by a Palestinian commando unit. The searchlight focused on me and stopped moving. I froze in the bright beam. As an army jeep started slowly driving down from the hill towards me. I realized in a panic, that I did not have my *hawiyyeh:* my Israeli-issued ID card, which all Palestinians must carry. Here I was, a lone Palestinian on the beach, and suddenly the area felt almost like a military zone!

The Jeep drove straight towards me. I raised my hands above my head. The soldier barked something in Hebrew, and I responded by repeating in a sing-song fashion, a phrase I had just learned that morning.

Ani Talmid bi Ulpan Akiva. Ani Lomed Ivrit bi Ulpan Akiva. "I am a student in Ulpan Akiva. I am learning Hebrew in Ulpan Akiva."

The soldiers broke up laughing, as I'm sure my Hebrew sounded forced and awkward. But it did the trick. One gestured to ask me if

I had a light for his cigarette, and I shook my head. They were still laughing as they drove away.

The last week I was there I was invited for a little chat by the venerable lady who had founded the ulpan. She was reportedly quite famous for fighting against the British and the Arabs in Israel's War of Independence in 1948. She was considered one of the founders of the State. Her invitation surprised me, and I was curious.

She asked me how I was doing, and I said fine. She said she was glad I was taking the course, since she was a strong believer in Jewish-Arab coexistence. Then she asked me about the nature of my relationship with Lisa, one of the foreign Jewish volunteers at the ulpan. I told her that we had had a couple of interesting political conversations, all in Hebrew.

"Yes," she said, "but Lisa is new here and does not quite know the situation in Israel."

"You are quite right about that. I am in the process of educating her about the political reality," I replied.

"But what about the romantic interest?"

I assured her that I had no romantic interest in Lisa whatsoever.

"Even if you do not, Lisa might have her own ideas," she replied. "I cannot have any of that going on at my *ulpan*. I have seen how she looks at you. She is quite enamored with you. You are an intelligent and handsome young man, and she is quite impressionable. It would be tragic if you got romantically involved and ended up getting married."

I was taken aback. "Why is that?"

"Because you are an Arab and she is Jewish."

Now I grasped the reason for her invitation.

"We are both adults. What we do is nobody's business but our own."

"Ah, but it is," she said. "Not only would Jews object, but people in your own society would not like to see this happen either. A marriage between the two of you would be a catastrophe not only for you and your future children—but think of what it would do to all the wonderful work we are trying to do here to build Jewish-Arab coexistence. Our reputation would be utterly ruined."

I thought of the film *Guess Who's Coming to Dinner,* starring Sidney Poitier, in which a liberal, lily-white American family was surprised when their daughter brought home her African American boyfriend whom she was planning to marry. Apparently, this self-proclaimed liberal Zionist was eager for Arab-Jewish relationships . . . as long as they did not lead to intermarriage.

I assured her again that I had no intentions of the sort she feared and that I was leaving the ulpan at the end of the week anyway because my month was almost up.

I had received my warning that evening, but I was greatly disappointed by her attitude. It was an important lesson for me to remember, though—that even those who preach Jewish-Arab coexistence often had their own racism and prejudices.

Later I learnt that Ulpan Akiva, which also taught Arabic to Jewish students, was a basic recruitment location for Israel's intelligence agencies, whose interrogators needed to know enough Arabic to be able to interrogate Palestinian prisoners. So much for their interest in "Jewish-Arab coexistence."

After leaving the ulpan I returned to Jerusalem, where I had a truly ideal situation. As an MCC volunteer I had written my own job description, which in addition to learning Hebrew, included using my law degree to work on issues of justice and human rights. The Mennonite organization was dedicated to peace and development work. As such, it tried very hard to avoid the politics of the Palestinian-Israeli situation. They were initially involved in relief services for Palestinian refugees who had lost their homes and livelihoods in 1948, and now were active in small income-generating programs (needlework by Palestinian village women, for example) and technical assistance to farmers.

At that time, Harold Dueck, from Canada, was supervising an MCC program that helped farmers in the Jordan Valley remain on their land by teaching them how to maximize their limited supply of water. Israelis were strict about not permitting the Palestinian farmers to use any more water than they did in 1967. They were not allowed to dig artesian wells. At the same time, the Israeli national water company, Mekerot, dug deep wells in the same area, sometimes drying up natural water springs like Far'a Spring, which served the Palestinians. Mekerot used the water to generously supply the Jewish settlements, with their swimming pools and grass lawns, and even pumped it straight to Israel. Exact figures as to water usage were kept secret by Israel, but it was well known that Israel had full control over subterranean water and would not allow Palestinians to use any additional water for their agriculture than they had used before 1967.

With a very small budget, MCC was helping farmers adopt drip irrigation techniques, which allowed them to triple their vegetable production. Tripling farm production, however, created a second problem. Since the West Bank market was soon flooded with produce, the farmers could not obtain a decent price to cover their costs for harvesting their bumper crops. For a businessman like Harold, the solution was simple: Find another market for the products.

The Jordan Valley lies at the lowest point on the surface of the planet, and this creates a natural greenhouse effect, allowing farmers there to grow vegetables out of season. This meant that they had a potentially huge and lucrative market in Europe and could command good prices, since they produced their vegetables year-round.

The problem was that Palestinian farmers did not have access to European markets. The Israeli Civil Administration, which took over the functions of the Jordanian Ministry of Agriculture, had no interest in assisting the Palestinian farmers other than to direct them to sell their products to the Israeli semi-public agricultural company, Agrexco, and at low prices.

Harold decided to put on his business hat and teach Palestinian farmers how to access an international market with a fresh agricultural product which would be sold under their own name and identity. After all, MCC was a development agency, and assisting those farmers was precisely its job.

The first step was to train farmers to package and store their products in a uniform fashion that could be exported to an international market. This meant that instead of the traditional manner of randomly loading tomatoes or eggplants in boxes, with a few choice examples at the top, they instead organized the products according to uniform size, shape, and quality. They also prepared brochures describing their products in standard, universally accepted terms. Finally, they were taught how to make contact with markets in Europe, negotiate a price, and arrange to ship the product directly to them through Israeli ports.

On to the next hurdle.

Israel's largest agricultural marketer, Agrexco, a semi-governmental body, wanted to buy all Palestinian crops at reduced prices and export them to Europe itself, as an Israeli product, also pocketing the profits. Palestinian farmers, however, wanted to export directly under their own Palestinian label. Agrexco benefited from its relationship with the Israeli Civil Administration as well as the Israeli control over the borders. Under the occupation, no Palestinian product could be exported without a permit. In addition, the fertilizers, insecticides, quality seeds for specialty vegetables, and other necessary ingredients could not be imported without Israeli permits.

Under Harold's leadership, the MCC waged a valiant effort to break through these barriers and assist the farmers. He often told the saga of his attempts in a very informative and sometimes funny lecture for visitors which he titled, "What Happens when a Tomato Crosses an International Border."

Harold's biggest project was sending fifty tons of tomatoes to a European vegetable stores chain. After Israel refused to give permission for the shipment, the project captured the attention of high officials in Europe. They could not understand why Israel was being obstinate when the same buyers were also buying Israeli products and so benefiting the Israeli economy. When the efforts of European officials failed, they decided to trigger certain mechanisms in the bilateral agreements that allowed Israeli products to enter Europe. As a result, Israel began to lose literally millions of dollars in trade every week.

In the end, Israel relented and granted the necessary export permit for the Palestinian farmers in Jericho. The farmers were amazed. They had never imagined that they could have the power to insist on shipping their own merchandise under their own name and label.

Unfortunately, the story didn't end there. Even after Harold finally managed to overcome all these bureaucratic obstacles, the largest shipment of Palestinian tomatoes and eggplants was left to rot in the sun at the Israeli port of Ashdod. It arrived in Europe totally unacceptable for sale to European consumers.

This event made it more than clear to me that in addition to the competition over land and water resources, Israel was also exercising good, old-fashioned, colonial control, benefiting the colonizers at the expense of the colonized.

Apparently, some people outside the Israeli American milieu were catching on, seeing the truth, as well. The light was starting to dawn in the world at large as to our plight. Perhaps the propaganda that painted Israel as the innocent victim could be broken through. Still, it was an uphill struggle.

One of the agricultural engineers working with MCC was Ibrahim Matar, a Palestinian from Jerusalem. As he travelled around the West Bank dealing with farmers, he became increasingly aware of the impact of Israeli settlements upon Palestinian land and water. Before long, he became an expert on how the location, growth, and expansion of the Jewish settlements occurred at the expense of Palestinian farmers.

While Israel was claiming that it had no ambitions in the territories it had occupied in 1967, Ibrahim knew better. He started giving "settlement tours," in which he would educate visiting groups—such as dignitaries, journalists, and members of the diplomatic community—about the impact of the settlements in the Occupied Territories. He showed how Israel was directly benefiting from Palestinian land and water resources, while using a variety of methods to capture and keep as much land as possible, thus creating "facts on the ground." Israel would use its power as well as violence to confiscate land and build settlements, and then point to the lives of the settlers as established facts that could not be ignored. "This is the reality, and any peace plan or proposal needs to take that reality into account. You cannot simply uproot them and ruin their lives".

As I learned more about Israeli military orders, I was increasingly called upon to join Ibrahim on his settlement tours to explain the legal aspects of Israel's methods for controlling water, confiscating land, and otherwise restricting Palestinian development. It was amazing to me that Israel found a way to do all these things "legally," by providing a myriad of military orders specifically designed for this. Every aspect of Palestinian life and economy was subject to a regime of permits and licenses, which were granted or withheld at the sole discretion of the Israeli army and its civil administration.

Another of Harold's projects was to start a development bank that would provide microcredit and other services to Palestinian farmers and entrepreneurs. He brought together a group of economists, professors, businessmen, and others to explore the possibility. They enlisted my help as a lawyer.

"Will your bank be accepting deposits?" I asked them.

"We have no such plans," they replied.

"Will it be issuing checkbooks?"

"No," they said. "We will only be giving loans on a concessionary basis to help development."

"Do you need to call yourself a bank to carry out your proposed activities?"

"Not really," they conceded.

Since they were not calling themselves a bank and were not accepting deposits or issuing checks, I got an idea. We would establish the proposed entity and register it as a nonprofit company in Jerusalem under Israeli law.

That was how we established the Economic Development Group (EDG), which, in time, was able to obtain millions of dollars in grants and provide solid development loans to farmers and businessmen in the West Bank and Gaza—all without needing permission from the military authorities. Harold felt that this particular project was one of MCC's most important. With a miniscule budget compared to other development organizations, the Mennonites were having a considerable impact on economic life in the West Bank. And I was proud to be part of that effort.

What we did was not without its consequences, however.

While the MCC tried to carefully structure its activities as a development agency that assisted needy people, there was no escaping the political ramifications of the organization's work in Palestine.

Their stance in nonviolence and peacemaking would also have a direct impact on Palestinians resisting the occupation.

For all these good efforts, the MCC was rewarded by having the Israel Civil Administration keep a wary eye on them, often accusing them of being "too pro-Palestinian". But since the MCC had been doing development work in the West Bank before the occupation began in 1967, and since the Israeli Civil Administration itself was not providing much assistance to Palestinian farmers, they allowed their activities to continue. Catholic Relief Services (CRS) as well as Swedish Organization for Individual Relief (SOIR), World Vision, and the Lutheran World Federation were also active in the West Bank, and they often coordinated their activities with MCC. This created a strange situation where the Israeli civil administration was wielding all governmental power and was responsible for the people of the West Bank, yet it viewed them as enemies and had little incentive to serve them or provide them with services, beyond simply allowing the organizations already serving them to continue to do so under their watchful eye.

In time I would complete my volunteer service with MCC and open my own law office, continuing to cooperate with these groups. Some of them eventually became paying clients.

CHAPTER 7

WHILE I HAD BEEN WORKING with the MCC, I simultaneously worked with Raja and Charles, continually building our human rights organization, Law in the Service of Man (later called Al Haq). We had no model or template to go by: we were learning as we went along.

One day some of our friends and supporters joined us for an event where we were planting olive trees at Al Jeeb, a village north of Jerusalem. Israeli settlers came in a bulldozer, so we stood between it and the newly planted trees. Roger Heacock, a professor at Bir Zeit, actually climbed into the bucket of the bulldozer in order to prevent its use. The settler lifted him high in the air, though nothing terrible happened. Fortunately, there were only a few settlers, and the event was quite peaceful. After we left, however, the settlers returned and uprooted all the trees.

THE TRUTH SHALL SET YOU FREE

We later discussed the incident at our offices and decided that in the future any such activity should only be carried out by people from LSM in their individual private capacity.

While we were clear about the illegality of the settlements, our role should not be that of an activist organization. Our mandate was clear and narrow: we were to focus on documenting human rights violations, research, and publication of materials about the rule of law. As individuals, we had our political views, and many of us were active in nonviolent resistance to the occupation. But as LSM, we needed to maintain our objectivity and our high standards of work. Our main target was the outside world, particularly the human rights organizations and activists worldwide.

Ultimately, we hoped to bring some action before international courts, but for the time being, merely documenting human rights violations and publicizing them was a big enough job for us. We were fully aware that the Israeli military government could arrest any of us for our activism. The terrible truth was, they would not need to prove anything. We could be tried in military court or simply placed under administrative detention without any charges or trial, just like thousands of other Palestinians who were languishing in Israeli jails. Certainly, the Israeli army would not be happy with our work documenting its human rights violations.

To avoid or minimize our risk, we decided to follow a two-pronged approach.

First, we deliberately avoided membership in any of the Palestinian factions. This was highly unusual since almost all Palestinian activists and concerned, public-minded people like us belonged to one or another of the political parties. But we knew that mere membership in any of them would have been illegal under the existing military orders. So, we had to carry out our work in a truly independent fashion and hope to stay under the radar, at least initially.

Second, we would continue to build up our international contacts, especially among international human rights organizations, so that if we were arrested, we would have many important individuals and organizations who would take up our cause and intervene on our behalf with Israel. It helped that Justice Haim Cohen, then presiding justice of Israel's High Court, was himself one of the Commissioners of the International Court of Justice.

If we were arrested, then, Israel would have a hard time explaining their reasons for it, since our activism was centered on human rights and research into the military orders and justice system. As such, we were not really "political."

This was not merely a tactic. We truly believed in human rights as a value. It was clear to us that human rights are universal and should be upheld worldwide. For example, if torture is wrong, it is wrong worldwide, regardless of who the victim or perpetrators are. I am proud to say, years later, that the organization we created continues to apply the same standards fearlessly to the Palestinian Authority and our own society, and not only to Israel.

Some of the cases we encountered were heartbreaking, and the world needed to know about the victims.

An early case that made a big impact in our office was that of Sabri Ghrayyeb, a new client from a small village north of Jerusalem. He had recently approached my law office for help because Israelis were trying to confiscate his land to expand the

settlement of Hadasha. They had already confiscated about twenty-five acres and had put up a wire fence around it, claiming it as
"state land."

I had already learned that this type of action was one of five
different legal machinations the Israelis use to rob the Palestinians
of their property. By declaring it to be "state land," the burden of
proof was suddenly placed on the farmer. Such cases were taken
out of the regular courts and placed in military "objections committees," where the primary method that Palestinian farmers had to
use to prove ownership was demonstrating ten years of continuous
agricultural use. If the land had lain fallow for some of the time
during any ten-year period, the farmer would have a very difficult
case indeed. Once it was declared state land, it would revert to the
government and be given to Jewish settlers.

The problem for Sabri was not just the court case, but the constant harassment from the settlers who coveted the rest of his land
and wanted to chase him away. Sabri's home was at the very edge
of his village where he was more isolated and totally defenseless
against the incursions and attacks by the settlers. They had thrown
stones at him, tried to burn his house down, and otherwise harassed
him and his family members in many other ways. Defending his
property was becoming a full-time job.

As an ironic sidenote, Sabri's name means "the patient one".
He certainly needed a lot of patience for his lifelong struggle to
stay on his land.

When Raja and I went out to visit Sabri, we were in the process
of creating LSM and we felt that the documentation of human rights
violations was the most powerful and efficient method of dealing

with settlers, the army, and their daily harassment in the lives of Palestinians. How we would handle this, we weren't sure, as we were still experimenting with our ideas and methods. But the need for legal help was critical.

On this trip, we decided to bring Sabri a small camera and film. We told him that the next time settlers attacked him, he should take pictures of them so that we would be able to take detailed affidavits of their illegal actions. Without solid evidence, we could not even file a police complaint. The police would simply say that they did not know who the violent settlers were, and therefore they could not investigate it. But with photographic proof on our side, we could attempt to follow up with formal police complaints. Settlers knew that we could not seek any redress against them if we did not know their names and addresses. A camera would at least help us to identify who the attackers were and to demand legal actions against them.

Theologically, as a Christian and a pacifist, I felt that such actions were using "the weapons of light" against the forces of darkness. The words of the Apostle Paul made sense since evil thrives in the dark. In secular terms, I knew that to the extent we could bring the actions of settlers into the light, it would be harder for Israel to justify them.

When we met him, I told Sabri that he should not consider any violence whatsoever, since it would only justify the vastly superior violence of the settlers against him and his family.

"Think of the camera as your weapon and the film as its ammunition," I told him. I was in fact teaching him some of the basic principles of nonviolent resistance.

Sabri took this lesson to heart, and the next time I visited him, I saw the result.

When a group of settlers came over from the settlement to harass him and throw rocks at his house, he came out of his home with his wife at his side. He showed me how he had taken out his camera/weapon and stood legs akimbo. Holding the camera in both hands, he pointed it straight at them and clicked off a few shots. The settlers continued to come closer, and likely would have grabbed his camera and taken it with them to destroy the evidence against them. But Sabri handed the camera to his wife, who stuck it into her ample bosom. Now the settlers could do nothing without physically assaulting the woman. Instead, they fled.

This was a neat tactical addition to my instructions, and certainly served the purpose. I also decided that on the next trip to the U.S., I would buy a foghorn—of the type used in boats—so that he would be able to alert the rest of the village if the settlers attacked him at night.

For years after that, Sabri and his family continued their struggle as the Israeli settlement grew. Eventually, it surrounded his home on all sides, while he and his family valiantly hung on to their house. When he passed away, he was honored by Al Haq as one of our earliest cases, another peaceful warrior who continued to resist non-violently to the very end.

Our decision to build a team of well-trained field workers was triggered by one event in particular—a very harrowing one.

A fourteen-year-old Palestinian boy had been kidnapped by settlers, beaten up, and kept in a makeshift prison in the nearby settlement for three days before he was released.

The incident had not been reported in the local papers, and the story was so unusual that we decided to investigate. We knew that settlers had no legal authority to arrest or detain any Palestinians—though they were known to attack and shoot at Palestinian children, whom they accused of throwing stones at their cars. But they had absolutely no legal basis to independently arrest or keep Palestinian children or adults overnight. Furthermore, as far as we knew, there were no jails in any Israeli settlement at the time.

Turmus Ayya, the village from which the boy was kidnapped, was a Palestinian village north of Ramallah. We were warned to go during the daylight hours since the villagers did not have power and their generators only produced electricity for a few hours every night. The military government was not allowing them to hook up to the Jerusalem Electric Company, an Arab-owned company which had held the mandate and monopoly for providing electricity in the West Bank since Jordanian times. Israel had cut off their connection to the Jerusalem Electric Company and was pressuring Palestinian villages to hook up to the Israeli national grid instead. Many villages, including Turmus Ayya, were resisting. They saw the measure as designed to promote and speed up annexation into Israel.

Once in Turmus Ayya, we found the boy, Hani, with bruises on his face, lying in bed. He told us that he had been playing in the street with friends when settlers in two cars stopped and started chasing them. Hani was the only boy they caught. After they beat him up, they took him to the nearby settlement, where they kept him for three days in a small storage room with one small window. He was never turned over to the Israeli army or charged with any offense. Just beaten up, illegally kidnapped, and held for three days, then released.

Hani was clearly traumatized, but his physical injuries did not look too severe. In all other respects, this would be a very routine story, except for one critical difference: the perpetrators were not Israeli soldiers, but settlers. As civilians, the settlers had absolutely no legal authority to arrest or detain anyone. What they had done was assault and kidnapping of a minor.

After we listened to the boy's story, we also heard from his uncle about the family's efforts to get him released. We took detailed notes and prepared affidavits to be signed by the boy and his family.

If we were to challenge these practices, we realized, our first task would be—as we had told Sabri—to collect credible evidence and to shine the light of truth on what was clearly illegal and unacceptable. But given the outrageousness, or even (for many outsiders) the almost unbelievable story of this incident, we would have to present the clearest proof for the world media to even consider our story. We would be under intense scrutiny, and the credibility of our entire organization was on the line.

From the very beginning, therefore, we decided that our most important task in this new organization we were establishing (LSM/ Al Haq) was to provide accurate documentation of human rights violations. We would only accept courtroom-quality evidence. As we investigated each alleged violation of human rights, we ourselves would act as skeptical attorneys for the other side.

To gather as much data as possible, we would also have to train a cadre of field researchers. Their job would be to collect only the most credible evidence possible for each incident or category of human rights violations that they encountered. Our field researchers would have to be trained in proper collection of documentation and in the rules of evidence that would be followed in a court of law. They would collect physical evidence where it existed—such as medical reports and spent bullets—but the most important issue was insisting on a very high level of witness credibility. We taught our field workers to ruthlessly critique their witnesses, as we felt this is the only way we could build our credibility and ensure that our evidence would be trusted.

Our standards had to be extremely high.

Our researchers had to learn to be very skeptical of everything they heard, and only collect the most accurate affidavits from the most reliable eyewitnesses. They had to be trained how to question witnesses, how to spot and reject instances of exaggeration, rumors, and willful lying. They were instructed to question each witness separately, and to cross-examine them and grill them as a hostile lawyer in a courtroom would. They had to avoid hearsay statements and only accept sworn statements under oath. They were to seek supporting witnesses and documents wherever possible.

Witnesses were repeatedly warned to only give statements about the absolute facts of what they saw personally, and not what they heard from others. They were to give details as to the exact unit of army, jeep, border patrol, or civilian settlers who committed the violations. They were to state with precision where they were located when they witnessed the events and what may have led up to them. They were to refrain from inserting their own opinions or drawing their own conclusions.

For example, we would not allow them to make a statement that a person was shot by a dumdum bullet, since they were not munitions experts. Even doctors, at best, could only say that a person was shot by "a bullet which exploded into pieces inside the body."

Our part-time field researchers—each in one area of the West Bank—were well-respected and connected in the Palestinian community. Each was required to report to us on a weekly basis. The types of human rights violations included collective punishments, house demolitions, deportations, administrative detention (without charges or trial), shootings, beatings and abuse by soldiers, settlers, or Palestinian collaborators, and all other manner of abuses and humiliations of the local population.

When field researchers brought their affidavits to us once a week, Raja or I would grill them again and only accept affidavits when we were certain they could stand up to scrutiny. At that point we would give the affidavit a number and translate it into English. Then we would microfiche it and hide the original at a safe location away from the office. From that point we worked only with the copy and its translation, because we were afraid that Israeli military would raid our offices and steal and destroy the original evidence.

These affidavits would later serve as the basis for our publications and possible intervention with the authorities. In the back of our minds, the hope was that ultimately the evidence that we collected would someday be used to bring justice to the Palestinians in a proper court of law or perhaps an international tribunal or criminal court.

In the meantime, we would have sufficient evidence to permit us to speak with authority as to the actual human rights situation in the occupied territories. We felt that our credibility was our most valuable asset, and we would go to great lengths to preserve it. Our by-word was that we should always be understated and let the facts speak for themselves, rather than make sweeping statements which we could not adequately support.

One issue where this policy was clearest was the matter of torture.

CHAPTER 8

IT WAS WELL KNOWN throughout Palestinian society that the Israeli military was routinely torturing Palestinians, but it was hard to prove because the Israelis were experts at using torture techniques which left no physical marks on the bodies of Palestinian prisoners. They also ensured that torture took place "in the dark"—that is, during periods where a prisoner was denied any contact with the outside world, attorneys, or family visitors.

The Israeli system also isolated the torturers from other Israeli officials who might conceivably have to testify in court. The person who would take a prisoner's confession usually was not the torturer himself, but a different policeman. A prisoner who had been tortured, broken, and finally confessed would be taken to another policeman who would treat him nicely and take down his "confession." If he refused to sign it or recanted his confession, he would be sent back to the torturer until he was ready to confess and sign.

The policeman who would testify in court could truthfully say that he never tortured the prisoner, but in fact treated him nicely and even offered him a cigarette or a cup of coffee before he took down his "voluntary" confession.

We faced a situation where our only source of information on torture was the unsupported testimonies of prisoners. Israel could argue that such testimonies were biased, and that those who gave them were lying to avoid being convicted or perhaps to simply tarnish Israel's reputation. To decry this torture without doing the difficult work of actually proving that it took place would only hurt us. It would allow others to label us as nothing more than anti-Israeli propagandists. If we were going to prove it, we would have to be careful about making unsupported public accusations. We decided to proceed slowly and carefully to build our case that torture was taking place, and that it was a systematic practice that was an integral part of the military court system, not merely the actions of a few bad apples and individual rogue cops.

For this reason, for almost five years we largely refrained from even using the word "torture" in any of our publications. We collected evidence until we were confident enough to publish a report (jointly with the ICJ—the International Commission of Jurists) about torture in Israeli prisons. It was a carefully worded document that started with the definition of torture under international law and then described the indispensable function of signed confessions in military courts. We also listed the substance of Israeli denials and attached a number of affidavits of victims of torture.

In order to combat rumors of torture, Israel had often protested that they allowed the International Committee Red Cross (the

ICRC) access to its prisoners during interrogations. They neglected to say, however, that the ICRC traditionally does not openly publish their reports for the world to see, but only shares them directly with the country involved. This is how the Red Cross manages to have access to prisoners and prisoners of war and to do their humanitarian work around the world under all sorts of circumstances. Therefore, we ended our document with a challenge to Israel to publish the secret reports provided to it by the ICRC. If the reports exonerate Israel, as they claimed, why not make them public?

Another publication soon followed, which dealt with mistreatment and torture of prisoners in Far'a prison. Our publication was quoted extensively by the representatives of Algiers, Syria, and the PLO at the UN headquarters in Geneva.

The Israeli ambassador replied with an attack, saying LSM was a hostile organization and a mouthpiece for the PLO. He said our report was full of lies, falsehoods, and exaggerations. We were making a mountain out of a molehill, he claimed, and our statements should not be considered truthful at all. Since the publication in question had been jointly published by us and the ICJ, Niall McDermott asked us to respond, so I wrote one of the finest letters I think I ever penned. I said that the charges made by the Israeli ambassador were very serious indeed. We were an independent human rights organization and not a mouthpiece for anyone. The ambassador knew very well that mere contact with the PLO was illegal under Israeli military orders. To call us a "hostile organization" was also a very serious accusation, making us subject to penalties of up to ten years in prison for us and anyone who associated with us.

Furthermore, I said that we were committed to the strictest standards of accuracy and truthfulness. If he—or anyone else—could show our statements to be materially inaccurate, we promised to retract such statements and to publish the retractions as widely as possible. This commitment was a standard that we promised to apply not only to this particular publication but all of our publications. The ICJ loved my letter, and after failing to get a response to it from the Israeli ambassador, printed it in full in their monthly newsletter.

Several years after our report was published, the Israeli High Court admitted that torture had been systematically used during interrogations, after an Israeli journalist published credible pictures and reports that contradicted the story of the Shin Bet (the Israeli internal intelligence agency) regarding the confessions they had obtained.

An official Commission of Inquiry was established, which found that Shin Bet interrogators systematically lied under oath regarding their methods of obtaining confession. They felt that it was their duty to torture prisoners and get confessions in order to protect the security of the state. If they told the truth about many confessions being obtained under torture, they reasoned, the confessions would be thrown out and dangerous terrorists would be allowed to walk freely. Therefore, they felt it was their duty to lie.

The court was concerned about the ethical dilemma that the interrogators faced, which forced them to lie under oath. Instead of being outraged at the torture itself, they decided to solve that ethical dilemma by permitting certain forms of "coercion." Interrogators would henceforth be allowed to use psychological methods as well as "moderate physical pressure" to obtain information and confessions. It stated that certain methods—which it listed in a secret appendix and declined to make public—would henceforth be allowed for interrogations, so that Israeli interrogators would not need to lie about them anymore.

In this way, the Court legalized torture. I was shocked and appalled. As I tried to understand how Israelis can justify such actions, I frequently came across this type of convoluted morality.

Eventually, it would become widely known and acknowledged that Israel used torture systematically during its interrogations. The Israeli human rights organization B'Tselem even issued a booklet which—with illustrations—described the methods used by interrogators, including position abuse, violent shaking, sleep deprivations, hot and cold treatment, as well as threats and blows.

Another of our early publications was a critique of the U.S. State Department's "Annual Report on the Human Rights Situation in Israel and the Occupied Territories." Such an annual report is published every year with respect to each country that receives U.S. foreign aid. Yet the reports, which were initially prepared by the U.S. Consulate in Jerusalem, would be watered down and "beautified" several times over before they were finally issued from Washington. We decided to critique the published report on Israel and the Occupied Territories by pointing out the true picture of human rights and the specific violations that were ignored or minimized. As always, we used full and careful documentation in our critique.

As a result, we began to receive visits from the Consulate and delegations from the U.S. State Department. The conversation was always the same: They wanted to know our sources and methodology. It was clear they were fishing for any information that would allow them to discount our materials and would justify their ignoring our documentation. I loved those meetings, because they gave me an opportunity to explain our methodology and emphasize the systematic way we critiqued our own information. I would explain that we were interested in patterns and systematic behavior rather than merely occasional anecdotal materials. Each violation also had to be linked to a specific violation of international law.

In addition to all of that, we also tried to address any possible Israeli explanation or excuse for the incident in question and made sure to refer to it. Invariably each such delegation would thank us and leave, until the next delegation arrived to ask the very same questions again.

The process itself was very useful to us. We were facing what we knew to be a hostile Western media and official establishment. Their scrutiny reminded us that in order to be taken seriously, we needed to be meticulous about our procedures. The ultimate effect was that LSM/Al Haq eventually became quite respected internationally.

Recently, at our fortieth anniversary celebration, we had a chance to take stock of what we had achieved. We received many plaudits from Amnesty International, Human Rights Watch, and many other organizations, many of which gave us or our workers international awards for human rights. Propaganda organizations funded by the Israeli government (like the so-called NGO Monitor) continued to attack us and claim that we are part of terrorist organizations. They tried to pressure European countries to cut our funding or withdraw any prizes they give us.

Fortunately, in every case, we could provide solid documentation and credible materials to justify the honors we received and continue to receive. Raja and I always told our staff that our good name and credibility were our most valuable assets, and must be maintained and protected rigorously.

Yet, despite all our efforts, the torture continued unabated.

One day I asked a friend, Father Dennis Madden, a Catholic priest, and professional psychiatrist who later became the bishop of Baltimore, if he would assist us in writing a booklet to help young people deal with the pressures of an Israeli interrogation. He was fascinated by the idea and asked to meet with former prisoners who would describe the interrogations.

I took Father Madden to the Qalandia refugee camp, where almost every young man had at one time or another been imprisoned and interrogated by the Israelis. We met with Khalil Abulleil, who described his experience to us. Father Madden asked me to translate exactly what was being said, so that he could capture the nuances.

"They came at night, about three AM, banged on the door of my house, and dragged me out. They tied a plastic handcuff so tightly around my wrists that my fingers became numb. They blindfolded me and threw me into the back of an army jeep where they kicked me and kept their boots on my back and head.

"Then they took me into a prison yard at the Russian compound, put a filthy bag smelling of urine over my head, and left me tied to a water pipe. I would hear the boots of soldiers and policemen as they passed me. Some of them would slap or kick me or yell at me.

"After several hours, it became daylight, and someone came and took me inside to the interrogation room. Several policemen kicked and slapped me until I saw the noonday stars."

"What?" Father Madden looked at me inquisitively.

"I am just literally translating what he says so that you can get the full impact." Abulleil meant that he saw stars from being struck in the head.

Abulleil continued.

"Someone made me sit on a low stool with uneven legs, which quickly got me really cramped. Then the interrogator who called himself Captain Avi came in. He said, 'We know who you are and all about your activities. You had better start talking. I do not want to waste my time with you. You are just a small fish. Tell me the names of the others in your Fatah cell.' I said, 'I am not in Fatah.' He slapped me and said 'Liar! You are and we know this.'"

The description of the beatings and interrogation went on and on.

Father Madden interjected. "How do you cope with this? What do you do while this is happening?"

Abulleil did not understand the question.

"Do you, for example, pray?"

"How could I? I was handcuffed and tied down!"

For a Moslem, prayer is the physical action of genuflection and repeating the formal prayers five times a day. Abulleil could not "pray" in the required Moslem manner while he was handcuffed and immobilized.

I had to explain all this to Father Madden, and I realized how little Westerners know about Islam and Islamic culture. An Arabic word like "pray" can be accurately translated to English, yet totally fail to convey the true meaning. What Father Madden had in mind was the type of communication when a believer speaks conversationally to God, which could be done silently, at any time and in all situations. A Moslem might in fact speak to God that way, but this type of dialogue with the Almighty is called by different names. It could be a heartfelt *munajah* (a highly spiritual, soulful communication with the Almighty) or a *du'a'* (a prayer of request and supplication). Moslems, however, do not refer to these as prayer in the Christian traditional sense.

It was clear to me then that Father Madden, lacking a deep knowledge of the culture, could not help prepare a booklet for training Palestinian children on how to cope with interrogations. It was difficult to believe it had come to this—and I'm sure my American friends would be shocked and some even disbelieving, but it was the terrible truth.

I later gave a speech to high school boys about how to deal with interrogators, including what their legal rights were and methods for not allowing themselves to be intimidated by what they might be subjected to during such an experience.

To my surprise, the speech was quoted at length in the Israeli newspaper, *Ha'Aretz*.

Clearly, we were being watched.

Would our efforts have a good and lasting impact? Or would we be shut down? Was our work hanging by a thread and we didn't know it? How could we expand our influence, with so many set against us and the people we represented?

Meanwhile, as part of our continuing effort to build up our international contacts, and further establish our credentials as human rights activists in the international community, I accepted an invitation to a conference organized by UNICEF in Utrecht, in the Netherlands on "The Rights of the Child."

At this conference I had an opportunity to speak for a few minutes from the floor and inform the attendees of our new organization and of the military orders that were severely restricting the human rights of Palestinian children and subjecting them to various forms of abuse at the hands of the military authorities.

Unbeknownst to me, some international advocates were attending the conference in order to bring together a group of activists and experts in international law. They wanted to create an entirely new organization by the name of HURIDOCS (Human Rights International Documentation Systems). HURIDOCS would act as a technical hub for coordinating, standardizing, and streamlining the documentation systems and practices of human rights organizations around the world.

Since we already had determined that accurate documentation of human rights violations was a central element of our new organization in Palestine, I was excited to meet others who were working on similar problems. I was also interested in the possibility of joining the new organization.

On the last day of the conference, I had just returned from jogging and was sitting on some stairs chatting with the head of Amnesty International, whom I had just met. I was approached by a young Algerian lady who asked to talk to me. She told me that there was intense political maneuvering as to who would be on the initial board of the new organization which would be launched the next day. There was interest in keeping it geographically representative, and one seat on the proposed board was implicitly reserved for the Arab countries of the Middle East and North Africa.

She said that she was clearly the most qualified person for that position, as she was very active and energetic. However, her rival was a certain Mr. Abdurrahman El Youssefi, a Moroccan diplomat and human rights lawyer who had worked with UNICEF for many years. (Years later, he became the Prime Minister of Morocco.)

Further, she said, he was vigorously challenging her and using his old boys' network to deprive her of the position. She said that she had heard me speak at the conference and thought it would be wonderful if that position were filled by a Palestinian.

"In order to deny the position to Mr. Youssefi, I would gladly withdraw my candidacy in your favor."

I said I would consider it, though I was not a candidate and was not lobbying for that position.

Within five minutes, Mr. Youssefi himself showed up while I was sitting still on the steps. He also wanted to talk.

After introducing himself, Youssefi told me that he was canvassing for the position of representing the Arab world on the board of the new organization that was being formed. He was clearly the most qualified for that position, he claimed, given his extensive experience in international organizations, but there was a certain young Algerian lady—who actually lives in Paris, and not in the region, he said—who was competing with him. He said it would be a disaster if she got that position. He had heard me speak at the conference and thought it would be wonderful if Palestine was represented on the board of the new organization. In fact, he would gladly withdraw his application in my favor if I would consent to it.

So, without even trying, I was unanimously elected to the position. It turned out to be an extremely valuable experience; I even ended up drafting the constitution of the new organization. We met every six months, usually in Geneva. Through this organization I met and maintained contact with many organizations and activists in human rights throughout the world. Best of all, LSM continued to gain more international support and connection.

We would very much need this support and association in the days ahead, which would become even tougher.

CHAPTER 9

AT THE SAME TIME, I was working hard to start LSM/Al Haq, I was also preparing to start my law practice. I was still a volunteer with the Mennonite Central Committee, while also apprenticing in the law office of the Shehadeh firm under advocate Aziz Shehadeh, Raja's father.

As my volunteer term with the MCC came to an end, Ustaz Aziz, Raja's father, asked me into his office. During my time with the MCC, I had apprenticed with his law firm in Ramallah. I did not yet have my license to practice law in the West Bank. The Israeli officer who—by military order—was in charge of the judiciary in the West Bank was dragging his feet. His position was powerful. In addition to heading the West Bank judiciary, he also exercised the functions of Minister of Justice, Head of the Bar Association, the Registrar of Companies, and several other functions in the West

Bank. Initially, he had told me that with my U.S. law degree, I only needed a six-month apprenticeship to get my West Bank license. But after almost two years, he had yet to grant it. Apparently, he had learned of my human rights work, and was deliberately dragging his feet, and might indeed never grant me the license. I had a plan, however, to circumvent him altogether.

An obscure military order allowed Israeli lawyers to appear in all West Bank courts, including military courts. I would redouble my efforts to learn Hebrew and join the Israeli Bar Association. I would take advantage of my East Jerusalem residency (since Israel annexed East Jerusalem and considers it part of Israel) to join the Israel Bar Association as a foreign attorney, and practice indirectly in the West Bank. Actually, I might never need a West Bank license to practice there. As it turned out, it would be three years and six months before I finally got my license from him.

Aziz Shehadeh was an Anglican who served as the Vice President of the Synod of the Episcopal Church in the Middle East. He asked me if I would be willing to take the position of chancellor of the Synod. In return for a salary of five hundred Jordanian dinars a month (around a thousand dollars), I would oversee the church properties.

"You can still pursue your license, and even start taking up Israeli military court cases on your own if you wish," he told me, "But this position will give you a chance to earn some money and begin to build your practice while you await your West Bank license."

I agreed. This would indeed begin to give me an opportunity to practice directly, while continuing to familiarize myself with the law. I was not taking any salary for my human rights work, and this position would provide a way for me to earn some money.

My new position provided me with an office in the complex at St. George's Cathedral in Jerusalem. The complex also housed the offices of the Diocese, the residence of the Bishop and St. George's College, as well as St. George's High School, which I had attended before I went to the United States.

Since I was working there, I decided to attend the Anglican Church, as well. There were two Sunday morning services: one in Arabic for Palestinian locals at ten, and the second, in English at eleven. The Anglican Church was very different from the simple evangelical church I grew up in. It was far more formal and ritualistic. The robes, candles, and even the use of incense reminded me of Catholic or Greek Orthodox churches. I was not totally comfortable with the liturgy, which was new to me. While I was used to my father's lengthy sermons, Reverend Naiim Ateek, who was the pastor at that time, preached for exactly eleven minutes. He half-jokingly told me it was an article of faith in the Episcopal church never to exceed that time limit for a sermon. The short sermons were not necessarily the main event of the service, but they tended to be interesting and to the point.

More importantly, Reverend Naiim believed that the gospel should be relevant to our daily lives. His view of theology was what he called "incarnational." While being very orthodox in his teaching, his theology was a contrast to that of my father, where "saving souls" and personal piety were central. Reverend Ateek's views were closer to the Sojourner community that I had encountered in the United States. He often said that the gospel means nothing if it does not address the reality we live in—especially the occupation and the daily challenges that it brought to our lives.

Reverend Ateek started a practice of holding discussions in the church parish hall after each service, most of which eventually centered around the political situation—especially the most recent outrages, curfews or restrictions. We also frequently engaged in heated discussions on how we Christians should relate to the Jews who were ruling us, as well as to the Moslems who were the majority of our Palestinian people. If a lot of foreigners happened to be at church, the discussions would be held in English. A number of the regular attendees, like me, were not Anglican, but Reverend Ateek treated us all as his parishioners.

I loved these meetings. It was like being in college again and engaging in discussions about God, the universe, angels, war, nonviolence, and peace: what we all had in common was the desire to make our faith relevant to the current situation. We were amazed to discover that, regardless of our denomination, we shared the same concerns and perspectives on the issues of the day.

These meetings also enabled Reverend Naiim to develop his own version of Liberation Theology that was Palestinian in nature. He felt that religion should be good news. That is what the word *gospel* means, after all. He saw little point in preaching about a heaven to gain after death while not engaging with the pressing issues we were living under. What did God have to say to those who suffered under systematic injustice? Reverend Naiim felt that if we did not present a gospel that was truly good news for Palestinians, Christianity would become increasingly irrelevant in our land.

Therefore, he emphasized the Bible verses that taught that God was on the side of the poor and the orphans, and he wanted to see justice "roll down like a mighty river" (Amos 5:24). "What does the Lord require of you? Act justly, love mercy and to walk humbly before your God" (Micah 6:8).

When he retired as pastor of the Anglican Church, Naiim Ateek told me, "I'm thinking of starting a new ecumenical center for Palestinian Liberation Theology. What do you think of that?"

"I think liberation theology is a Catholic movement from Latin America, and it's Marxist. Would that work for Palestine?"

"It is true," he said, "that in Latin America some priests and theologians are indeed quite extreme in their views, and some of them have even joined the guerrilla movements and fought against dictators and other oppressors. What is remarkable about them, however, is their emphasis on justice. They believe that religion is often used by the rich and powerful to legitimize support for oppressive rulers and unjust economic and political systems. That is why Marx and others said that religion was the opium of the people."

"My understanding of Jesus and his teachings is one of pacifism and nonviolence," I replied. "How does liberation theology fit with that revolutionary value?"

"It fits exactly!" he said. "In our context what is more radical and truly beneficial than to say that Jesus represents peace and nonviolence? He was the Prince of Peace, but he never promoted inaction. In fact, he was crucified for the political crime of challenging the rulers of his day. His charge was that he insisted that God, not Caesar, deserved ultimate obedience. It was the religious establishment of his day that was his greatest enemy."

It occurred to me that Reverend Naiim was constantly referring to the "prophetic function" of the church. What he meant
by that term had nothing to do with foretelling the future. It
meant playing the true prophetic role of calling out oppression
and urging people to repent from individual and social evil. He
was also concerned with finding the right hermeneutic to help
him interpret some of the dangerous and toxic stories in the Old
Testament, which seemed to justify violence and even ethnic
cleansing.

Everything that Reverend Ateek was saying sounded very much
like the discussions I'd had with the Sojourner community in the
United States. They, too, had spoken of the prophetic witness of the
church, though I did not remember them referring to it as liberation
theology.

"All it means is that how we practice our religion and read the
Bible should be relevant to our lives," said Reverend Ateek. "The
gospel should liberate, rather than enslave us. After all, Jesus said
'I came so that you might have life and that you might have it more
abundantly.'"

✧ ✧ ✧ ✧ ✧

Soon after, Naiim Ateek introduced me to Marc Ellis, a Jewish
liberation theologian. Marc was quite sympathetic to Naiim and to
the Palestinian cause in general. He had his own critique of Zionism
and the state of Israel, based on his ethical and moral understanding
of Judaism. He agreed with much of what Naiim was saying, based
on his own views of the Hebrew scriptures.

"You see," Naiim told me, "Liberation theology is not limited to Catholicism. There are even Jewish liberation theologians. Your work with human rights, for example, is an expression of your faith that God has created all people in His image, and that they are worthy of dignity, respect and human rights. That is also liberation theology."

Slowly the elements of a uniquely Palestinian liberation theology were beginning to emerge. Once I understood it, I was totally on board.

In the end, we established Sabeel, a Palestinian ecumenical movement that explored liberation theology from a Palestinian perspective. The Arabic word *sabeel* refers to "the path", or "the way." It is also a word for a "spring of water" from which passersby can get a refreshing drink on a hot day. One of the clearest elements of Palestinian liberation theology was its ecumenism. Palestinians from different denominations shared the same fears, concerns, and interpretations of Christ's teachings as they related to their experiences under occupation.

Our interests were not only political: we also yearned for the unity of the body of Christ, which was divided along denominational lines. In its effort to actively bring Christians together, Sabeel began to host a monthly breakfast for priests and leaders from different churches and even sought to arrange for them to occasionally exchange pulpits. Another element of reform that Sabeel was concerned with had to do with the tensions between the church hierarchy and the laity. Naiim was an Anglican canon—a ranking member of the clergy in the Episcopal Church. Many other priests and ministers from different denominations joined in the activities of Sabeel. Yet most of the heads of all de-nominations in Palestine were far removed from the concerns of their flock. While trying to remain respectful to the denomi-national leadership, Sabeel was clearly reflecting the interests and concerns of the laity and lower clergy of all the churches in Palestine.

A third and vital element for Sabeel was dealing with Chris-tian Zionism and its brand of theology. Naiim considered it to be a heresy. He felt that, in a sense, we were defending God himself against theologies that turn Him into a racist who favors one nation or tribe over others. We insisted on the Christian doctrine that God loves all mankind equally, regardless of race or ethnicity, and pointed to an important scripture in the New Testament: "For God so loved the *world* that he gave his only begotten son, that *whosoever* believes in him shall not perish, but shall have eternal life" (John 3:16). Christianity was not only universal in its appeal to all people, but also in its insistence that God is the Lord of the universe and is not restricted to a small piece of land in the Middle East. In that sense, the insistence on the sanctity of the land or the centrality of the Temple were elements that Christianity did away with twenty centuries ago, and it was heretical to revive them as Christian Zi-onism seemed to be doing.

My involvement with Sabeel spurred me to renew my contact with Jim Wallace and Sojourners. I shared with him, when he visit-ed Jerusalem and when I visited the U.S., about my work and about Sabeel. I also had an ulterior motive. I asked him to make me the correspondent for *Sojourners* magazine in Palestine and to issue me a press card as their correspondent.

While I did not do much active journalism on their behalf, there were times when I could whip out my journalist card at checkpoints or to get out of a mess, particularly before I finally got my Israeli Bar Association credentials.

During these years, many other new civil society organizations were being created, all of which were helping Palestinians deal with the occupation in one way or another. In addition to Sabeel, I helped to provide legal advice and structure to several other organizations.

Dr. Ron Sider, one of my professors from Messiah College, remained a close friend. During one of our many discussions about peace, nonviolence, and the Israel/Palestine situation, we talked about setting up a brigade of Christian peacemakers who would go into conflict situations like the Occupied Territories. They would use their presence to de-escalate violence in places of tension, even standing between combatants. The idea was fanciful and fantastic, but we both felt that if Christians were serious about peace and nonviolence, they should lead by example and put their lives on the line for peace. We lamented that the world never gave nonviolence a chance, because they did not see it in action nearly enough. Demonstrations, leaflets, or lobbying efforts for nonviolence and military de-escalation were no match for the military industrial complex which had massive resources in personnel, money, training, equipment, weapons, and war strategies.

A few years after our initial discussions on the subject, Dr. Sider decided to broach the subject publicly at the Mennonite World Conference. He challenged Mennonites, Quakers, and other Christians from the Anabaptist tradition to set up Christian Peacemaker Teams which would be sent around the world to "get in the way" of those who were fighting and to provide a Christian witness of peace, justice, and reconciliation. These Christian Peacemaker Teams (CPT) would follow Jesus in radical obedience.

"We must take up our cross and follow Jesus to Golgotha," said Ron. "We must be prepared to die by the thousands. Those who believed in peace by the sword have not hesitated to die. Proudly, courageously, they gave their lives. Unless we are ready to start to die by the thousands in dramatic and vigorous new exploits for peace and justice, we should sadly confess that we never really meant what we said, and we dare never whisper another word about pacifism to our sisters and brothers in those desperate lands filled with injustice. Unless we are ready to die developing new nonviolent attempts to reduce conflict, we should confess that we never really meant that the cross was an alternative to the sword."

The idea took root. Teams were eventually created and dispatched to a number of trouble spots including Colombia and Iraq, but also to Hebron in the West Bank.

I was contacted by CPT and asked for my involvement and advice. I readily agreed to be their attorney and to discuss all aspects of their activities with them. As far as the West Bank was concerned, I suggested that they not try to register as a local organization, but to enter as tourists on three-month tourist visas. If any of them were deported, others could take their place.

One of the first to arrive in Palestine with CPT was Art Gish, the author of The New Left and Radical Christianity, a book which had quite an impact on me at Messiah College. Together with a small group of volunteers whose number fluctuated between three and seven, the team took up residence in Hebron. Their initial goal was to observe and document the behavior of Israeli settlers, and to provide physical accompaniment to children going back and forth to school in Hebron's Old City and the nearby village of Atwan, in the south Hebron hills. School children were particularly vulnerable, as Jewish settlers would often attack them, beat them, or otherwise harass them.

CPT felt that their very presence as foreigners would provide a measure of protection, as the settlers would be less likely to attack foreigners who were peacefully walking with the children.

The organization was deliberately Christian and viewed their activity in that light. In addition to their own nonviolent methodology, they sought to teach the same to anyone else who would listen, whether Palestinian or Israeli. They also tried their best to be somewhat neutral, seeking to see the humanity of the settlers and to view their behavior as mistaken and in need of reform, rather than an evil which should be challenged. At the beginning, they would not even use their cameras to take photographs of human rights violations on the Sabbath, in order not to hurt the sensibilities of religious Jewish settlers. Over time, CPT's methodology evolved, and they saw the need to confront and challenge oppressive behavior rather than only seeking to timidly mediate and protect victims of oppression.

The settlers, on the other hand, never accepted or trusted CPT. They felt that CPT was a troublesome presence, so they tried to intimidate them by attacking them verbally and physically. They called them Nazis and terrorists. They would also spit on them, throw stones at them, or hit them with chains, sticks, and iron bars. The team members were trained to try to de-escalate such violence

THE TRUTH SHALL SET YOU FREE

by physically and nonviolently "getting in the way." They put their bodies on the line, meekly accepting the blows and anger of the settlers rather than retaliate with violence.

My own role with CPT started with taking a power of attorney from each member upon their arrival in Israel, so that in case of their arrest, I could demand to see them as their representative. This would happen frequently, though they were usually released after a few hours.

Whenever I got a phone call that the Israelis had arrested a member of CPT, I would quickly jump in my car and travel to Hebron. Often the CPT member would have been taken to the police station in the settlement of Kiryat Arba'.

One of the first cases I handled typified my ongoing interactions on their behalf with the Israeli police. When I arrived at the police station, I demanded to see my clients and asked what the charges were against them. The police officer said, "Assaulting a policeman."

I laughed out loud. "CPT is known worldwide for their insistence on nonviolence. They have come halfway across the world specifically because they *reject* violence. If you plan to charge them, you have to come up with something better than that charge, because you'll be laughed at and ridiculed even by your own judges." I also knew that it is standard police policy worldwide: when police arrest peaceful demonstrators, they usually tack on the claim that the demonstrators were resisting arrest and perhaps even assaulting the police. This is used to justify whatever force they use against demonstrators and helps to explain any bruises they may have given to them.

From time to time, Israel felt that they needed to take harsher measures against CPT. Sometimes members of that group were not only arrested but also deported. Other times they were identified at the airport and denied entrance to the country altogether.

In one such case, the police arrested a CPT volunteer in Hebron and decided to deport him. It just so happened that the previous day, this very same volunteer had jumped in front of an Israeli soldier to protect him from a Palestinian teenager who was coming at him with a knife. It was insane that the Israelis would want to deport him. I convinced the Mennonites that they should challenge the deportation and allow me to take the case to the High Court.

The position of the Israeli government was that he was a foreigner on a visitor's visa. As such, they had the right to cancel his visa and deport him any time they wished if his activities were not to their liking.

I argued that while the discretion of the Minister of Interior was indeed very broad, it had to be exercised reasonably and not arbitrarily. I argued that it was not rational to deport a man only because he consistently practiced peace and nonviolence—especially one who was willing to risk his own life to prevent an attack against an Israeli soldier.

While waiting for the case to be heard, I managed to get him out on bail, something almost never granted to a detained Palestinian. The case dragged on for many months. Eventually the CPT volunteer wanted to travel, and I managed to obtain an order to allow him to travel abroad with the proviso that he could return any time until the High Court ruled one way or another on his deportation decision. The Israeli government agreed, and he left the country.

Several months later, when he tried to return, he was denied entry. By then, the Mennonites were not interested in pushing the case any further. They had been reluctant to go to court in the first place and did not want to continue to fight the case now that the volunteer had left the country.

CHAPTER 10

AS I BEGAN TO ESTABLISH my practice, and was no longer a volunteer with MCC, I had to figure out my own position on money.

This was because I had grown up believing that money was evil. My father would often remind us that, "It is easier for a camel to go through the eye of a needle than for a rich man to go into heaven" (Matthew 19:24). In my mind there was a dichotomy: The love of God entailed self-denial, sacrifice, and frankly, poverty. This was contrasted with the ways of the world, which included the materialistic love of money.

I was raised to be suspicious of wealth and to trust God to supply all our needs. Landrum Bolling, an American Quaker and the head of the Tantur Ecumenical Institute, often called on me to talk to groups of scholars or visitors about the legal and human rights situation in the occupied territories. Tantur is a post-doctoral ecumenical extension of Notre Dame University. It sits on a lovely property at the entrance of Bethlehem. Because it was annexed into Israel when the Jerusalem municipality was enlarged, it became a convenient place for Israelis, Palestinians, and foreigners to meet and hold discussions, seminars, or lectures.

Landrum wanted me to meet a friend of his, a wealthy American-Catholic philanthropist named Jim Ryan. I wasn't sure what the meeting was about, but I agreed.

Before we got together, I learned that Jim made a lot of his money building modular homes with the Ryan Homes Corporation. He also raised racehorses. He had a particular gift for teaching management techniques to nongovernmental organizations. I got to know and love Jim and his wife Linda. They gave me a great appreciation of how God works with Christians of all denominations, and not just my own narrow evangelical church. They also helped me appreciate how money can be a great blessing. He used to say that money can be a vicious and cruel master, but it can also be a wonderful servant.

When we met, Jim started out talking cautiously to me, but soon launched into an aggressive diatribe about how the Catholic Church should be doing more for charity.

He said, "The Catholic Church is a very wealthy institution."

"Yes, it is," I readily agreed, and told him about the extent of their possessions and wealth in Palestine, including the Tantur Institute where we were meeting. It was sitting on valuable property which had been purchased by the Vatican and was greatly underutilized.

"The Catholic Church," he said, "is not doing nearly enough to alleviate the suffering in the Middle East, or the poor worldwide."

"I totally agree," I replied.

By the look on his face, I could tell he was surprised and relieved that I was sympathetic to his approach.

"I think," he said, "that the Church should be supporting several projects I have heard about in the Holy Land. As a good Catholic, I would be willing to participate and match the Church's contributions on a number of projects for up to $100,000, or maybe more."

"That's lovely," I replied.

He looked puzzled. "Have we agreed? Then let's do it!" He offered his hand for me to shake.

I was mystified. "Who, me?"

He said, "Yes, of course. You're the Apostolic Delegate from the Holy See, aren't you?"

I threw back my head and laughed out loud.

"Oh, no, I am not, Jim. I just left my MCC position where I was making twenty-five dollars a month. And now I'm just starting my legal practice. I'm a poverty-stricken lawyer. I'm in no position to match your generous contributions."

We became good friends on that day after another good laugh.

Jim and I were involved together with many humanitarian projects such as Operation Smile and the Qalandia Health Center. I also frequently translated for him when he gave lectures on management techniques.

This dovetailed perfectly with one of the persistent themes of my work, which was the need to communicate across language and cultural barriers. It was not an accident, therefore, that I would often be called upon to translate, and not only for Jim.

The results were sometimes hilarious.

When Gene Sharp, Harvard professor and expert on nonviolence, would give lectures to Palestinians, I would be called upon to translate for him. He would stand in front of his audience and speak in his flat crisp Boston accent, hardly moving his lips or lifting his head from his notes. By contrast, I would be translating in an agitated, expressive tone, gesticulating, using my hands and body, and often adding qualifying or interpretive phrases to bring the true meaning across. My translating sometimes took a bit longer than his sentences would warrant, and he would turn and look at me questioningly.

"I said all that?" he would sometimes ask me, amazed.

Another wonderful friendship that helped me rethink my views on wealthy Christians was a man named Robin Wainwright. He was an evangelical Christian who called me one day with a strange request. He wanted to marry his fiancée, Nancy, at the Church of the Nativity in Bethlehem. He had asked for help from the State Department, the American embassy in Tel Aviv, and the American Consulate in Jerusalem, but nobody could tell him how two American Christians could legally marry in Bethlehem.

Someone at the Consulate in Jerusalem, however, directed him to me. As a U.S. attorney who also practiced in Palestine, they thought I may be able to help him. As it turned out, I was probably the only person who knew the complicated interaction between the ecclesiastical and civil legal systems in the US, Israel, and in the occupied territories.

The couple were not young. They each had been previously married, and both had adult children. But they were clearly in love and wanted to marry in Bethlehem. I not only found a way for them to get married at the Lutheran church there, but also got the Greek Orthodox priest of the Church of Nativity to allow them to repeat their vows in his presence while he gave them his blessing.

I also played wedding planner. Even though the wedding took place at the height of the First Intifada, with frequent strikes and demonstrations, I found a place where they could rent a wedding gown and have it fitted for the bride. According to the traditional Palestinian wedding custom, I drove them throughout the deserted streets of Bethlehem in my own car while loudly honking the horn. In short, we became very good friends and continue to be so to this day.

The Wainwrights were big philanthropists and had a heart for the Middle East. Nancy had inherited a substantial sum from her father, who had made his money from a patent for a crucial valve used in hydraulic and oil-drilling equipment. They used the money to establish the Catlin Foundation, which supports various schools and other non-profit initiatives, with a special emphasis on the Middle East. They truly enjoyed blessing others generously with their wealth. It was a further lesson to me on how wealthy Christians could indeed be a blessing to others, and how my own warped views on money and wealth needed to change.

While I was taught that it was difficult for a rich man to enter heaven, the verse continues that with God, all things are possible. The Wainwrights and Jim Ryan were true examples of this.

Their behavior also contrasted with the views of many evangelical Christians who hardly knew we existed, and who, if they ever gave us a thought, would have stated that we did not even have the right to remain in Israel because God had granted it to "His people, the Jews" and not to "those violent Palestinians."

As a Christian and someone committed to truth, knowing that my brothers and sisters in the West were being deceived by a very skewed presentation of certain facts while having other facts hidden from them entirely, was a constant frustration.

CHAPTER 11

SOME YEARS LATER, at the approach of the turn of the millennium, Robin Wainwright had the idea of reenacting the Journey of the Magi from Iran, through Iraq and Syria, into Jordan, and across the Allenby Bridge crossing into the West Bank. As a modern pilgrimage, the group would travel by foot, camel, and donkey, arriving in Bethlehem around Christmas. His idea was that a group of modern pilgrims would retrace the original journey as much as possible. They would also bring gifts to share with ordinary people in the towns and villages they passed through on their way to Bethlehem, as a way to showcase the message of the Prince of Peace who was born there two thousand years earlier. Like the wise men who brought gifts to the infant Jesus, the modern Magi would also bring gifts such as helping to open kindergartens, clinics, digging wells, or meeting other needs of villages and communities they encountered along the way.

THE TRUTH SHALL SET YOU FREE

It was a beautiful, crazy idea.

They would need people in every country along the way to help them, not only with the logistics of maneuvering across the different borders, but also identifying hosts along the way who would benefit from gifts they brought with them. The Wainwrights planned to use some of their own wealth through the Catlin Foundation, as well as funds they hoped to raise from other philanthropists and royalties from a film they planned to shoot during the journey.

The group set out on foot, led by local guides as they made their way through each nation. They also hired camels, horses, or donkeys as they made their way across the various regions. They created quite a stir. Robin had a long white beard, and a flowing robe and carried a walking staff that made him look like an Old Testament prophet. He also had banners made with the ninety-nine names of God, according to Moslem tradition. Each day, the group would lift a banner with one of the names of God in beautiful calligraphy in Arabic and English as they marched, sang, prayed, and meditated their way all the way to Bethlehem. They planned to arrive on Christmas Eve, 2000. It was good to see an evangelical Christian who was also comfortable with and open to Moslems. Rather than treating Moslems as pagans whose God was anything other than the Hebrew-Christian God we know and worship, he was showing them respect and appreciation, while also sharing his own faith with them.

I was responsible for the permits and the logistics in Israel and the West Bank. I even joined the group in walking the last few miles into Bethlehem, joining, among others, my nephew Sami Awad, who had done most of the journey with the group.

One important spin-off from this modern-day Journey of the Magi was the strong relationship that developed between Robin and Nancy and Sami. They urged him to establish a new organization, the Holy Land Trust, which would serve the people of Bethlehem in a Christian spirit and carry out the nonviolence message and activism for which his uncle Mubarak had been deported. Robin, Nancy, and I helped establish the Holy Land Trust, and I became the chairman of the board, while Sami became the executive director.

Sami had a unique flair in his nonviolence activities. Like his uncle before him, he was totally committed to nonviolence. He was also creative in reaching audiences, both in Bethlehem and in the wider Palestinian community, as well as with Israelis and foreigners.

While his message was clearly Christian, he was very open to other traditions as well. In his personal life, he was much influenced by the spiritual message of mystics, Sufis, Buddhists, and even secular people. He had quite a few Jewish friends and was unafraid to start dialogue even with settlers.

One of the early activities of HLT was to commemorate the Massacre of the Innocents. This event in the traditional church calendar is rarely commemorated in the West. It falls on December 28, three days after Christmas, and recalls the tragedy of the hundreds of children massacred by Herod in his attempt to kill the baby Jesus (Mathew 2:16-18).

Sami was remarking how the children in Palestine are truly the innocents of today. They are bearing the brunt of fighting the occupation and suffering Israeli reprisals. As a result, they are very politicized and feel the need to be free of the occupation. They took

THE TRUTH SHALL SET YOU FREE

upon themselves the burden of resistance, which the adults are not up to carrying. One could admire their bravery and self-sacrifice, but on the other hand they were still children; they should instead be playing and enjoying their lives.

Palestinians are sometimes reluctant to celebrate Christmas and its joys, when so many of them are living out tragedies relating to the occupation or if their family has had a recent martyr. Sami thought that the occasion of the Massacre of the Innocents provided a good opportunity to commemorate the sorrow and the tragedy of lost childhood, and at the same time remember the message of the Prince of Peace, perhaps by providing some relief and fun to the children of Palestine. We wanted to bring them a message of hope and peace rather than sorrow, grief, and bitterness.

Holy Land Trust obtained permission from the Bethlehem municipality to carry out a number of events on that feast day. We erected a field of markers in Manger Square, each with the name a child who had been shot and killed by Israeli soldiers or settlers, his or her age, and the year the child was killed. We commemorated the child martyrs in a solemn procession, but then followed up with a full program of games, clowns and entertainment with various plays and shows. We also offered gifts to all the children, in celebration and honor of their lives.

In many struggles around the world, demonstrations are marked by dancing and singing. Not so much in Palestine. Nonviolent activism in Palestine often concentrated on the evil of the occupation and the need to resist it, becoming too serious and somber. Here was a different approach: a way to protest, be active and relevant to the situation, yet at the same time be joyful and playful, and allow children to be children. Sami knew that, as activists, we needed to be joyful and full of hope. This was to be a central theme of his nonviolent activism.

One day Sami led a protest against the closure of Bethlehem during Palm Sunday. Because Israel had annexed East Jerusalem, Palestinians from Bethlehem could not go the few miles to Jerusalem to celebrate Easter or Palm Sunday without a permit. Sami organized a group of people and rented a donkey from a farmer. They marched in a procession, carrying palm branches and singing "Hosanna!"

When they reached the gate at the wall, the soldiers saw the large group of marchers and they fled their post as the crowd surged in and kept marching towards Jerusalem. They were careful to stay peaceful. No one threw stones or took any action that the army would consider threatening. Instead of shouting slogans, they sang hymns and praises to God.

Very soon, the army and police reinforcements arrived and arrested a few people before turning the group around. They even arrested the donkey. After a few hours, they released everybody, but they kept the donkey. The owner was not pleased, and it took two days of pleading with the police before they agreed to give us back the donkey after charging us a fine of two hundred shekels.

Another time, Sami, wearing a Santa Claus suit, was arrested while trying to enter Jerusalem again on Christmas without a permit. He was released after a few hours, but the local papers had a field day with pictures of Santa Claus arrested by Israeli soldiers and denied entry into Jerusalem on Christmas.

If only this had been really humorous. It really wasn't.

Confronting a settler bulldozer at the village of El Jib

Rev. George Kuttab, Frocina, and their 7 children.

Standing with Sabri Ghrayyeb. Steadfast against
settlement encroachment on his land.

Introducing the Dalai Lama to Jerusalem dignitaries.

Brother Sam Kuttab and Mubarak Awad unsealing a house
sealed by Israeli authorities in open civil disobedience.

Removing police barricade protecting settler tent.

Removing settler tent with hateful graffiti—"Death to the Arabs".

Uprooted Olive trees from Khrab El Lahem being planted in
Jerusalem Municipality Park to "honor" Martin Luther King Jr.

Arguing with police at protest action in Jerusalem.

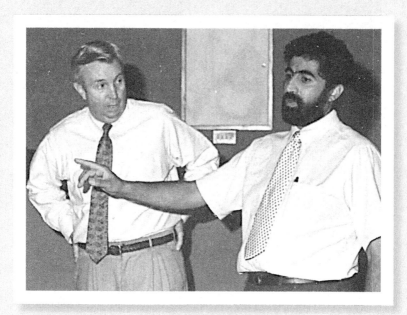

Translating for Jim Ryan.

CHAPTER 12

MY LAW OFFICE was in fact becoming the headquarters for a wide variety of public-interest projects, many of them having nothing to do with law *per se,* nor providing me any income either.

One such project was Operation Smile.

I was introduced by Jim Ryan to this wonderful project whereby plastic surgeons, mostly from the United States, would contribute their time and expertise to go on missions of one week or so to some developing country to perform free surgeries, particularly on children with Clubfoot, or Cleft Palate problems. Such children are usually born with such deformities, and live their lives in misery and suffering, their families rarely able to cover the cost of the surgeries needed to give them a quality life. Dr. Maghee, and his wife, who founded this charity, have developed a process to perform many of these complex surgeries in record time, completing each surgical operation in about 45 minutes, instead of the usual 3 hours it would ordinarily take and with fantastic results that brought smiles back to the faces of children. Funding from generous donors ensured that the expenses and materials were also covered, and the services were offered free of charge.

We certainly could use their services in Palestine, but the project required a lot of advance preparation to advertise the service, prescreen the cases, and prepare a local hospital so that when the surgeons arrived, they could immediately perform many surgeries in one week, and return to their own regular practices in the United States. They would also provide some training for local surgeons and nurses so that they could perform some of the surgeries and other services themselves in the future.

How could I say no? I immediately contacted several local organizations as well as the Augusta Victoria Hospital, a Lutheran hospital in East Jerusalem. I knew it was almost hopeless to get permission to perform these surgeries in the areas of the West Bank and Gaza under military government control, but since Jerusalem had been "annexed", I felt there should be no problem doing it there. I even wrote to the Israeli Health Ministry. Initially the Ministry said they wanted the project to be undertaken in West Jerusalem, at the Hadassah Hospital—which would have defeated the whole purpose, as Israel is not by any stretch of the imagination a "developing country". It has a well-functioning universal health system for Israelis and was not in need of Operation Smile. It was the Palestinian community that needed those services. So, we proceeded with our plans. I just made sure I wrote to the Health Ministry and kept them informed of the upcoming Mission. I got no reply.

I gathered a number of organizations to plan the first mission. There was a lot of enthusiasm, and they wanted to set up committees: One for contacting other hospitals, and preparing the cases; one for publicity; one for providing hospitality to families of patients, particularly those coming from Gaza or faraway villages; one to provide transportation for the Team from their hotel to the Augusta Victoria and back; etc... I knew at once that naming individuals to each committee, and providing "balance" to make sure everyone was represented would be a nightmare. Committees had to have geographic representation, as well as "political" representation of the different factions. I therefore proposed a different model: I proposed instead of committees that we use the "point person" method. We would entrust organizations, each one to appoint a "point person" for a specified activity-instead of a committee. That organization/person would draw on other members of the group as needed to carry out the functions entrusted to it. For example, the YWCA would oversee care for the families; Catholic Relief Services, whose headquarters was in Jerusalem, and who had access to vehicles, would coordinate transportation, and so on. It worked marvelously, and we were able to organize and process over 300 cases of patients to be operated upon.

One week before the Operation was to start, the Israeli Health Ministry contacted the Augusta Victoria saying they cannot have the operations, and would send policemen to the hospital to prevent the operations from taking place. Under Israeli law, they said, no person who is not licensed by them as a doctor can operate anywhere in Israel without violating the law. They would allow a duly qualified foreign surgeon to operate in Israel with a temporary license but only at a "teaching hospital" like Hadassah. Not at the Augusta Victoria!!!!

I went into full activity mode. As in other situations I knew I had to use the law, diplomacy, lobbying, and the threat of publicity to try and get the "approval" of the Israeli authorities. I pointed out that I had informed the Ministry of Health months in advance, and even sent them a reminder two weeks before the arrival of the team but got no answer from them. I used Israeli contacts in the Knesset, and the Labor Party to pressure the Minister of Health. I pointed out that the surgeons of Operation Smile had impeccable world-renowned credentials, and that I had offered to send copies of their credentials to the Ministry of Health in advance. I told them that I had already enlisted ABC and CBS who were sending teams of TV journalists to report on the event, and that children with cleft palates would be very photogenic. Pictures of their distorted faces as they were turned away from the free services by Israeli policemen would not give Israel a good image on US Television. The Team had already left the US and was arriving that evening. Children were already prepped and had fasted in preparation for the operations the next day.

A famous Jewish doctor from New York, who was part of the Team and who had arrived the night before offered to go with me to the Ministry of Health. He said he and his family were big contributors to Jewish charities in the US and would have a difficult time explaining why Israel would not let him and his colleagues operate on Palestinian children.

In the end, the Israelis relented, and told me I should go to the Health Ministry and obtain a "temporary license" for the doctors from the health minister. They said that their only concern was that we do not claim that Israel was not capable technically of carrying out similar operations in Israeli hospitals.

As it turned out, the health minister was away in Latin America, so I was to meet his Deputy, who was an Arab. At that time, I believe he was the highest-ranking Arab serving in any government position in Israel.

I went to his office, and while I was waiting to be ushered in, his Jewish "office manager"' who seemed to have a lot of authority came over and sat next to me, and began in a transparently friendly manner, to question me. Who was I? and how was this medical mission organized? and why we were not holding the event at Hadassah or some other Jewish hospital? It felt very much like a Secret Service interrogation, but I had nothing to hide, and answered her truthfully. She seemed to be satisfied and allowed me to enter and meet with the Deputy Minister, after she first went in and talked to him, and presumably told him it was OK to give me the needed permit.

I met with the Deputy Minister, explained again why I needed the "permit". I said all I needed was a simple letter saying they do not object to this delegation of surgeons operating on a one-time basis on cleft palate patients at Augusta Victoria Hospital, and that this did not reflect in any way that Israel lacked the capacity to perform such services at its own hospitals in West Jerusalem. After he agreed to give the letter, I offered to do the typing myself, since I needed the permit in English and it may be easier for me to do the typing than his staff, who were quite proficient in Hebrew and Arabic, but perhaps not in English. He agreed, and in a few minutes, I had typed out the one paragraph letter on Ministry stationary.

I gave the letter to his secretary to take it in for him to sign, but the "Office Manager" intercepted the secretary and said in Hebrew (which she did not know I understood, since I only spoke to her in English) "He cannot sign anything before I see it. Let me see it first". Only after she read it, did she give it back to the secretary to take it in for the signature of the Deputy Minister. That confirmed what I thought from the minute I walked into his office. Even at that exalted level, he was just a token Arab presence. The real power, when the Minister was away, did not lie with him, but with his "office manager".

The Mission was a great success. About 250 children were successfully operated upon, and several nurses and doctors received practical training in the latest techniques for that type of surgery. The next year and the year after that, similar missions were conducted with equally good results. They also discovered that the greater needs in plastic surgery were for treatment of burns. Apparently, a lot of children and adults get severe burns from use of kerosine stoves in the cramped refugee camps, but such burns were far more difficult to treat, and required continuing care, and could not usually be handled by speedy operations from visiting plastic surgeons as in cleft palette cases.

The question arises from time to time. What was I doing with Operation Smile, or other such projects? They had nothing to do with law, really, or even human rights. Was this my way of dealing with the controversy of "social gospel, versus saving souls? In my mind, it was simple. I had the ability, the connections, and the vision to do something to help needy people. Whether they were victims of the occupation, or human rights violations, or poverty, or other suffering, I wanted to help. This gave meaning and purpose to my life. I saw it as God's work, even though the activities were not being done through the churches or with a boldly Christian motif.

The most immediate and pressing need however, was in fact in my field of expertise.

Palestinians have a very high rate of incarceration. According to Palestinian estimates, seventy percent of Palestinian families have had one or more close family members who served time in Israeli prisons as a result of activities against the occupation. About forty percent of all adult males in the West Bank have been arrested or detained at one time or another. Most incarcerated Palestinians are not in prison because they are criminals, but because the system itself is against them. Often it is the most honest, public-minded, and best elements of our society who end up in jail. Most of those who are in jail are honored by the community when they are released, because they are seen as people who were willing to suffer and put their lives on the line for freedom.

Palestinian and Israeli attorneys can do very little of a legal nature within the Israeli military court system. However, they are allowed to visit prisoners once they are sentenced. While the Israeli system occasionally allows for family visits under certain circumstances, such visits are rare and severely controlled. A lawyer representing a prisoner, however, usually has much easier access.

For this reason, one of the few things that a lawyer could do for a prisoner was to simply conduct a visit to provide prisoners with access to the outside world. We could bring them news of their family and take the prisoners' messages back home. Prisoners looked forward to such visits and referred to lawyers as their "lungs," bringing them mental, emotional, and spiritual oxygen.

I felt that we needed to set up a new organization which concentrated on the needs of prisoners. After seeing what they experienced while incarcerated, I was motivated by the teachings of Jesus concerning those who are incarcerated, because he said, "I was sick or in prison, and you did not visit me. Inasmuch as ye have failed to do this for one of those the least my brethren, you have failed to do it for me" (Matthew 25:36). It was as clear a mandate as any Christian could have. The Bible specifically says that on Judgement Day we will be asked whether we visited prisoners, the sick, and others of vulnerable status. If we did not, our Lord will tell us that we have failed him in his hour of distress.

I discussed this idea with Reverend Naiim Ateek as well as one of my colleagues, Ahmad Assayyad. They were both very supportive. The result was the creation of a new non-profit corporation, which we called the Mandela Institute for Palestinian Political Prisoners. Because the fight for freedom and equality is universal, we named it after Nelson Mandela who was still incarcerated in South Africa at the time.

In establishing the Mandela Institute, Reverend Naiim and I were both motivated by our Christian faith. Even so, the organization we created was secular—with Ahmad, a Moslem, and me acting as initial directors. Ahmed's wife, Butheina Duqmaq, also a lawyer, became very involved as well. She made serving and visiting prisoners her life commitment. In fact, she hardly ever went to regular courts, but determined to put all her energy into visiting prisoners.

Many an early morning found me picking up Butheina in my car. We would stop to gather additional supplies before making the long drive to Nafha prison in the Negev Desert. We would spend the whole day dealing with the Israeli Army bureaucracy, waiting, being searched and questioned, until we eventually succeeded in meeting at least some of the prisoners on our list. We would usually fax a list of twenty prisoners, the maximum allowed, ahead of time, although we would generally only have access to meet five or ten of them.

We never knew if the authorities would deny that some of the prisoners were at that particular prison. Sometimes they would state that no visitors were allowed for a particular prisoner. Other times we would be questioned as to the authenticity of our legal credentials or our powers of attorney. In the end we would be allowed to visit some prisoners, each for ten or fifteen minutes. We would quickly jot down notes about their situation, get the phone numbers of family members they wanted us to contact, and inform them of any packages we had left with the prison authorities for them.

I never ceased to be amazed at the morale and resiliency of the prisoners. Most could not even tell us what the specific charges were against them. They would just say "security charges" or name the organization they were charged with membership in—usually Fatah or Popular Front.

One man in Lydda prison was serving multiple life sentences. He arrived for our interview wearing three hats on top of each other.

Very curious, I asked, "What is your story?"

It turned out that the prison commander had once seen him wearing a hat in the prison yard and ordered him to take it off. He refused, so he was placed in solitary confinement for a week. When he went out, he wore two hats on top of each other. The prison commander again asked him to take his hats off, and again he refused. Off he went for a whole month of solitary confinement. When he was let out, he put three hats on and marched around in them. The prison commander finally gave up, and Ahmad started wearing three hats from then on. He may have been in prison, but his spirit remained free and his will indomitable.

On the long drive back from prison, usually in the late hours of the evening, I would dictate our report to Butheina, as well as letters to family members or interventions with the Red Cross on behalf of a particular prisoner. If we had a phone number, we would also make telephone calls to reassure the family about the conditions of their children in prison.

We would arrive at her home at ten or eleven at night and her husband, who later became the head of the Bar Association in the West Bank, would be waiting for us with a cup of coffee after having put their two children to bed. I was grateful that her husband fully appreciated and supported the efforts we were making.

Given the stereotypes of Moslems in the West, it would surprise many Americans to know that a Moslem man would allow his devout wife to spend the entire day alone with another man who also happened to be a Christian. But our friendship and mutual trust were very high, and we were determined to serve the prisoners above everything else.

It is customary during the Moslem Feast of Al Adha that authorities will allow packages, and supplies of olive oil, dry goods, and other canteen provisions to be brought into prison. Many Moslem charities take advantage of the feast holidays to bring in supplies which are much appreciated and needed by the prisoners, to supplement their miserable prison fare. I thought it would be appropriate if Christian churches also provided some assistance to prisoners during our religious holiday.

During the First Intifada, many Palestinians were being held in a tent camp in the Negev Desert. It gets very cold at night in the desert. As many as five thousand prisoners were kept in one such prison, called Ketzi'ot. Palestinians called it Ansar III. (Ansar I was the prison camp that the Israelis had erected in Lebanon, and Ansar II was the name given to their massive prison in Gaza). Most of these prisoners were administrative detainees, without any charges or trial. Quite a few were Christians from Beit Sahour, a town near Bethlehem.

I thought we could get Christian churches to donate woolen hats and scarves at Christmas, but I recognized that collecting the donations was only half the battle. The bigger battle would be to convince the Israeli prison authorities to permit the donation. Sure enough, when we managed to raise the funds for the scarves and hats, the Israeli prison authorities said they would not allow them in. We brought an action before the Israeli High Court and as a result we reached an agreement. We would be allowed to bring in the scarves, provided that they were of a certain length and one color—navy blue. The requirement for the hats was that they should be too short to cover the face. It was a compromise we gladly accepted.

In time, I would discontinue my involvement with the Mandela Institute, but by then it had become an independent organization, well respected in the Palestinian community. I am pleased to report that the organization continues to exist and thrive and serve the community and Butheina continues to be active within the organization.

Meanwhile, the cry for legal services continued—with many heart-wrenching cases to be dealt with.

I heard about one case in which a man was ordered to pay the equivalent of a $2000 fine, because his daughter was caught by settlers as she returned home from school. They alleged that she had been throwing stones at them. She was eleven years old, so even under Israeli military orders she could not be put in jail, as the age of criminal responsibility was twelve. Instead, they arrested her father, a baker, and ordered him to pay the exorbitant fine or go to jail for one month.

A new military order authorized the military government to order the parents of a child who threw rocks at soldiers to be fined for the actions of his child. If they could not pay the fine, they would go to prison.

This case was not unusual, as many Palestinians, who are largely unarmed, resort to throwing stones at settlers and soldiers. In turn, whenever stone-throwing occurs, the soldiers or settlers chase any children they see—sometimes, clearly, trying to provoke an incident. They arrest whomever they catch, whether they were throwing stones or not. So common was the imposition of fines for stone-throwing that Palestinians called it the "stone tax."

I felt that this particular military order went even beyond the

collective punishment authorized by the Emergency Defense Regulations, and that we needed to challenge the order itself at the
High Court.

While Israel does not have a constitution, it prides itself on
having an independent judiciary and a greatly respected High
Court. The High Court, we were told, is not reluctant to criticize and even annul illegal actions of the government and pieces
of legislation that it considers to be violating basic principles
of justice.

I decided to take the case to a law professor at Hebrew University, Dr. David Kretchmer, to discuss whether we could bring a
test case before the High Court and challenge the legality of this
military order.

Dr. Kretchmer was a kippah-wearing religious Jew from South
Africa, active in civil rights. He is very progressive in his views,
having left South Africa because of his opposition to apartheid. A
supporter of Peace Now, he later became the head of the Association for Civil Rights in Israel (ACRI) which is like the ACLU in the
United States.

Dr. Kretchmer said that while Israel never had a case where the
Israeli High Court struck down a military order, he thought that
ours was an excellent case. He opined that the standard of review
over military orders, which are treated as administrative actions
of the Defense Minister, would be more favorable to us than that
applying if we were challenging legislation of the Knesset. The military orders were the result of a decision by the military commander,
a mere agent of the Defense Ministry, whereas Knesset laws were
the result of a deliberative process by the democratically elected

legislature, and therefore could not as easily be overturned by the High Court. At least that was our reasoning. We also had an array of arguments under international law to use.

Nonetheless, Dr. Kretchmer warned me, the Israeli High Court had never done too well in issues relating to the rights of Palestinians in politically sensitive cases that could be labeled as related to "security."

"If this were the case of a commercial dispute between a Jew and an Arab over an unpaid bill, we could expect the Court to be strictly neutral and professional," he said. "But when political issues are involved, such as rights to land, legality of settlements, or actions by the Israeli army are concerned, we should temper our expectations."

While Israeli courts are independent and free from any pressures by the government, they can also be independently racist and fully supportive of a Zionist agenda. They can be even more creative than the government in finding legal justifications for its actions against Palestinians. Indeed, most Palestinians have little or no expectations from the Israeli courts, and many boycott them. In fact, when they learn of my work, they would often quote the Arabic proverb to me: "If your opponent is the judge, to whom do you plead your cause?"

I, on the other hand, felt that it was imperative to give the Israeli courts the benefit of doubt, and to challenge them to be as good as the ideals they purport to espouse.

If we failed, which seemed likely, we could at least say we tried, and could expose the lie about "Israeli justice" to the whole world. Failure to bring our case to the Court could send the message that we did not have a strong case. It would bolster the Israeli claims that they did not steal our land or oppress our people, since we never complained about it to the courts at all. Unless we could show that the courts themselves were part of the problem, Israel would continue to get away with everything it was doing, while claiming to be an orderly democracy. Israel constantly claimed that its actions were monitored and controlled by an independent judiciary, and that Palestinians had full access to its courts—so what was the problem?

The experience of bringing cases before the High Court provided an additional benefit for me. It helped me deal with my own negative feelings towards Israeli Jews and to see them as people, rather than reducing them to a faceless "enemy."

In addition to David Kretchmer, I came to know and like many other Israelis. But it was still shocking for me to realize that in a few years his son, Jonathan, would become a soldier. Jonathan was a sensitive and intelligent boy, a vegetarian on principle from a young age. I could not imagine him as a soldier who could very well end up doing his army service by patrolling in Bethlehem or Ramallah. How would I feel about him then? Very few Israelis refused to serve in the army, though some brave ones at least refused to serve in the occupied territories. Most Israelis, however, were not pacifist, and saw fighting in the army as their normal duty and an obligatory service to their nation. Baffling to me, they could not see that Palestinians felt the same need to serve and fight for their homes and lands and nation as well.

Nonetheless, I embraced my connections with Israeli liberals. I felt we could be real allies in fighting for justice, and for peace.

Law—even Israeli law—could perhaps be an instrument in that joint fight.

As expected, we lost that case and many others before the Israeli High Court. The court did not even bother to give an elaborate reasoned decision but simply said it did not see a reason to substitute its judgement for the judgement of the Military Commander who issued the Military Order.

CHAPTER 13

IN ADDITION TO THOSE High Court cases, there was still the daily grind of representing Palestinians in regular military courts, which is the bulk of the work of many West Bank lawyers.

Looking back now, I can say unequivocally that appearing before an Israeli military court to defend a Palestinian is one of the most frustrating experiences for a defense attorney. In reality, there is little or nothing that you can do on a professional level. The outward formalities of a regular court are maintained, and the burden of proof is supposed to be on the military prosecutor, who needs to prove guilt beyond a reasonable doubt. There is also the possibility of appeal to a higher military court. In real life, however, these formalities are a facade. A practically insurmountable burden to prove innocence is on the defense attorney. Appeals, if filed, rarely go anywhere. More often it is the military prosecutor who will appeal a judgement he finds too lenient. The structures of the military court system are fixed, they are neither objective nor neutral, and they do not produce any justice for Palestinian defendants.

In practice, no case is brought to court before the prosecutor has in his files "confessions" admitting to the alleged offenses at his disposal. He uses those confessions to prepare the charge sheet, and he lists the accusations simply by referring to the said confessions and matching them with sections of the military orders that the Palestinian is accused of violating. Rarely is any material evidence produced or witnesses heard and cross-examined, as one would expect in a normal trial. The prosecution file consists almost entirely of the "confessions" of the defendant, as well as the "confessions" any co-defendants who have implicated him. These "confessions" are handwritten in Hebrew by the interrogators.

At the beginning of my career, I sought to use every channel possible to challenge the confessions, knowing that they were extracted under torture. Those were the days before the knowledge of Israeli torture of Palestinians was in the open and "legal." The secrecy regarding the use of torture made these trials even more frustrating.

The law used in the military courts provides the basic right for defendants to have access to a lawyer, at least in theory. Nevertheless, the same law also permits Israeli authorities to deny lawyers access to their clients if they think that such access could disrupt an "ongoing investigation." As both defense and prosecutors in the military court system know, this "exception" became the rule.

It gets even worse. Defense lawyers are routinely denied access to their clients until their interrogation period is over—after they "confess." Statements of confession are invariably taken during the period of interrogation, when the defendant has no access to a lawyer, family, or other prisoners. Thus, the statement of the interrogator who takes the confession—the "technical witness"—cannot be seriously challenged.

In military court, defense lawyers have two choices: we can either accept the confession or try to challenge it. If one wants to challenge the admissibility of the confession, the first step is to insist on the presence of the technical witness/ interrogator in court. But if we make the challenge, our chances of success are minimal to none, and our client will receive a much harsher sentence. Prudent lawyers, as I was to learn, did not bother with this option.

In the beginning, though, I took the matter seriously and insisted on the appearance of the technical witnesses. After all, there are few other defenses that can be made to the court. I knew that my demand irritated the judges and prosecutors. Nevertheless, they would invariably comply and set a new date for the hearing when the witnesses would appear.

At the new hearing, I would ask the interrogators why the confession was taken in Hebrew since the defendant did not know Hebrew. I would remind them of their own laws: that the Israeli High Court had ruled that confessions should preferably be in the language—and even the dialect—of the defendant.

The interrogators would uniformly testify under oath that while they knew Arabic well enough to speak and translate, their written Arabic was not that good. The fact that the Supreme Court only strongly advised but did not require that the "confessions" be in the language of the defendant meant that they could safely ignore it. Thus, they only used Hebrew in writing down the purported confessions.

Unless I wanted to really escalate and challenge the admissibility of the confession itself, there was not much more I could do. The confession, whether of the defendant or someone else who implicated him in their confession, would be admitted and used as the primary if not sole basis for the judgment of the court.

If I insisted on challenging the admissibility of the confession, I would also need to ask for a mini trial (*mishpat zuta*) solely on the admissibility of the document. The mini trial is held in secret. The public is removed from the courtroom, and the court is held in private.

Such a mini trial would typically go like this: the defendant would testify under oath about the torture and physical abuse he had been subjected to. He would insist that the statements he made in the "confession" were untrue and were extracted after days of sleep deprivation, beatings, position abuse, and outright torture. He would explain how he would eventually break down, and "confess" to whatever the interrogator wanted. Then a different officer would come in and take down the confession statement and get his signature. If he refused to sign the statement, he would be sent back to the original interrogator, and his torture would resume, until he was ready to sign the document. The court would then listen to the soldier/policeman who took the confession, and who would deny the whole thing, and insist that the confession was voluntary. His testimony would be invariably preferred to the testimony of the prisoner, who would be viewed as a biased interested party trying to avoid a penalty and trying to besmirch the reputation of Israel and its army.

Defense lawyers are actively discouraged from asking for a mini trial. We are openly told that if our client should retract his confession in court, thus forcing a mini trial and the confession be nonetheless accepted—which invariably would happen, even after the mini-trial—that our client would get a much more severe sentence for wasting the time and energy of the court.

Therefore, as lawyers, our professional duty and obligation to our client dictated that we simply accept the confessions of our clients as such and try to get the best deal we could from the military prosecutor. The best we could do would be to negotiate a plea-bargaining deal, under which one or more charges would be reduced. Another possible tactic would be to agree to a specific sentence and then leave it to the court to confirm it.

To this day, this is how ninety-nine percent of all the military court cases are handled. There is no real trial. Even more discouraging, conviction is a foregone conclusion in virtually all cases.

As the role of torture in the whole process became clear to me, I was forced to accept that I could do little in the military courts themselves. Rather than hoping to obtain justice for my clients in Israeli military courts, I would need to expose the human rights issue of torture through meticulous documentation and analysis with Al Haq.

Nevertheless, we defense lawyers still needed to go to court to represent clients and to monitor what was happening there. Every once in a while, we would achieve a simple victory. We could not hope to get an actual acquittal, but we counted it a success if we were able to play the system enough to get a small reduction for one of our clients.

One such client, a middle-aged man named Mahmoud El Ramahi, (Abu Ayman) was arrested along with a number of young people from Jalazoun refugee camp, near Ramallah. He was active in many social programs at the camp, and therefore a target. He denied all charges, but his name appeared in the confessions of other members of the group. When I spoke with him, he told me that the Israeli Shin Bet officer in charge of the refugee camp was convinced that he was an influential member of Fatah. The officer told him that he was going to get him and throw the book at him.

He shook his head in disgust. "They think I am the head of Fatah at the camp. I have no idea what punishment they are planning for me. Just see what you can do. I have confessed to nothing despite being tortured for weeks. But they will use the confessions of others against me, I am sure."

The charge sheet indicated that Mr. Ramahi would be tried before a three-judge panel, which has no limits on the penalties it can mete out. This is in contrast to the usual single-judge panel, which was limited at that time to a maximum of five-year sentences. The charge sheet contained a long list of charges arising from an incident where a Molotov cocktail had been thrown at an Israeli army jeep near the camp. It contained charges of terrorism, membership in an illegal organization, conspiracy to commit murder, arson, damage to property, recruiting others, and more.

The first hearing at the military court was a routine technical hearing before a single judge. At this hearing, the judge was supposed to hear the accused person's plea and set the date for the actual trial, which would be held before a three-judge panel.

I noticed that the military prosecutor handling the hearings that day was clearly young and inexperienced. He had a pile of about forty files before him and appeared to be overwhelmed with work. That gave me an idea. I told Mr. Ramahi that we could surprise the military prosecutor by telling him that he was ready to change his plea on the condition that he be tried and sentenced that same day. I would not haggle over the charges nor request that they be reduced. Rather, we would simply plead guilty as charged, and accept the charge sheet.

"Look," I told him, "at a hearing before a single judge, the sentence usually consists of several components: an actual prison sentence and a suspended sentence to ensure that you will not commit any security offence after you are released. Maybe also a fine. A judge could sentence you to three years actual imprisonment and two years suspended. Or he could sentence you to four years actual and one year suspended. The maximum penalty is five years of actual imprisonment, without any suspended sentence. But as a single judge, he can do no more than that."

"What do you think would happen differently," he replied, "if we waited and had our trial before the regular court?"

"Well, the Shin Bet probably would want the court to treat the case as an attempted murder and terrorism. We both know that they will convict you, even though you did not sign a confession. It will be on the basis of the confessions they extracted from other people, which are in your file. They may send you away for fifteen or twenty years. But if we move right now, the judge may not even look to other cases to determine the "going price" for similar offenses nor take any mitigating factors into consideration, such as the fact that no one was actually hurt, and it was a military target that was allegedly attacked. This is probably your best option."

"Fine," he said. "Go for it. I know they have it in for me, and who can stop them?"

I made the offer to the military prosecutor, who was a bit surprised that I did not try to bargain with him to reduce the charges. I told him that my client just wanted to get this over with. The prosecutor agreed and presented the plea bargain to the judge, who pronounced the conviction and then ordered a brief recess to consider the penalty. I presumed he was going to consult with the Shin Bet before he ruled on the penalty. Even though it was highly improper for him to do so, we all knew that that is what happens. He came in five minutes later, clearly agitated, and glared at the prosecutor before giving Mr. Ramahi the maximum sentence of five years of actual imprisonment and no suspended sentence.

But that was not the end of the story. After her husband was put in jail, Mrs. Ramahi visited my office and told me that the authorities had sealed off their small home in the Jalazoun refugee camp. It was an additional punishment for his alleged crimes.

Since their home was small and in the midst of the densely populated refugee camp, the Israelis could not dynamite it, so they sealed it off instead. Mrs. Ramahi told me the new situation would be a great hardship because her daughter, Samah, had a kidney problem. She needed good hygiene and constant medical attention, which was very hard to provide in the make-shift shelter to which the family moved.

I told her there was nothing I could do as a lawyer, since the Israeli High Court had ruled again and again that such actions, whether house demolitions or sealings, were valid administrative actions and within the discretion of the Military Commander. They did not require any court action or even proof of guilt.

This type of collective punishment was one of the issues where Israeli law clearly departed from international law and norms of justice. It was perfectly fine to punish the family, neighbors, or whole communities for the alleged transgressions of one member. In contrast to this approach, I remembered the teaching of the Bible: "No longer shall it be said that when the fathers eat sour grapes, the teeth of the children will be set on edge. Everyone will be responsible for their own transgressions" (Jeremiah 39:21).

Mrs. Ramahi said, "I know you cannot help me as a lawyer, but Samah, my daughter, needs a very rare medicine that is only available in one pharmacy in West Jerusalem. Now that my husband is in jail, I will never be able to get a permit to go to West Jerusalem to get this medicine. Do you think you can get it for us?"

From that time on, my wife and I would obtain the monthly medicine for Samah and visit her family in Jalazoun refugee camp frequently.

Collective punishment turned out to be another of the main issues that we tackled in Al Haq as a human rights violation. But as a lawyer, just as with the issue of torture, there was nothing I could do about it in Israeli courts.

The path of my life from this point on was becoming clear. My Christian commitment to serve was fully synchronized with my national commitment to resist the occupation. I would do so as a lawyer, not just in the courts, but more importantly through my human rights work with Al Haq. I did not seek to become rich but in fact enjoyed great fulfillment, as I felt that I was doing important work that served God as well as my country. My ability to explain our situation to foreign journalists as well as visiting dignitaries was an important part of my mission. I could explain, from my own experience and legal practice, exactly how the system worked, and could complain about the injustice in international human rights terms. My job as a lawyer was not going to get any easier, but I could still find positive and rewarding things and not get bogged down in the despair that military courts can engender.

CHAPTER 14

▬

ONE DAY I RECEIVED A CALL from World Vision, an international Christian charitable organization. One of their Palestinian employees had been arrested by the Israelis and they wanted me to defend him. I made some calls and discovered that he had been issued a six-month administrative detention order. There would be no charges or trial.

Administrative detention is a frustrating aspect of defending Palestinian clients in the military courts. Under these orders, issued through the Emergency Defense Regulations, a Palestinian can be detained without charges for up to six months. The sentence is renewable indefinitely at the discretion of the military governor.

Nevertheless, Israel does have a legal procedure to object to and seek redress when a person is issued an administrative detention order. I decided to try it.

On the appointed date, I traveled to the Israeli military base in the Negev which housed the military court where the hearing was going to take place. I brought the country representative of World Vision and a translator who would be interpreting for him with me, since the hearing would be in Hebrew. After waiting for a long time, we were ushered into the courtroom. As usual, I went to the left side of the courtroom where the lawyer for the defendant in a military court usually sits. When I got there, I was told that I was in the wrong place, and that I should be on the right side because I was the person who was initiating the procedures.

The court clerk, a Druze soldier who doubled as the court translator, had a smirk on his face.

"This is not a trial and there are no charges," he said. "You are the one who is challenging the administrative detention order. Therefore, you are the one who needs to start the procedures. You need to sit on the right with your client."

As I picked up my papers to move, he continued. "The representative of the army will sit on the left and will defend against the action you are bringing."

It was easy to see that the army representative was actually a Shin Bet officer in plain clothes.

Soon the judge, who was a military officer, came in. We stood up as one would in a regular court. He appeared to be kind and intelligent. He took his seat, waved for us to sit down, and then looked straight at me. "Mr. Kuttab, you may proceed. What do you have to say?"

I stood. "What do I have to say? I have nothing to say. My client is innocent. He has done nothing. I see no reason why he is in jail, and I have no idea what we are doing here today at all. There is no charge sheet and there is no evidence. I do not know what he is accused of, and I cannot refute what I do not know." And I sat down again.

The judge nodded and turned to the other side. The prosecutor stood, holding a thin file that appeared to contain only one sheet of paper—probably my objection. "What I have to say, I want to say to the court alone," he said. "Not in the presence of the objector or his attorney."

I jumped to my feet. "This is ridiculous! How can I defend my client if I don't even know what the charges are against him or why he is being imprisoned? If the prosecutor thinks that my client met with an enemy agent on a particular date, perhaps I could show that he was somewhere else on that date, or that the person he allegedly met with has been dead for fifteen years. If the army believes that he has written slogans on a wall, I may be able to show that he is illiterate and cannot write at all."

The judge said, "But your client is not being accused of violating any law or military order. This is just an administrative detention."

"Well, I need to know why he is being detained so that I can disprove or otherwise convince you that he should not be in prison. For all I know it could simply be a matter of a mistaken identity," I replied.

"I totally sympathize with you, Mr. Kuttab," said the judge. "It is like boxing in the dark. However, this is what the law says, and we have to obey the law."

I had recently learned from an attorney in South Africa that even there they did not have such a procedure. What we experienced in the occupied territories would not even pass muster in the courts of apartheid South Africa.

THE TRUTH SHALL SET YOU FREE

"It is a shame to have such a law in the occupied territories. Even in apartheid South Africa, there is no such a law!"

"Ah, but we also have a similar law in Israel. This is not just a matter for military courts and the occupied territories."

"It is a shame for Israel, then, as well."

"That is why we have a hundred and twenty men and women in the Knesset who write the laws in Israel. We are a country of law."

"It is a shame, then, for each and every one of these hundred and twenty men and women."

"It is what it is. I hereby order that the proceeding continue *en camera*. Please leave the room with your client. Everyone else leave the courtroom, as well."

"Are you going to be presenting arguments in my absence or just secret evidence?"

"Both," answered the Shin Bet officer with a smile.

There was nothing that could be done. We all left the room, together with the World Vision representative and my client.

In five minutes, we were recalled and I returned to my seat on the right side. The judge looked at me.

"Now, what do you have to say, Mr. Kuttab?"

What could I possibly say? My objection was denied, and the detention order confirmed.*

Much of my practice, however, was before military courts defending ordinary Palestinians. What Israelis think of as dangerous

---

* As of this writing, there are over eight hundred and thirty Palestinian administrative detainees in Israeli jails. They are usually prominent members of society against whom the Israelis could not even get a trumped-up charge. They just languish in prison until released. At the height of the First Intifada there were as many as five thousand administrative detainees, mostly housed in the Negev prison Ansar III.

fanatical terrorists are basically ordinary Palestinians. Actually, I only met one religious fanatic among all the clients I represented in military courts. His case was so different from the typical cases I take that it has stuck with me for a long time.

It started when the plumbing contractor who once worked on our kitchen extension in Ramallah came to my office asking me to represent his son, who was in jail. "He is the one who carried out the operation in the settlement of Halamish," he told me. "Have you heard of it?"

"No," I confessed, "but I will take the case."

"I will pay you what I can," he said. "Your wife has been very kind to me when I did the work in your kitchen. She offered me coffee and cake and inquired about my family."

"No need to pay. I will gladly take the case *pro bono*. Let me go see him."

As I recall, his name was Mahmoud. On my first visit, I introduced myself and said his father had sent me to be his lawyer. He was quiet, soft-spoken, and seemed to operate on a different plane of reality. His views may have been fanatical, but he was not wild-eyed and did not look at all crazy.

"Thank you, but I do not need a lawyer. I cannot afford one anyway."

"I am not taking any fees," I said.

"That is what you lawyers say. Then you will suck the blood out from our families."

"I will do no such thing. I know your father because he did some work for us in our kitchen in my apartment in Ramallah. He asked me to come. That is why I am here today."

Suddenly his attitude changed. "You have an American wife, right?"

"Yes. How did you know?"

"My father told me about you. He told me that you and your wife are good people. I will sign your power of attorney."

That was a strange conversation, but I was glad he was willing to trust me based on his father's interaction with my wife.

"Okay," I said. "What faction are you affiliated with?"

"I am not affiliated with any faction. I work alone. It's just me and God."

"Are you a member of any group in your village?"

"There are no true Moslems there."

"Is there no Hamas there?" I asked, referring to the Islamic resistance group.

"Do you call them Moslems?" He laughed derisively. Clearly his standards for true Moslems were much higher.

"Can I get you a book to read? Maybe a Qur'an or a Bible?"

"No, do not do that. This is a filthy place. I would not want the Qur'an to be defiled and desecrated."

I'd never represented someone like him and was curious about his background.

"Tell me your story."

"I was the first in my class in the last year of high school. I read a lot, and I used to be a Communist. I then started to read the Qur'an and decided I could not be a Communist any longer. You see, there are three basic ideologies in the world: Communism, Capitalism, and Islam. After the collapse of Communism, my choices were Capitalism, and who wants that? This left Islam. So, I sought to be a good Moslem and follow God's commandments."

(Note: I did not know it then, but I learned later that very pious Moslems fast every Monday and Thursday of every week.)

My client continued.

"One Thursday when I was fasting, I decided to carry out an operation against the settlers of Halamish, the settlement near our village. I took gasoline and matches so that I could burn the evil outright. I also took a pickaxe as a weapon. I set some stones as a barrier in the middle of the road and waited for a car to come so I could attack it. For a long while, no car came. This was a new settlement with only a few families living there. Over an hour later, a car finally arrived. When they saw the stones, they stopped. I was making my way towards the car with my pickaxe, when I was interrupted by a car approaching from the other side. It was another settler. He stopped his vehicle, jumped out and came towards me pointing his Uzi submachine gun. I turned from the car and went towards him. He was shooting at me, but I kept walking towards him since it says in the Qur'an, 'Do not turn your back to the enemy'."

He paused for a moment, then continued with the dramatic story.

"So, I kept facing him and walking towards him, as bullet after bullet struck me. Eventually, I fell. I had nine bullets in me. I woke up much later with this heavenly face looking down on me. I thought I was in Paradise, but then I saw the golden Star of David around her neck, and I realized I was in the hospital and being attended to by a Jewish nurse. I had wanted to be a martyr, but God did not find me worthy of that honor."

What could I say? I usually thought of religious fanatics as wild-eyed monsters. This fanatic was soft-spoken, polite, and humble, but he still seemed clearly divorced from reality and operating within his own sphere. I also realized that most of the other religious Moslems I knew, including clients who were members of Hamas and active in the resistance—people whom Israel and the Western world viewed as fanatical terrorists—were really quite ordinary and sane. I hoped his ideas would change, as I could see him having trouble dealing with other prisoners if he thought that even Hamas , and Islamic Jihad were not genuine Moslems.

As with other prisoners, there was little I could legally do for him. There was no need to torture him into confession, as he readily and proudly admitted that he intended to harm the settlers. As usually happened in these cases, his trial ended with a plea bargain. During his trial, I emphasized that no one other than himself was actually hurt, that he acted alone, and that he was not a member of any terrorist organization. I did not mention that this was only because he was too fanatical to join any of them. He was sentenced to fifteen years in jail.

Another unusual case I took was for a young man from Gaza.

Abdel Hadi Ghnayyem had just carried out a bloody operation against Israel. While riding on a bus, he had wrenched the controls from its driver and sent it careening into a ravine. The bus exploded into a firestorm, killing sixteen of the passengers and wounding many more, including himself. Israel was in an uproar, with the families of the dead soldiers demanding revenge. He needed representation, and Gaza lawyers were afraid to take up the case. I said I would be willing to do it. As far as I was concerned, there was a clear distinction between a lawyer and the activities of his client. Even though I was a pacifist, I had no trouble defending Palestinian militants who were considered by the Israelis to be terrorists. I was also very curious about this case for a number of reasons. I wanted to meet this fellow and discuss them with him.

When I visited him in jail, I found a thin young man with a red beard. I introduced myself and told him I had been hired by his family to represent him. After he signed the power of attorney, I proceeded to ask him my questions.

He told me that he was not a member of any Palestinian group. His family home had already been searched and demolished by the Israelis. His family members had all been arrested, questioned, and then released. They were clearly not involved in his activity and did not seem to be politically involved. Likewise, no organization or faction had claimed responsibility for his actions. He also maintained that he had acted alone.

"I am curious," I said. "Your operation was so out of step with the Intifada and the directives of the PLO. We are in the beginning of a major popular uprising that has been largely nonviolent. The PLO made it clear that Palestinians are not to use any firearms. Only stones are acceptable as weapons. Furthermore, activities are to be limited to the West Bank and Gaza, to indicate to Israelis that we are willing to accept a Palestinian state in the Occupied Territories. The intent was to *not* attack Israel itself. Yet you carried out this attack, killing many people inside Israel. Isn't this against the directives of the PLO and the Intifada?"

He said, "I do not care about the PLO, the Intifada, or Palestine, for that matter."

I was shocked. "What do you care about then?"

"My friend," he answered.

"Who is your friend?"

"I have this friend who was my bosom buddy. We grew up together. You would always find me at his house or him at my house. We were inseparable. One day, we dressed up, put on some aftershave, and went for a nice time on the town. We saw some demonstrations on one street and saw that the Israeli soldiers were responding with tear gas and live ammunition, so we took another street that was parallel to it. We were not political and had no desire to get mixed up with what was happening there. As we were walking down the parallel street, I saw my friend suddenly fly into the air and land on his face . . . *with a bullet lodged in his spine.*"

My chest tightened, and I saw tears in his eyes, which he fought back.

"For months I stayed by his side in the hospital, but there was little that the doctors in Gaza could do. He could be treated in a specialized hospital in Italy though. His family arranged for everything. Unfortunately, he needed an exit permit to travel to that hospital and Israel refused to issue it. Since he had been wounded by their soldiers, they assumed that he had been participating in the Intifada. They had not arrested him, which they would have done if he had actually been involved at all, but still, they did not grant him a permit to leave and get medical care abroad.

"I tried every possible way to get his exit permit, including giving bribes to collaborators, but nothing worked. We lost all hope, and I was frantic. I could not face that my friend was now doomed to be a paraplegic. How could I live and look him in the face? I felt that I had to do something.

"So, without much of a plan, I put a knife in my bag and went to the Tel Aviv bus station. There was a group of soldiers there getting on to a bus that was heading to Jerusalem, so I joined them. I honestly did not know what I was going to do once we were on the bus together. I thought I might grab the wheel and drive the bus into the side of the hill or into a ravine.

"Suddenly we were near Deir Yassin."

Deir Yassin is the site of a horrible and infamous massacre in 1948, when Israeli soldiers slaughtered innocent, unarmed Palestinian men, women, and children.

"When I saw the deep ravine on the right-hand side of the road, I jumped from my seat, and then I do not know what happened. I blacked out and woke up in the hospital.

"The reports are that you yelled 'Allahu Akbar!', yanked the steering wheel from the driver, and turned the bus towards the ravine."

"That is probably true, but I do not remember any of it."

"What if there had been children on the bus?"

"I would not have done it."

"What if there were civilians and women and others?"

"I would not have done it. They were all soldiers—male and female, but all soldiers."

This case was unlike any other. Rather than the military court, it was being tried in the District Court in Jerusalem. In light of the large number of casualties, there was a lot of pressure from the families to revive the death penalty for my client.

THE TRUTH SHALL SET YOU FREE

Israel had used the death penalty only once, against Adolf Eich-
mann, the Nazi responsible for tens of thousands of deaths in the
Nazi concentration camps. The nation prided itself on not using the
death penalty, though it was still on the books. I knew there was
little I could do for him, but I thought if I could get the prosecutor
to agree to take the death penalty off the table, I could plead guilty.
This would avoid the media circus of a lengthy trial showing all the
grisly evidence.

Luckily, the prosecutor agreed with me and said he had been
instructed by his superiors to stay with the same policy and not
demand the death penalty.

The trial was short and consisted of me entering a plea of
guilty to the entire charge sheet, which listed sixteen counts of
first-degree murder and twenty-four counts of attempted murder,
one for each of the wounded who survived the attack. The presiding judge asked my client if he had anything to say before
sentencing.

To my surprise he stood up. Through the court's Hebrew
translator, he delivered his message sentence by sentence to the
courtroom.

"We wanted to make peace with you. We stretched out our
hand to you, but to no avail. We offered you a chance for a two-state
solution, but you do not want peace. You want a war. So be it."

He closed by quoting an Arabic proverb. "The initial aggressor
is the one to blame."

Then he sat down.

The chief judge listened in stony silence. After a brief recess,
she announced the verdict and judgment: sixteen consecutive life

sentences, plus 480 years on top of that, twenty years for each of the wounded victims.

Abdel Hadi was taken to prison and was kept in solitary confinement, referred to by prisoners as the dungeons, for the first three years, with visits rarely allowed. I was able to visit him several times. He looked scary, with a long disheveled beard, and I was the only person who ever visited him. I met him once three years later, when he was taken out of solitary confinement and allowed into the prison population. He told me that after his years in solitary, he felt he was now in paradise, being able to interact with other prisoners. He now proclaimed himself to be a member of Fatah.

Several years later, I learned that he was released in a prisoner exchange and sent to Gaza. I never saw him after that.

I often thought about Abdel Hadi. He had killed more Israeli soldiers than anyone I knew. Yet he was no terrorist, no fanatic, and not even very political. The harsh occupation had turned him into what he became. Even after his friend had been shot, it was the cruel refusal to give him a travel permit to seek medical care abroad that pushed Abdel Hadi over the edge and made him seek his senseless revenge.

Israel sometime claims that Palestinian schools or parents teach their children to hate Jews. I know better. The most effective teacher of hatred is the reality of an occupation that daily creates anger, despair, frustration, and hatred. I had to work to rid myself of the hatred I had felt as a teenager before I left for the United States. If I had not found fulfillment and satisfaction in working for human rights and nonviolence, I myself would have succumbed to hatred and violence, as well.

CHAPTER 15

WHILE I WAS BUSY TRYING to get my legal credentials, learn Hebrew, and begin my studies of the Israeli legal system, and starting my legal practice, my cousin Mubarak Awad had also returned from the United States to Jerusalem, where he established the Palestinian Counseling Center.

He was full of energy and wanted to change society. Like me, he was also a firm believer in the power of nonviolent resistance, but with a greater emphasis on activism. We gravitated towards each other, even though we were opposites in many ways. I was careful, conscientious, and risk averse—a "good boy" who followed the rules. He was a totally fearless troublemaker who had little respect for authority. I weighed my words carefully, while he brashly said whatever came to his mind, regardless of consequences. He shunned neither politics nor controversy. He was not terribly religious and had his problems with the Church, but there was no question that he was deeply moral and ethical. Like me, he had absorbed the ethics of service and sacrifice that we both grew up with. He met with Israelis often and would travel on his motorcycle to different villages in the West Bank to talk to villagers.

One of the things that cemented our working relationship was this extremely important fact.

Mubarak told me that, just after the occupation started in 1967, he had a discussion with some of his friends at the basement of the Ritz Hotel in East Jerusalem. He told them that we needed to fight the occupation nonviolently.

His friends thought he was crazy.

"Nonviolence is nonsense. The only reason you talk about non-violence is because we have no access to weapons. What we really need is armed struggle."

Mubarak pressed them. "Then why do you not engage in armed struggle?"

"We would, but we have no weapons, and no way of getting them."

Mubarak laughed. "You get your weapons like every other liberation movement in history—from your enemies."

"What do you mean?"

"I will show you."

He left the group, walked outside, and found a young Israeli soldier walking in the street.[**] Mubarak grabbed the soldier—gun and all—in a bear hug and dragged him down to the basement. The soldier was too frightened to resist.

[**] At that time, the situation was very different from what it is now, and Israelis roamed freely throughout the occupied territories.

"Sit down", he said "and put your gun on the table."

The soldier silently obeyed.

Mubarak motioned to his friend. "Get him a cup of coffee!"

The ashen-faced soldier sat there, paralyzed with fear, as the coffee was set before him.

"Drink!" Mubarak ordered.

The soldier picked up the cup in shaking hands and as ordered, gulped down the coffee.

"Now take your gun and get out of here!"

The soldier grabbed his gun and quickly ran out of the room. Apparently, he never reported the incident to anyone because Mubarak never saw the soldier again. Obviously, the young soldier could not believe his luck.

That incident describes my cousin well. He was just as fearless as he was totally committed to nonviolence.

Mubarak told me he wanted to set up a series of talks to teach Palestinians about the power of nonviolent resistance. I suggested that we first start a center for that purpose and call it "The Palestinian Center for the Study of Nonviolence." That would make it sound more like a research center than a political activist organization. If the center was based in East Jerusalem, which Israel had illegally annexed, it would allow us to take advantage of Israeli civil law, which was broader than the military law that was applicable in the rest of the West Bank. As with Al Haq, my idea was to try to stay under the radar as much as possible.

Mubarak had other ideas.

The first public meeting was held in the YWCA in East Jerusalem. To my horror, the first words out of Mubarak's mouth were bold and clear. "This is a political meeting. Our goal is to get rid of the occupation!"

I wanted to crawl under my seat.

He then told the audience that the only reason the occupation existed was because we wanted it to exist. "The occupation would disappear if we withdrew our consent to be ruled by the Israelis."

The audience was stunned, but they were also angry that his accusation was directed at them.

Mubarak had recently discovered a book by Gene Sharp, a Harvard professor and authority on the subject of nonviolence. The book listed three hundred different tactics of nonviolence that had been used in different times and countries. Professor Sharp's theory was that every oppressive regime depends on the consent of the oppressed. This consent is obtained either by terrorizing, frightening, or bribing them. Once people lose their fear and are willing to pay the price to withdraw their consent, the oppressor can no longer operate and his regime will collapse.

This theory of nonviolence was not based on spirituality, religion, or the sanctity of life, as was the nonviolence of Mahatma Gandhi and Rev. Martin Luther King, Jr. Rather, it was very practical and pragmatic, based on understanding the dynamics of power between the oppressor and the oppressed. The idea was that if masses of people could make the cost of the oppression/occupation/dictatorship high enough, the regime would eventually collapse. Nonviolent resistance might well lead to greater retaliation by the oppressor, but that suffering would only strengthen the resistance and speed up the fall of the regime.

This was particularly interesting for me, since the majority of Palestinians were not Christian, but Moslem. While they respected Jesus and his teachings of peace, it would not be easy for them to accept the option of nonviolence. They would have to be convinced that it was not merely an easy or cowardly way to avoid conflict, but instead, a powerful tool that could help them fight for their freedom. The nonviolence had to be assertive, even militant.

When I realized what Mubarak was advocating, this approach suited me just fine. It dovetailed beautifully with my Christian pacifism, and I was glad to put my energy behind Mubarak and his activities.

Without bothering to get Gene Sharp's consent or considering the copyright aspects, Mubarak lopped off one or two chapters from his book, which he thought were too technical, and had the rest of the book translated into Arabic. He printed it and quickly began to circulate it to anyone who cared to read it.

Gene Sharp, who was a professor at Harvard, later met Mubarak and bitterly complained to him about the copyright infringement. Mubarak was astonished. "I thought you would be glad and proud to have your ideas translated, read, and followed by Palestinians!" Eventually, Gene and Mubarak became the best of friends. Before he passed away, he moved his entire library on nonviolence from his Harvard offices and donated them with all his papers to Nonviolence International, the organization that Mubarak and I would later start in Washington, DC.

Mubarak's actions were often spontaneous and contrary to normal practices. Once, as he rode a bus from Bethlehem to

Jerusalem, the bus was stopped by Israeli soldiers for a second time to inspect the passengers' IDs.

But Mubarak was fed up; he refused to show his *hawiyyeh* card. The soldier was stunned and did not know what to do. My cousin said, "You have a gun. Shoot me!"

Palestinian passengers were also shocked and begged Mubarak to show his ID. He refused. "They already saw my *hawiyyeh* at Rachel's tomb two miles back. It is ridiculous to make me show it again. I refuse to do it. He can shoot me if he wants to."

The young soldier relented, and sheepishly left the bus.

Whether Mubarak sensed that this particular soldier did not have it in him to deal with a defiant Palestinian or whether Mubarak had just had his own Rosa Parks moment, I will never know. But this was Mubarak. You never knew what he would do next.

Another time, while giving a speech about nonviolence, he was challenged by a Palestinian politico.

"But the PLO Charter specifically says that armed struggle is the path to the liberation of Palestine. What you say is the opposite of what the PLO teaches."

"Yes, it is. So what?"

There was an audible gasp from the audience. Open defiance of the PLO and of its Charter was close to political blasphemy in this crowd. Mubarak was not only lacking in politically correct speech, but the ease with which he did it was breathtaking. For him, it was nothing to contradict the Charter, or the PLO, or to deviate from what political activists considered the sacred party line.

Around the same time that Mubarak and I started the Palestinian Center for the Study of Nonviolence, my brother Daoud and some of his friends formed a new theatre group that they called Al Hakawati (The Storyteller). Daoud had also recently returned from the United States and eventually started what would become a brilliant career as a journalist. This theatre troupe had several actors who were Arab-Israeli citizens, as well as people from the West Bank and East Jerusalem. I was a part of the group for a while, while also acting as their lawyer.

We took over an unused building across from my office that had once been a movie theater. After renovating it in a very frugal but artistic fashion (using plastic bottles for lamp shades and the like), we started writing and performing our own plays.

Our first play, "Mahjoub, Mahjoub"—roughly translated, "Hidden, Hidden"—was a tragi-comedy featuring the adventures of a Palestinian Arab from East Jerusalem called Mahjoub. The theater group planned to perform the play not only in the newly renovated theatre in Jerusalem, but also in Arab schools in northern Israel in the Galilee.

But then we ran into a problem.

The Israeli Committee on Films and Theatre decided that the play was too incendiary and provocative. They would not allow it to be performed in Israel.

I was shocked. I didn't even know there was such a committee or that there were any restrictions on art and theatre in Israel. I knew for a fact that progressive Israeli Jews often produced very brave, provocative, and politically daring plays and films, many of them sympathetic to Palestinians. These plays, however, were usually in Hebrew.

As a lawyer, I decided to challenge the decision. I read up on the regulations on this issue. The regulations governing the Committee on Films and Theatre provided for a right to appear before the Committee and appeal their decisions. I wrote a letter demanding to meet with them and received a reply saying that the Committee would be willing to hear my appeal. In fact, they were willing to come to Al Hakawati Theatre in East Jerusalem and hold the hearing there.

On the appointed date, the Committee, which was composed of about twenty-five people, came to the theatre. Most did not appear to be government bureaucrats. Apparently, they were mostly volunteers, and many were themselves artists.

I stood before them on the stage as they filed into the front section of the seating at the theatre. I asked permission to speak in English, since my Hebrew was not good enough.

After summarizing the play for them—since the text we had provided them was in Arabic—I told them that I was not sure what their problems were with it.

"We are a law-abiding group," I said, "and will accept the judgement of the authorities." Certainly, the authorities have the power to ban our play. However, since this was an original play written by the actors themselves, we had great flexibility.

"If there is a particular scene, act, or phrase that you feel is illegal from a security point of view, we will be willing to remove it."

A gentleman sitting directly in front of me was apparently the only one on the Committee who knew Arabic. He appeared to be a representative of the Secret Service (Shin Bet) and spoke to me in Arabic.

"Mr. Khattab, (he mispronounced my name), this play is in Arabic, and is meant for an Arab audience. The hero of this play speaks, among other things, about house demolitions and deportations. How do you think an Arab audience would react to such subjects?"

I realized at once that he was probably the only one who read the play and that the rest of the members of the Committee had simply gone along with his recommendation that the play was inciting and harmful. So that was how an otherwise liberal committee would routinely censor Arab plays in Israel.

I decided to break his monopoly and force the rest of the Committee to take a position independently.

As he fixed his gaze upon me, I did not answer him in Arabic, which I suspected was what he wanted. Instead, I turned to the rest of the Committee and continued the conversation in English.

"Let me repeat what this gentleman said to me in Arabic. He objects to the use of the words 'house demolition' and 'deportation.' He is concerned with the possible effect of addressing these subjects before an Arab audience. As an international lawyer and a human rights activist, I believe these practices are illegal under the Geneva Conventions. As an Israeli lawyer, however, I know they are commonly used by Israel, and are perfectly legal according to Israel's own laws. They occur all the time and are used routinely against Arabs. It is true that an Arab audience knows about these practices because they constitute part of their lives.

"If your committee, however, declares that it is illegal to talk about them, we are perfectly willing to abide by your decision. We will remove these words and any reference to house demolitions or deportation from the play. We will not let our hero, Mahjoub, refer to them directly or indirectly. This is, after all, a country of law. We will not violate the law but will strictly abide by your decision."

The Committee was clearly uncomfortable. When put this way, they could not say that original art is not allowed to address current issues in the community just because they were uncomfortable for the government. They also realized that their much-flouted democracy was experienced very differently by Arab Israelis, and that their committee was in fact part of the power structure which enforced this discrimination.

They told me they would review the text again and reconsider the matter.

Soon after that, we received a letter from them saying that the Committee had reversed its decision. The play could be shown according to the text we had previously shared with them, without any alterations.

I was beginning to see that, in many ways, Israeli Jews themselves did not know the reality of the occupation. Thus, they could maintain a wonderful view of themselves as a liberal democracy, while systematically oppressing others. I was determined not to allow them that luxury. They needed to see themselves as Palestinian Arabs see and experience them. The rest of the world also needed to see them as they are, and not as they wanted to be seen. The hope was that, like this committee, perhaps some or most of them would be embarrassed and change their behavior.

The Al Hakawati theater was literally in the yard behind my office. I could look outside my window on the third floor and see what was happening there. I often saw the border patrol, a military adjunct to the police in Jerusalem, loiter outside the entrance, checking ID's and intimidating those who entered and exited. They even closed the theatre at times to prevent gatherings and events that they deemed "against public order." The police were there so frequently that the theater would sometimes call me in on a weekly basis. I would have to put on my lawyer's hat and come down to see what was going on and try to do something about it. Usually, there was little or nothing I could do, but still, I would go and argue. Even when the authorities allowed an event to take place, the presence of soldiers armed with machine guns at the entrance scrutinizing all who entered was quite intimidating.

While I could not spare the time to play an active role as a member of the group, its members continued to be good friends, and we would share many meals and discussions as they lived their Bohemian artist lives in Jerusalem. It was interesting to see how life goes on, and even art and theatre can thrive while events continued to play out against Palestinian people—and on a greater scale.

One day Mubarak dropped by my office. "Why do you think the settlers are always uprooting Palestinian olive trees? Is it to deprive them of their livelihood and force them to leave the land?

Land that has olive trees not only provides a family with food and income for generations, but it is also living, physical proof of continued agricultural use. An olive tree requires several years of careful tending before it begins to yield its fruit."

I thought for a moment, and replied, "You remember the story we were taught in school about a king who once saw an old man planting olive seedling? He asked the farmer if he expected to live long enough to enjoy the fruits of his labor. The old man had replied, 'They planted, and we ate. Now we plant so that they can eat.'"

The obvious lesson was that he planted for the benefit of his children and grandchildren, just as he had benefited from the work of his parents and grandparents. Some olive trees are so old they are referred to as *"Rumi"*—meaning, from the time of the Romans. The olive trees in the Garden of Gethsemane in Jerusalem are reputed to be from the time of Christ. The existence of the cultivated olive trees all over Palestine is a testament to the continued use of the land by the people who lived on it for centuries.

Switching from my professorial mode, which Mubarak had tolerated with mild amusement, I told him, "Legally speaking, it is even trickier than that."

My poor cousin had to endure another lengthy lecture.

"Israel has decided to revive an old Ottoman law which says that land, outside of city boundaries, that is not used for agriculture for ten continuous years can revert to the Emir. Land that is used for vegetable or wheat production is sometimes allowed to rest for one year out of every seven. It might also lie fallow when there is a drought, or if there is an illness in the family or some other personal reason. Regardless of the reasons why any land might be lying fallow, it is very vulnerable under this Israeli interpretation of the Ottoman law. Aerial photographs could be introduced as evidence that the land was not used in a particular year, and the farmer would lose it. But if it has olive trees growing on it, it is clearly being used continuously."

"Wonderful!" said Mubarak. "Let's start a campaign of nonviolent resistance by urging Palestinians to plant more olive trees, particularly in lands near the settlements or where settlers or soldiers have uprooted trees. I can get the Mennonites or Quakers to donate money for hundreds of olive seedlings which we can offer to villagers and help them plant them in areas facing confiscation."

I thought it was a wonderful idea.

Mubarak started going from village to village telling people that they could protect their land from confiscation by planting trees on it. He told them that he would organize groups of foreigners, Israeli peace activists, and others to join them as they planted olive saplings on their lands. There were only two conditions. First, they would not throw stones at the soldiers; it was important that the activity be totally nonviolent. The second was that they would not run away when the soldiers came.

"Nonviolence is not an option for cowards," he said. "It requires as much if not more courage than armed struggle."

I accompanied Mubarak on many of these trips, which were also fascinating examples of joint Arab-Jewish cooperation for peace and justice. I would explain the legal aspects of what we were doing to the farmers and be there as a legal witness when the army or settlers would try to stop the activity. There was much debate in Palestinian society about whether throwing stones at heavily armed soldiers, which routinely happened during political demonstrations, is actually violence. Mubarak insisted, however, that even the appearance of violence should be avoided during the activities he was organizing.

"If the army comes while you are planting trees, drop the hoes or pickaxes from your hands. You do not want to give the soldiers any excuse to use violence against you. If you throw stones," he said, "the soldiers can claim that they were afraid of your 'weapons.' Nonviolence requires you to understand how the soldiers think and to realize that many of them, however incredible that sounds, are actually afraid of you."

One day, we got a call from villagers in Khrab el Lahem, near Qatannah, a West Bank village. They said that the army was cutting down and uprooting hundreds of old *Rumi* olive trees from their lands which were in no-man's land and on the West Bank side of the old '67 border.

Mubarak and I organized a group of foreigners and Israeli peace activists to go to the village. Sure enough, it was a scene of devastation. Israeli bulldozers and heavy equipment had been hard at work for several days cutting off the olive branches, and then uprooting the remaining trunks of the trees. The villagers were devastated. Some of the older ones were in tears, mourning over the trees like their own children.

We had brought a pickup truck full of olive saplings, and so we immediately got busy digging holes about ten feet apart and then planting and watering the seedlings, while the villagers prepared a meal for everyone.

Soon, two jeeps filled with Israelis showed up. One was from the army and another from the Nature Preservation Authority. They told us the land in question was State land since it was near the old border between Israel and the West Bank. It no longer belonged to the villagers, as the Jordanian Army had taken it previously and used it. Further, they stated, Israel had declared the land to be a "national park reserve" and we were not allowed to be there at all.

I stepped up and challenged their statements.

"This land belongs to these villagers, and they have the documents to prove it. As a lawyer, I personally inspected and found their documents to be authentic. Furthermore, if you are so concerned about nature and nature preservation, why are you allowing them to cut down fruitful trees?"

They had no answer. They said, again, that the land was now government property, and we were trespassing to even be there.

We all knew that this was just another method commonly used to take land from Palestinians. It was all an excuse, but they would fight very hard to maintain the fiction. It was important to them that the outside world—and even Israeli society itself—should project an image of democracy, liberalism, and the rule of law.

One of the officers from the Nature Preservation Authority was particularly aggressive and was going around pulling out all the saplings which the volunteers were planting.

Mubarak ordered that each tree should be protected by three people: a Palestinian, an Israeli, and an international expat.

The soldiers and so-called nature preservation personnel saw that they were outnumbered. Though they were armed, they could not deal with people who were refusing to obey their commands.

Eventually, we agreed to leave based on their promise to leave the seedlings unharmed. After they left, we celebrated and enjoyed a meal with the villagers, many of whom had never broken bread or shared a meal with Israeli Jews before. It was a beautiful moment.

Sadly, we learned that the Nature Preservation Authority jeeps came back after two days, with heavy army reinforcements, and pulled out all the saplings we had planted.

The story did not end there, however.

It came to our attention that about twenty of the uprooted olive trees had been replanted in West Jerusalem, at a small park that was dedicated to the memory of Rev. Martin Luther King, Jr.

Irony of ironies.

We were outraged at the hypocrisy and decided to hold a demonstration at the site of the new park. We tied yellow ribbons on the branches of the replanted trees and put up signs saying, "Take me back home to Khrab El Lahem."

We tried to get some newspapers to cover the event. We also took pictures and sent a lengthy letter to Coretta Scott King, the widow of the late Martin Luther King, Jr., explaining the situation. We told her that if her late husband was alive, he would probably be demonstrating with us rather than accepting accolades from our oppressors. I explained that the Palestinian Center for the Study of Nonviolence was inspired by the example of Dr. King and that we hoped they would send a letter from the King Center in Atlanta, explaining to the Israelis and to the Jerusalem Municipality that their actions in uprooting the olive trees was a desecration of the memory of her husband and everything he stood for.

Weeks passed, and we heard nothing. We did not receive any acknowledgement of the letter, and no reply whatsoever. One person opined that the King Center in Atlanta could not afford to alienate some of its Zionist donors and funders and would rather not deal with the problems this issue presented for them.

I found that hard to believe, and said they probably never got the letter. In the end, I looked up the telephone number of the Martin Luther King Center in Atlanta and called them.

I told the receptionist that I was calling from the Palestinian Center for the Study of Nonviolence in Jerusalem and would love to speak to Mrs. King. The receptionist said, in a heavy Southern accent, "Is theees about them treeeees?"

They had clearly received the letter.

Unfortunately, Mrs. King could not be reached and nobody else was available to discuss the issue with me. They promised that she would call back, but she never did.

Two years later, after Mubarak was deported, he visited Mrs. King in Atlanta. The visit resulted in a one paragraph letter from Coretta King "thanking the villagers of Qatanna for donating trees to be planted in memory of her late husband."

We were very disappointed.

Given all of these serious injustices, and the dismal non-support from the West, I continued to work to keep my spirits up.

The contrast between the actions of the Israeli government and the image it had in many Western circles was bewildering for me. I knew that part of it was the result of ignorance, which was fed by the failure of Palestinians to make their case in terms that Westerners would understand. Another part of it, however, was the effective influence of Zionists who systematically presented their case powerfully and convincingly. They knew how to manipulate the levers of power throughout American society, whether it was in the media, Congress, the arts, or even the churches. They also effectively utilized the position, reputation, and power of the Jewish community. Such was their effectiveness that it lent credibility to anti-Semitic charges of "Jewish control." The more successful and effective their efforts were, the more they fed the stereotypes and anti-Semitic conspiracy theories.

By now, I knew clearly the difference between such effective advocacy and influence and nefarious tropes about "Jewish control," but many of my fellow Palestinians were not as aware of this distinction. They were convinced that the United States had no power to act even in its own interest where Israel was concerned. That is how they interpreted what they saw.

CHAPTER 16

OVER TIME, my cousin Mubarak and I developed a close relationship. I would continue to be the conservative lawyer, working on human rights and explaining the legal situation while he would be the fearless activist. Both skill sets would be needed as events escalated.

Mubarak was very good at making creative trouble for both the Israelis and the Palestinian "politicos" who did not understand him. He spoke in a language that was different from all the established Palestinian career politicians, and his actions made many of them uncomfortable. They always were sure to mouth the accepted formula for nationalist positions, but Mubarak had no time for such drivel.

"The PLO is our sole legitimate representative."

"Revolution until victory."

"Armed struggle is the sole method for liberating Palestine."

"The legitimate rights of the Palestinian people include a Palestinian state with Arab Jerusalem as its capital,"

"The eternal and inalienable rights of the Palestinians to statehood, Return, and self-determination."

I suspected that, initially, the Israeli authorities were not worried about Mubarak. They were eager to promote anyone who would appear to challenge the authority of the PLO, and so perhaps they saw him as useful in that regard. He certainly did not constitute a "security threat" by any stretch of the imagination, as, like me, he was emphatically nonviolent.

Some Israelis thought that this might be an opportunity to create a local leadership other than the PLO, but Mubarak made it clear: we were not trying to start a new political party. We accepted the PLO as our sole legitimate representative and felt that if Israel truly wanted peace it should negotiate with Arafat and the PLO.

Despite that stance, Mubarak was just as willing to criticize the PLO and Yasser Arafat as he was the Israelis. Though he did not belong to any of the political factions, he was willing to work with any of them, including Hamas—which was just beginning to become a force. More importantly, he was willing to work with ordinary Palestinians regardless of political affiliation. He was also willing to talk with Israelis of any stripe who would listen to him. It was impossible to put him into a box.

With his bravado and my skills as a lawyer, we made a good team. We must have been a real puzzle to the Israelis, who preferred to think of all Palestinians who resisted their occupation as violent terrorists.

The Palestinian Center for the Study of Nonviolence was right next to my law office in the Cinema Nuzha building, and Mubarak received a never-ending stream of visitors there—including Israelis, Palestinians, foreigners, journalists, and undercover secret service agents. I often joined him for these discussions. Whenever he decided to carry out some new action, I would usually discuss it with him in advance, considering the legal ramifications and helping him write any instructions or press releases to be issued later.

The Israeli military authorities could not accuse him of any "security offence" without admitting that all these "offenses" were basically political in nature. He had already made a name for himself as an advocate of nonviolence, so they could not credibly pretend that he was fomenting violence or accuse him of terrorism. He seemed to be having more coverage and interest among foreigners than among Palestinians. Nevertheless, they were concerned and kept a close eye on him, often arresting him for minor offenses. These small arrests did not deter Mubarak in the least.

I was with him as his lawyer when he was arrested at one of the tree-planting activities near the settlement of Sussia. This settlement in the Hebron area was home to some of the most fanatical settlers. It became infamous among Palestinians later when a settler was filmed shooting a Palestinian prisoner who had just been arrested. The man was blindfolded, handcuffed, and lying on the ground helpless when the settler came up and shot him dead. Needless to say, these particular settlers were very ideological and radical.

When the military governor of the Hebron area learned that a group of Palestinians, foreigners, and Israelis were planting olive trees in order to protect the land from seizure, he came out with soldiers and began to shout at us. When he saw that Mubarak, the leader of the group, was a U.S. citizen and that there were plenty of journalists there, he just ordered us to leave the land. But not before he took Mubarak's passport and ordered him to report to the Russian Compound in Jerusalem the next day. This was clearly not a typical demonstration, and he thought that the regular Israeli police in Jerusalem would know better how to handle such a high-profile troublemaker.

The next day, I went with Mubarak to the compound, which used to belong to the Russian Orthodox Church before 1948. Israel had converted the place into a police station and prison. I instructed Mubarak not to speak to the police without my presence and to let me answer on his behalf when he was questioned. The police would not agree to my presence, so I repeated my instructions to him not to speak in front of them and waited outside.

After fifteen minutes or so, the interrogator came out and told me I could be present. Mubarak had adamantly insisted that he would not talk to them without his lawyer. He threatened to go on a "no-talking strike." The interrogator did not know what to do. The policeman tried to coerce him to speak by saying, "I know who you are. Don't worry. I will not hit you, because I know you will hold a press conference and tell everyone about it." Mubarak nodded his head but would not answer. In the end, the interrogator gave up and allowed me inside the room. This was highly unusual since the police always interrogated Palestinians in the absence of lawyers.

Once inside, the interrogator took my Jerusalem ID card and my Bar Association ID and laid them on the desk in front of him. He then proceeded to ask Mubarak a number of questions about who he was and what he was doing at Sussia. I replied on his behalf, as the police officer busily wrote down my words in Hebrew.

At one point, the interrogator said, "We are also looking for another fellow who was with you. A certain Jonathan Kuttab. Do you know where he is?"

With a straight face I replied, "A lot of people joined Mubarak in this event, including foreigners, Israeli Jews, and Palestinians. He will not give you any names or information on any of them."

All this while, my picture ID with my name on it was on his desk! We would have a great laugh afterwards that Israeli Intelligence is not always what it is cracked up to be.

In the end, they closed the file and released him, warning him to stop carrying out such activities.

Of course, everyone knew that that would not stop Mubarak.

Regardless of how most Israeli authorities may have seen him, the Jewish settlers did not think that he was so harmless. They were very vocal in demanding that he be arrested or at the very least deported. He was a real pain for them. The rightwing Rabbi Meir Kahane, founder of the Kach Party, which advocated for the mass expulsion of all Arabs, publicly said he would personally shoot Mubarak if he had the chance.

Would some radical pick up the challenge? We had no way of knowing who might be out there waiting for him at any public event or even when he chanced to walk down the street.

One day, Mubarak went to the Knesset as a guest of a Knesset Member, Yossi Sarid, from the left-wing Meretz Party. While he was there, Yossi Sarid asked if he would like to meet Meir Kahane, who was in the hall at the same time.

Mubarak walked over to him and said, "Hello. My name is Mubarak Awad. I understand you want to kill me. I think that before you kill anybody, you should look them in the eye, so here I am."

Kahane smirked. "You are just a tourist to me. You do not belong here."

"Actually, you are just a tourist to me, too. I don't think you belong here either, but I do not want to kill you. So as one tourist to another let us shake hands!"

Kahane was outraged and started shouting. "How dare you! You come into the Knesset and tell me I am just a tourist here?"

And as he flew into a rage, Knesset guards stepped in between them, and then whisked Mubarak away.

Yosi Sareed said, "They look at you and they see no fear, and that scares them to death."

His words were prophetic.

The essence of Mubarak's message of nonviolence was this: *We needed to conquer our fear.* Once we do that, the occupation would be in trouble.

Yossi was also right in his second observation—that the Israeli authorities would not tolerate Mubarak much longer. Soon after that event, Mubarak was arrested again.

This time was different. It was what we called "the big one," leading to his deportation from the country.

By the time of Mubarak's final arrest, it was already too late— in the sense that the non-violent resistance he had advocated and taught for years had turned into a full-blown movement that was already being referred to as an "Intifada." It had been in full swing for a few months at the time of his deportation and was continuing to pick up more momentum. Despite the best efforts of the Israelis, it seemed unstoppable.

I remembered Mubarak's first public lecture, when he told his audience that the occupation would collapse if we would withdraw our acceptance of it. And it was true that the West Bank and Gaza were being ruled at the time by a very small number of Israeli soldiers. I heard the figure of five hundred soldiers in Gaza and another five hundred in the West Bank was all it took. What would happen if the entire population suddenly refused to abide by Israeli dictates and chose to rise up and challenge the occupation? How many tens of thousands of soldiers would then be needed to keep the population under control?

The Intifada was essentially a mass expression of Palestinian refusal to continue to give our "acceptance" to the ongoing Israeli occupation. It was a genuine attempt to "shake off"—that is what *intifada* means—the yoke of occupation.

I first learned about the breakout of the intifada while lying in a hospital bed in early December at the Mount David Hospital in Bethlehem. I was there for a twisted ankle and had been discussing politics with the male nurse who was taking care of me. He was from Gaza. I noted that the demonstrations that were taking place in Gaza had continued daily for weeks. They started after an Israeli vehicle plowed into a group of Palestinian workers, killing several them. Some demonstrations were also taking place in the West Bank.

The nurse surprised me by saying he thought the demonstrations would continue until Land Day, on March 30th, which was over three months away.

Land Day is an annual event that commemorates the anniversary of the killing of six unarmed Palestinians—Arab Israeli citizens who lived in the Galilee—in 1976. During protests over massive land expropriations, six were killed, over a hundred were wounded, and many more arrested. Arab Israelis had reconciled long ago to the existence of Israel and rarely committed actions against the State. On Land Day, however, they always went on strike to remind themselves and Israel that they are still Palestinians who have legitimate grievances against Zionism and the State of Israel.

For most of the Palestinians in the Occupied Territories, our goals were more pressing: we needed independence and statehood. The creeping annexation, the Jewish settlements, the military government, the confiscation of land, and the denial of freedom were a daily struggle then and now. We had gradually and reluctantly accepted that the State of Israel was here to stay. For several years now, the hope was that in return for our giving up our claims to 78 percent of Palestine, and which was now the State of Israel, the occupation would be ended, and we would be allowed a Palestinian state in the West Bank and Gaza.

It took a long time for the PLO leadership to accept this position and even longer to express its willingness to abandon armed struggle in favor of negotiating a peace agreement that would lead to two states living side by side. As Palestinians, we felt that time was running out to achieve such a compromise. Every additional settlement seemed to carry the threat that unless we made peace soon there would be nothing left to negotiate over.

I was personally very much in favor of such a compromise. While I felt that our people had suffered a great injustice in 1948, I knew that realistically, compromise was necessary. The two-state solution seemed to be the best idea. I was very pleased to see the PLO leadership slowly move in that direction and eventually accept UN Resolutions 242 and 338, which encompassed that principle.

The Intifada, which was gaining strength right before our eyes, seemed to be a vindication of all the trends that Mubarak, myself, and others had been advocating for years. The nonviolent activism, along with work in human rights and international law, was all based on the principles of justice, human rights, international law, and self-determination.

The demonstrations not only went until Land Day but continued for months and years after that. Young people were no longer afraid. They were willing to face the strongest army in the region with nothing more than stones. We were no longer waiting for Arab armies to rescue us, nor were we waiting for armed resistance by the PLO, whose leadership in exile seemed as surprised as anyone else at the intensity and effectiveness of the demonstrations.

Unfortunately, Mubarak would not be there to share in the experience for which he had worked so tirelessly for years. It was only about a month after Land Day that Mubarak was arrested.

After his arrest, he was placed in the Mascobiayya jail: the Russian Compound. I was able to visit him pretty regularly. The Israelis did not immediately charge him with any offence but insisted—as Meir Kahane had—that he was merely a tourist whose visa had expired. Thus, he had no right to stay in Israel and should be deported.

The local and international press was showing a lot of interest in his case. Mubarak prepared a statement, which I read out to them. He said it was clear that Israel was only objecting to his nonviolence activities. He argued that they wanted to get rid of him precisely because he was interested in peace, and they were not.

Soon after he was jailed, he went on a hunger strike. He had many friends among the Israeli Left, who could not understand why Israel would want to get rid of a person who was clearly nonviolent, moderate, who argued for a two-state solution, and was working for the peace that they all desired.

One of his most enthusiastic supporters was Professor Edy Kaufman from the Hebrew University. Edy was not terribly active politically at the time, but he was shocked that Mubarak was going to be deported. As a Jew, he had emigrated from Latin America under the Right of Return and enjoyed full Israeli citizenship. He could not justify why someone like Mubarak, who was born in Jerusalem and who so clearly belonged in this land, would be denied the right to live in it, when he himself could freely settle here.

When he learned that Mubarak was on a hunger strike, Edy decided to join him. He set himself a small carpet outside the Mascobiyya jail and put up a sign in Hebrew saying he was on a hunger strike in solidarity with his friend Mubarak Awad, a Palestinian peace activist who was on a hunger strike inside the jail.

The location of the Mascobiyya compound is in the center of Jerusalem, and cars passed by the location frequently. Poor Edy was subjected to much abuse as people yelled at him from out of their car windows, sometimes shouting obscenities and even spitting at him. His own son, an Israeli Air Force pilot, felt the need to appear in uniform with his father to protect him from abuse by passing Israelis.

Nonetheless, Edy persisted day after day.

This had a tremendous effect on both Mubarak and me. We were used to Israeli Jewish leftists talking about peace and coexistence while not necessarily taking a concrete position which would actually cost them anything.

Mubarak said, "I have many arguments with Edy, but I will never forget this. Please tell him to stop his hunger strike. He has made his point."

But Edy would not stop his hunger strike as long as Mubarak was continuing with his.

Mubarak said, "Look Jonathan, I have quite a bit of fat on me and can last many weeks. The last time I was arrested, it took three or four Israeli soldiers to carry me when I refused to move. But Edy is thin; he cannot last long. For his sake, I will stop my hunger strike. Please tell him to end his strike and go home."

After being held in jail for several days, Mubarak's case was first heard at the Magistrate's Court in Jerusalem. He used his trial to share his political views with the judge and any press people in the room. When the prosecutor asked him what the message on his answering machine was, he cheerfully answered, "Happy Intifada!"

He went on to explain that the Intifada—contrary to the messages portrayed in the Hebrew press—was a positive movement for freedom and peace. It was meant to throw off the yoke of occupation and pave the way for a Palestinian state side by side with Israel. He pointed out the predominantly nonviolent nature of the Intifada, and the fact that it deliberately avoided using weapons and killing Israelis.

When asked about stone throwing, he answered that when faced with heavily armed soldiers, tanks, armored vehicles, helicopter gunships, and worst of all, bulldozers, stones were more an act of defiance than a lethal weapon. He conceded that he would not personally throw stones, as he was totally opposed to all forms of violence, but that he would not condemn a Palestinian child for using stones to express his rejection of the occupation.

At one point the judge was so intrigued, he started asking him questions that clearly had nothing to do with the ongoing trial, but more about his political views.

"What would you do with the settlements if there is a two-state solution?" the judge asked him.

Mubarak said they would be put to good use to accommodate returning Palestinian refugees. "We will call them victory cities," he said, "because peace is a victory for both parties."

As his lawyer, I continually emphasized that Mubarak was in favor of peace and a two-state solution. I reminded the court about his consistent dialogue with Israelis and the way he urged Palestinians to use nonviolence rather than armed struggle. I also boldly demanded that Israeli Prime Minister Shamir be brought to testify since he had publicly called for Mubarak's deportation.

The judge declined that demand.

In the end, the judge ruled that Mubarak was indeed a tourist and in the country on a tourist visa. While he did not personally feel Mubarak was a security threat, he said that this particular determination was not his to make. The security services were the ones charged with security matters, and they needed to make the call. Israel was a sovereign country that had full authority to determine what foreigners could enter the country and for how long. Because Mubarak's visa had expired, the judge would do nothing to reverse the decision of the security services to deport him. He said that arguments about what rights Mubarak had as a Jerusalemite were beyond his competence. Therefore, the judge granted leave for us to go directly to the High Court of Justice, which is also in Jerusalem, to debate that issue.

At the High Court, the discussion took a different turn. The legal issue there centered around what sort of rights people like Mubarak had under Israeli law. Mubarak had been born in and grew up in Jerusalem. When Israel annexed East Jerusalem and applied Israeli law and administration to it, Mubarak was listed in the census and issued a blue ID card as a resident. That was a different status from the orange ID cards issued by the Military Government to the residents of the rest of the West Bank and Gaza.

The Court rejected all the arguments based on international law. They did not accept that East Jerusalem was part of the occupied territories, since it had been annexed by Israeli law. They stated that East Jerusalem was no longer part of the West Bank or the Occupied Territories but was now part of Israel proper and thus Israeli law applied to it. But in that case, what exactly was the status of East Jerusalemites?

In the end, the Israeli Court held that the law which annexed Jerusalem had a *lacuna*, a gap, in that it did not grant citizenship to people who lived in East Jerusalem, nor did it specify what their status should be, and the government representative had no answer when asked by the court what is their status.

So, the High Court decided to fill this gap in the law.

It opined that residents of East Jerusalem should be governed by the Law of Entry into Israel of 1955. That law applied to non-Jewish foreigners who were allowed to enter Israel as immigrants. After several years, they could become permanent residents with the eventual possibility of applying for citizenship. However, they would lose that residency status if they (a) obtained another citizenship, (b) obtained another permanent residency, or (c) resided outside Israel for seven years. In any of these cases, the residents could then be treated as total foreigners whose entry and residency would be at the sole discretion of the Ministry of Interior.

The irony, of course, was that Mubarak and the other East Jerusalemites did not "enter Israel" in 1967. On the contrary, it was Israel and its forces that entered East Jerusalem and imposed their laws upon the people who were already living there.

As a non-Jew, Mubarak's birth in Jerusalem and his family ancestry in the city which went back for untold generations did not give him the right to live in Jerusalem or Israel whatsoever. That right, however, did belong to Jews under the Law of Return.

The decision of the Court in Mubarak's case became the official decision defining the status of all East Jerusalemites from that point on. The Court ruled that Mubarak had lost his status in accordance with the Law of Entry into Israel when he went to the U.S., resided there, and obtained U.S. citizenship. Having lost his status, he could now only enter Israel as a "tourist." But since his tourist visa had expired, the Ministry of Interior was clearly permitted, at its own sole discretion, to refuse to extend his tourist visa. The ministry also had the right to order his deportation and deny his entry into Israel for any reason or for no reason whatsoever.

As Mubarak was led from the court in handcuffs, he paused at the steps of the High Court and spoke to the many journalists who had gathered.

"I stand here as a Christian who was judged by a Jewish court. I was given no justice here. I am being banished from my own city and homeland simply because I am Christian and not a Jew."

I cringed a bit as he said this. I am always careful when referring to Israelis. I was sensitive about using broad terms which attribute the behavior of the State of Israel to Jews generally. I felt that this sort of talk could easily sound anti-Semitic. But in this case, there was no denying the truth of what he said. The Israeli High Court was expressing the same Zionist ideology that insists that Israel is a Jewish state which by its very nature grants rights—including residency rights—based merely on whether you are Jewish or not. If you are Christian or a Moslem, you are always viewed with suspicion. You are seen by many as a person who does not truly belong in the country. If, on top of that, you claim the country to be your own, then you are seen as a definite existential danger to the State. This is true even if, like Mubarak, you happen to be a most moderate person, totally dedicated to peace and coexistence, and a champion of non-violence to boot.

Mubarak was flown out of Israel the day after the court's ruling. It was the middle of June. He later told me that even though he was led in handcuffs to the plane, once it left Israeli airspace the pilot came back, shook his hand, and invited him to the first-class cabin as his personal guest. At least the pilot and the rest of the world treated my friend as a hero rather than as a criminal.

Sadly, Mubarak would never again live in Palestine. From the moment of his deportation, he could only return to his homeland by Israeli permission, and then only as a tourist. After the Oslo peace process, he did still occasionally manage to visit Palestine: by special permission to visit his family who still lived there. This permission had to be given in advance by the Israeli embassy in the U.S., and Mubarak was only granted a tourist visa.

For me, Mubarak's departure was one more Palestinian tragedy. All Palestinians struggle to stay in their homeland. Mubarak and I were more creative in how we would survive while retaining our dignity. We were fully aware of the amazing schizophrenia of Israeli society. They could be so racist and fascist and cruel, yet they could also be so enlightened, democratic, and liberal. We were making our mark (and our survival) by cleverly tiptoeing our way between these two opposing features of Israeli society.

But in the end, Israeli society could not tolerate my cousin. I wondered how long they could tolerate me. Choosing the path of nonviolence was not enough. They wanted us out, not because we were violent, but simply because we were Palestinians.

CHAPTER 17

MUBARAK'S DEPORTATION validated the effectiveness of his ideas. In fact, he became something of a hero in Palestine. Many who had previously expressed skepticism and doubt about the efficacy of non-violent activism now realized how effective it was. It was clear that Israel took such actions seriously as a true threat. In response, Palestinians continued to organize myriad forms of non-violent resistance across the Occupied Territories.

Palestinian flags, which were strictly forbidden by the military government, were appearing everywhere. Palestinian youth risked their lives to raise the Palestinian flags on rooftops, electricity poles, and high trees. They also painted them on walls. Israeli soldiers would rouse older people from their homes and force them at gunpoint to paint over the offending graffiti.

And the leaflets continued to arrive. On a regular weekly basis, leaflets would appear out of nowhere, signed by "The Unified

Leadership." They stated the aims of the Intifada and listed the times and activities to be carried out that week. Each person who found a leaflet would quickly copy it and distribute it further. Within a short time, the entire population would know the contents of the leaflet and would carry out its instructions to the letter.

One of the earliest actions instructed by the leaflets was a general commercial strike. To break the strike, Israeli soldiers would go through the main street of a town or village, break the locks on all the shuttered stores, and open them. With each store now wide open, its contents were available to be looted by anyone. Strangely, however, no looting took place. Instead, small bands of young people would discreetly follow the soldiers, close the shutters, install new locks, then take the keys to the merchant at his home.

After a while, the Israeli soldiers gave up and stopped trying to break open stores. That particular battle of wills was won by the Palestinians. And through non-violence.

The strikes continued, however. The Unified Leadership, realizing that economic life needed to continue in some fashion, began to regulate the hours when shops could open up. The weekly leaflet would indicate, for example, that stores were to open between two and four PM on Tuesdays and Thursdays, and everyone would dutifully comply.

Next, the Unified Leadership began to call for a boycott of Israeli goods for which there were local substitutes. They would specify goods and brands to be boycotted. When the population began to participate in the boycotts, it forced the merchants to comply and stop selling the offending items. Since many farmers had abandoned their fields and sought work in Israel, the Unified Leadership urged people to grow their own food in home gardens, like the British did with their "victory gardens" during the Second World War.

During the intifada, most local policemen who were working under Israeli command resigned from their positions. Other than the military courts, which were run by the Israeli army, all of the Palestinian civilian courts stopped operating as well. They were rather ineffectual to begin with and were run under the authority of the Officer in Charge of the Judiciary (the same officer who delayed giving me my license). Israelis thought that with the local courts and police no longer functioning, chaos would prevail, and criminal elements would take over. Instead, as the courts closed and the local police resigned, popular committees rose up in each community that acted to resolve all disputes amicably and to provide an alternative method of conflict resolution between Palestinians. Instead of leading to anarchy and chaos, the absence of courts and police led to a heightened sense of civil and community cooperation and solidarity. Crime rates fell to almost zero. Even drug addiction became much less of a problem, after a volunteer rehabilitation program was started near Jericho.

Despite the suffering, hardship, and severe repression, there was a celebratory and triumphant feeling all around. Because the PLO leadership was abroad and no one knew who the Unified Leadership was, every person seemed to feel individually responsible for the success of the national program.

This led to some humorous stories.

A friend in Jerusalem shared the following story with me. A well-to-do lady was shopping at an upscale minimarket in Beit Hanina, a suburb of East Jerusalem, when the owner asked her to hurry up as it was almost four PM. He would need to close the store at that time, according to the instructions of the leaflet. She answered, "And since when are you so careful in your timekeeping?"

"Oh," he said, "I got a written warning from the Intifada."

"Really?" She was quite intrigued. Everyone was eager to see anything that related to the Intifada and its elusive leadership. "May I see it?"

"Sure," he said, taking a crumpled piece of paper out of the drawer. "It says, 'It has come to our attention that you are not following the instructions of the Unified Leadership. You must comply strictly—or else! Signed, the Cubs of the Intifada.'"

"That handwriting looks familiar to me," she said.

After scrutinizing it a bit more, she realized that it was actually the handwriting of her own eleven-year-old son, Tareq, who had taken it upon himself to send the note and so ensure proper compliance with the Intifada.

One day the army announced that they had captured the Unified Leadership and found the printing press where the leaflets were being printed. The next week the leaflet appeared on time, and the Intifada continued. Palestinians found great delight and amusement in this.

The army retaliated against these unified measures with increasingly harsh treatment. Whole villages and neighborhoods were placed under curfew. Yet soldiers could not be everywhere at once. Youth roamed the streets, and when there were no soldiers around, they would burn tires and raise the "illegal" Palestinian flag in order to attract the army. When the army arrived, they would pelt them with stones. The soldiers would open fire and a martyr would fall. His funeral would be the source of another massive demonstration, and so on.

In response to these actions, Defense Minister Rabin directed the soldiers to break the bones of all the stone throwers. "Killing them only makes them martyrs," he said, "but if we break their bones, they will become crippled, and a burden to their families and soon they will stop." Even after the army started a policy of breaking the bones of Palestinian children, though, that did not stop the Intifada.

The army then ordered the closure of all West Bank/Gaza schools, since students would meet after class before marching out into demonstrations. The community responded by holding classes in homes, mosques, and churches, and so the demonstrations continued. A new military order was issued, prohibiting such homeschooling. But nothing could stop the intifada. It was no longer an issue of days, weeks, or months of organized protest. The entire population of the West Bank, including East Jerusalem, and Gaza was in revolt.

At one point, the army cut off electricity for the Jalazoun refugee camp near Ramallah to punish them for their acts of resistance. I thought it would be a great idea if churches were to buy a huge supply of candles for the camp. We collected a thousand dollars from churches. I took the money to a Greek Orthodox candlemaker in Bethlehem who normally supplies candles for the Church of Nativity and the Church of the Holy Sepulcher. When I told him why I needed a thousand dollars' worth of candles, he said he would gladly supply me with double the amount I needed and that he would only charge for his supplies, which consisted of the wax and string for the wicks.

"This is my contribution to the Intifada," he said. "I would like the residents of the refugee camp (who are all Moslem) to know that the Christians of Bethlehem stand with them. Jesus said, 'I am the light of the World.' He also said, 'Let your light so shine before men, that they may see your good works, and glorify your Father which is in heaven'. It is important that our fellow Palestinians know we all stand together in these difficult times. I do this for the glory of God."

I was initially surprised, but it was a good reminder to me that all Christians—and not just evangelicals, as I had been raised to believe—read the Bible and took it seriously.

The city of Beit Sahour, a Christian town that lies adjacent to and south of Bethlehem, became famous for its creative resistance during the Intifada. Several churches are located there in the "Shepherd's Fields," where the angels appeared and announced the good news of the birth of Jesus in nearby Bethlehem.

I had many clients from Beit Sahour, as well as some very good friends. When I was young, I had often accompanied my father during his ministry ventures there. Over a hundred kids would crowd into a rented room where he held Sunday School once a week. He used a flannel board to tell Bible stories, as well as teach hymns, Bible verses, and generally entertain them for an hour or so. Their mostly Greek Orthodox parents did not mind, since the program was not held on Sunday. The Greek Orthodox Church did not provide any kind of religious instruction for children. Even for the adults, all the services were performed in Greek rather than

Arabic. My father thought that was terrible. People should have access to the gospel in their native tongue. Despite his best efforts to evangelize their parents by holding Bible studies or inviting them to his church in Bethlehem, he met with little success in luring them away from the Greek Orthodox church, but he did have the opportunity to teach their children Bible stories at Sunday School. Many of them still remember his teachings to this day. Decades later I met a successful Palestinian businessman in Honduras, who warmly shook my hand and told me he still had wonderful memories of my late father teaching him hymns and Bible verses in Beit Sahour.

Residents of Beit Sahour are highly educated and very civic minded. During the Intifada, their town quickly became the center of nonviolent struggle against the Occupation. They were among the first to set up local committees to take care of the needs of the town. They resolved disputes and kept the peace in the absence of any police or courts. They also pioneered home gardens, to promote self-reliance and a boycott of Israeli products.

Much of Beit Sahour's economy is based on handicrafts in olive wood and mother-of-pearl artifacts which are sold to tourists. As the Intifada progressed, they began to feel the effects and hardships of the curfews, commercial strikes, loss of jobs in Israel, as well as the drop in tourism. Thus began a pioneering campaign around the refusal to pay Value Added Taxes (VAT).

VAT had come about in this way. Israel had issued a military order amending one of the Jordanian laws on customs. But the Israeli order simply gutted the Jordanian law entirely and replaced its text with the verbatim provisions of the Israeli VAT law.

VAT is a complex structure for taxing every element of commercial transactions, culminating in a whopping 15% tax imposed on the final consumer. For example, a carpenter would buy raw wood (with a 15% tax added to the price), cut it into appropriate pieces, and sell the pieces to an artisan at a higher price. (He would add the 15% tax to the price, but deduct, or claim, the 15% paid on the raw materials). The artisan would carve the wood, and sell it in bulk to a painter, at a yet higher price (to which he would also have to add a 15% tax, but deduct or claim the VAT he paid for the pieces of wood). The artisan would paint the pieces and then sell them in bulk to a souvenir shop (again, adding another 15% to the selling price, but also deducting or claiming the VAT he paid for the figurines and the paint). The shopkeeper would then sell each of the figurines at a higher price and add 15% to the consumer, but deduct, or claim the VAT he paid to his supplier.

For the process to work, each step in the transaction had to be meticulously documented, and each shipment or transaction recorded as mandated in the law to enable the authorities to collect the VAT taxes, and presumably give credit for taxes paid out by each merchant. Any mistake in the books would lead to heavy fines and arbitrary imposition of taxes. The VAT system required monthly reporting as well as detailed bookkeeping and retaining all invoices and receipts for every transaction. It was very complicated and time consuming, far beyond the normal capabilities of many businesses and shops, especially in an underdeveloped economy like the West Bank and Gaza.

Borrowing the famous slogan of the American Revolution, "No taxation without representation," the people of Beit Sahour declared a VAT tax strike against the Israeli military government. The army moved quickly and imposed a total curfew on the whole town, prohibiting anyone from entering or leaving it. They began an aggressive campaign for collecting the taxes.

Soldiers and officials from the Civil Administration moved from house to house trying to collect heavy taxes, which the residents refused to pay. In punishment for non-payment, they would confiscate the entire possessions of each house in turn: television sets, computers, and appliances as well as clothes and furniture. They took everything.

In one house, an old lady tried to appeal to the humanity of the army officer in charge of the operation. She said, "Look, you can take everything, but please leave the refrigerator. There is a nursing baby here, and we need the refrigerator for the milk for the baby."

The officer saw this as an opportunity to break the will of the strikers. He said, "I will help you. I will let you keep not only the refrigerator, but all the furniture of the house if you will only pay a small tax. All I want is one hundred shekels (about thirty dollars)."

The lady said, "I am not here to argue politics with you or to negotiate and bargain. I am appealing to your humanity, for the sake of the baby."

"Okay, I will make it only ten shekels."

The old lady stuck to her beliefs and refused to budge. The army took the refrigerator, television set and all the furniture, loaded them on a truck, and left. Later the woman said, "I felt like Jesus on the Mount of Temptation, being tempted by the devil himself. When Jesus was hungry, the devil took advantage of his hunger and then offered him all sorts of inducements, but Jesus rejected temptation and maintained his position."

The town did not budge, and the tax revolt continued. Nobody would pay any taxes, large or small.

As a result of all this, the Israeli military courts were inundated. They could not keep up with the influx of prisoners. Therefore, they decided to rely less on military courts and began instead to make increasing use of administrative detention. Since this was a popular uprising, prominent citizens were active in the many aspects of intifada leadership and organization. They could not be as easily accused of specific security related activities, but virtually any activism or leadership could be enough of a reason for administrative detention.

Several of my close friends ended up in administrative detention.

One such friend was Dr. Jad Ishaq, who was from Beit Sahour and very active in the nonviolent revolt. Jad was a committed and creative individual. As a scientist who cared fiercely about his community, he had started the Applied Research Institute of Jerusalem (ARIJ). He was experimenting with growing hydroponic plants and mushrooms with little or no soil and was researching ways that Palestinians could obtain greater energy independence by using solar energy. He once asked me what I knew about international water law. I told him that I had taken a couple of courses on riparian law at the University of Virginia Law School, but I knew very little on the subject." We have been invited to the first Israeli/Palestinian conference on water to be held in Geneva," he told me, "and I want you to be our expert. I will get you some books and we can jointly write a paper on the subject." (We actually did end up writing such a paper).

When the Intifada started, Dr. Ishaq became very active in working for economic independence, as we boycotted Israeli goods and sought alternative sources for food. He started a plant nursery to help people grow their own vegetables. He was also active in the local reconciliation committees. It was therefore perhaps not surprising that the Israelis arrested him, issued him an administrative detention order for six months, and sent him to Ketziot Prison in the Negev Desert. At the height of the Intifada, there were five thousand prisoners kept in tents at that prison camp. I often visited him there. Every time I did, I came back fully energized and happy.

What Jad and the other prisoners had done at Ketziot was amazing. Since many of the administrative detainees were prominent citizens, well-educated and respected professionals, they organized themselves and started conducting courses for the other prisoners, each in his chosen field or profession. Before long the entire prison camp was buzzing with constructive classes and student activities. These were not a defeated people, but true leaders.

Jad would often laugh. "We almost have a college here! If this goes on much longer, maybe we should consider issuing diplomas, certificates, and degrees."

Another friend who was arrested during the Intifada was Dr. Mamdouh El Aker, a very gentle physician and urologist. Originally from Nablus, he was also our neighbor in Ramallah. Like so many others, he was arrested under "indefinite detention" with no charges filed against him. While in prison, he was interrogated at length. He told me that he was kept standing for hours with a filthy, urine-soaked burlap bag over his head. When he was eventually brought in to the interrogator, Mamdouh smiled and said, "I don't know what I must have done in a previous life to deserve my treatment. I am a urologist and spend all my working days with urine, and now you have to give me a urine-soaked bag over my head!"

The young man interrogating him actually blushed and apologized. His interrogation turned into a lively political discussion about the conflict and the prospects for peace. The interrogator had to admit that his prisoner was a very affable and grandfatherly doctor, far more intelligent and sympathetic than he had ever expected, and not a terrorist or evil conspirator at all. He was eventually released after a couple of weeks and ended up being part of the negotiating team that went to Madrid to negotiate with Israel on behalf of Palestinians.

Another friend who experienced indefinite detention was Sari Nuseibeh, who was arrested some years later, during the First Gulf War. Sari was an Oxford-educated philosopher and intellectual—the future president of Jerusalem University—and well-known among the diplomats in Jerusalem. When he was arrested, several embassies intervened on his behalf and demanded to know why. They made it clear that Sari had better be charged and tried for a specific security offense and not merely held in administrative detention, as that would be unacceptable to them. The fact that he was a Jerusalemite also helped his case. Because Israel had allegedly annexed Jerusalem, it therefore needed to use Israeli law there, not military orders as it did in the rest of the Occupied Territories.

So, the Israeli authorities told the Americans that Sari had been spying on behalf of Iraq. They claimed he was monitoring the Scud missiles being fired at Israel during the war, reporting the *Ihdathi-yyat* (coordinates) of the location where the missiles fell so that the Iraqis could fine tune their accuracy.

As his lawyer, when I first visited him in prison, Sari asked me, "Please don't tell anybody I asked this, but what are *ihdathiyyat*? What are coordinates?" He truly had no idea what the Israelis were even talking about: he was a philosopher, not a spy nor a military man. He was eventually released a few months later, never charged with anything.

One way I helped Sari while he was in prison was to bring him books. He wanted to read the books of Douglas Adams, such as The Hitchhiker's Guide to the Galaxy and Life, the Universe and Everything. I was only allowed to bring him one book at a time, so I would pass one to him to read while I read the others. I had not previously been familiar with Douglas Adams, but I enjoyed what I read and ended up reading all his books.

Being a political prisoner was a badge of courage in the Palestinian community. Somehow, I managed to evade that particular honor. I always remained careful and calculating in dealing with the Israeli authorities, and while I often faced the prospect of arrest, I always managed to keep out of jail. But individuals can be placed under administrative detention without having to violate any law at all. Perhaps I evaded arrest because I did not belong to any political parties, and so the easy charge of membership in an illegal organization could not be thrown at me. Surely my status as a Hebrew-speaking attorney who held an American passport helped. It also did not hurt that I had extensive contacts with journalists and foreigners, including the diplomatic corps in East Jerusalem.

And of course, being a Jerusalemite, I was personally subject to Israeli civilian law, even though most of my activities were in the West Bank and under Israeli military law. I'm sure that all of these were contributing factors, but in the final analysis, I suspect the real reason may well have been the prayers of my mother for divine protection. My mother, like my mother-in-law, was a true prayer warrior, and she prayed daily for each and every one of her children and grandchildren.

But I wasn't afraid to go to jail. In fact, I even tried to get arrested once. (That is another story) But being a lawyer, it was clear that I could accomplish much more outside of jail. Mubarak once told me there is a different role for everyone. "You may be able to only type one letter at a time in Arabic, but your secretary can type sixty or eighty words a minute," he told me. "It would be a poor use of your time to peck away at an Arabic typewriter. You be the lawyer and let me and others go to jail."

As the Intifada continued, Israel realized that it was eventually going to have to negotiate with the PLO. For the important cause of solidarity, all Palestinian factions, organizations, and individuals had announced that the PLO was our sole legitimate representative. It was still illegal for Palestinians to have any contact with the PLO, whether direct or indirect; yet it was clear that Israel was going to negotiate with them sooner or later.

I was contacted by Jad Ishaq, who had finally been released from prison in the Negev. In preparation for the meetings that were sure to come, Jad felt that we should organize some experts who could prepare working papers on all subjects that might come up during the negotiations. He wanted to make sure that the PLO negotiators were armed with current and accurate information, facts, studies, and maps that they would need in order to negotiate properly and effectively on our behalf.

And this was indeed a real problem. The PLO leadership, which was situated outside of the Occupied Territories, had little detailed information about the current situation on the ground. They were all living in exile and had been conducting their armed struggle from outside the borders of the Occupied Territories. Many of them had been refugees all their lives and had not set foot inside Palestine for decades. Thus, while they conducted an international diplomatic and armed struggle for the liberation of Palestine, they had little direct information on what was happening there. Their perspective tended to be merely political or military.

"What do they know about the needs of the people here?" questioned Jad. "Do they know how many wells or trees we have here? Do they understand how much water we need? Do they have any statistics on the agricultural products or the villages, roads, schools, hospitals, or education?"

Jad was worried that the PLO would be eaten alive by the Israelis if they were not supported by a competent group of technical experts from the inside who could feed them with the pertinent information.

Working as much as possible under the radar, we began to set up secret "technical committees," which reflected all political factions as well as independents like me. We prepared technical papers with facts and statistics. We discussed all aspects of life under occupation, including the amounts of water used, the numbers and composition of schools and hospitals, of industry and agriculture, and the types and nature of soil, land, products, roads, springs, and of the number and nature of the different settlements, as well as the legal structures and military orders.

The energy and vitality of the Intifada was such that without any central leadership or instructions from abroad, we the people took it upon ourselves to carry out such ambitious projects. I was privileged to play my part in it, even without being a member of any of the political factions.

CHAPTER 18

ON MAY 20, 1990, right in the middle of the Intifada, an Israeli soldier stopped a bus going to Tel Aviv and asked all the Arabs on the bus to get out and line up against a wall. Eight Arab workers obeyed his orders. He checked their ID cards to ensure they were indeed all Arabs. Then he shot them all, one by one.

The soldier was arrested, and the Israeli authorities said he was probably mentally unstable. Everyone in the West Bank was in an uproar. Palestinian anger only increased when, during the demonstrations that followed, fifteen more Palestinians were shot dead. The heightened feeling among Palestinians was that we were all extremely vulnerable. Any Israeli Jew with a gun (and almost all Israelis Jews have guns, since they serve in the army) could massacre us for any reason—or for no reason whatsoever. An Israeli who commits such crimes can easily escape punishment. And if brought to trial, he is often either allowed to get away with it or given a joke of a sentence.

Several of us gathered at the offices of Faisal Husseini at the Arab Studies Center in Jerusalem to decide what to do. Faisal Husseini, the unofficial representative of the national movement in Jerusalem, declared that this was the last chance for us to keep the Intifada nonviolent and to show that nonviolence can in fact achieve results. We decided to hold an open-ended hunger strike, appealing to the international community for protection of the Palestinian civilians in the Occupied Territories.

About forty people from different areas of the West Bank and from different political factions joined in this hunger strike. I joined it as well, foolishly thinking I would be able to continue with my regular life, visiting prisoners and going to the office while fasting.

After the first two days of the fast, it was decided that we would be more effective if we held a sit-in on the grounds of the International Red Cross headquarters in Jerusalem, while staying in makeshift tents. We felt that somehow, we would be safer there and less likely to be dispersed or arrested. As someone who knew a little about the subject, I offered to give daily lectures to the group about the philosophy of nonviolence and the use of hunger strikes as a historic part of liberation struggles and campaigns for freedom and equality.

I called my cousin Mubarak, now in his exile in America, to send me some materials on fasting and hunger strikes. Though I had been involved in other forms of nonviolent resistance, this was my first time to participate in a hunger strike. I knew that from time to time, Palestinian prisoners participated in hunger strikes to protest particularly egregious conditions or to demand more visits from their families, access to radios, or something else. Prisoners would tell me, "The right to read newspapers cost us x tons of human flesh." Their logic went like this: If a hundred prisoners lost an average of five kilos over two weeks, for example, it cost them five tons of human flesh altogether to get newspapers into the prison.

Hunger strikes had been practiced by Palestinians for many years but were not usually referred to as nonviolence. That was mainly because the strikers did not have the analysis of nonviolence strategies that were understood as such by Gene Sharp, Mubarak Awad, and others. What they called a hunger strike, I understood as fasting.

The discipline of fasting for religious reasons was not part of my evangelical Christian upbringing. Compared to others, I was not so much a teacher in this area; I had a lot to learn myself. My father used to sometimes speak disparagingly of some Moslems, whose fasting consisted of refraining from eating or drinking for just one day (from sunrise to sundown), after which they could gorge themselves throughout the night. He also didn't think much of the fasting of Catholics and Orthodox Christians, whose fasting consisted of refraining from eating any animal products (veganism, basically) during Lent. Instead, he taught me that "biblical fasting" was fully refraining from eating at all, and it should be combined with prayer. It is a spiritual discipline for the flesh and the spirit as well. He told me that fasting should be undertaken in times of crisis and spiritual wrestling, not as a ritual to be performed at specified times of the year. I do not remember my father fasting at all. To be sure, he also taught me that when you fast you should not let anyone know (Matthew 6:17-18), in order not to boast about it. So, it is possible that he fasted often, and I never knew of it.

After participating in the fast, I quickly discovered why it is such a recommended spiritual discipline. Being on a prolonged fast is an amazing experience. After the second or third day, you actually do not feel any hunger at all. I felt lightheaded and yet fully alert. I seemed to have a greater mental energy and clarity. My bodily motions slowed down and I felt like I was walking on air. It was a very powerful spiritual experience for me.

One of the strikers was Dr. Mamdouh El Aker. He warned us that we need to drink at least three liters of water a day. "You can go without food for weeks," he said, "but your body cannot do without water for more than three days." So we each walked around with a water bottle with our name on it to keep track of our water intake.

It seemed that fasting accentuated our qualities. Those in our group who were thoughtful became much more thoughtful; those who were helpful, were even more so. One person who was a bit arrogant and obnoxious became that much more irritable and obnoxious. I stayed away from him. Most of us, however, bonded well and became much better friends from that day on.

While most of the forty people who went on the hunger strike were Moslems, they were primarily secular, and their reasoning was nationalist and not religious. For them it was a hunger strike, not a fast. We sat around preparing press releases, giving interviews, contacting diplomats, and generally working hard on our campaign for international protection for the Palestinian people. Different groups of Palestinians would come to greet us, sit with us, discuss the situation, and sometimes even sing patriotic songs.

Though only two or three of us participating in the fast were Christians, I was particularly delighted when we were visited by

Bishop Lutfi Lahham, a bishop (and later patriarch) of the Melkite Catholic Church. After greeting us, he gave a wonderful homily on fasting. He actually preached to all those present from Matthew 4:4, which says that "man shall not live by bread alone." He said we were fasting because we wanted our rights and our freedom. We were hungry for justice. Food and other material benefits would not satisfy us. As people made in the image of God, we needed and deserved human rights and human dignity. He told us that our fasting for these rights was an affirmation of our humanity and our willingness to struggle for justice. As a Christian myself, he certainly reflected how I felt about this event.

Two days later Bishop Lahham visited us again and gave us another sermon, this time from Mark 9:29, where Jesus told his disciples about the evil spirits: "This kind shall not be driven out except by prayer and fasting." He said that our hunger strike was for a just cause, against the evil of the occupation and oppression and the dehumanization it entailed. By fasting, we were engaged in a spiritual battle. This sounded just like something my father would say.

The United Nations Security Council was preparing to meet. It would be facing a vote on whether to send international observers to the Occupied Territories to provide basic protection for the civilians there. Dr. Hanan Ashrawi contacted the U.S. State Department, in the hopes that a moderately worded UN resolution might even get US approval, or at least avoid a veto.

On the thirteenth day of our hunger strike, two events happened that upended our hopeful solidarity. First, a rogue Palestinian group tried to make a raid by boat against Israel. They were spotted and arrested as they landed on the coast near Tel Aviv. This event was a huge blow to us and the nonviolent message we were trying to project. Israel was now off the hook and the United States felt justified in supporting them. That same day the Security Council met. While it voted overwhelmingly in favor of our position, calling for international protection for people under occupation, the United States vetoed the resolution, and it did not pass.

We felt stabbed in the back and our message totally undermined. There was now no point in continuing the hunger strike, so we decided to end it in a public manner. First, we marched together to the Dome of the Rock where we offered prayers, and then to the Church of the Holy Sepulcher where we prayed again. We ended at Bishop Lahham's Melkite church near Jerusalem's New Gate, where we each ended our fast by sipping a bowl of onion soup and eating a small slice of toasted bread. I was amazed that I felt so strong and fresh as we marched to the Dome of the Rock and the church. Not only was I not hungry, but I felt that I could easily have fasted for another thirteen days without trouble.

I had not lost a lot of weight, but as I slowly returned to normal in the next few weeks, I learned to appreciate and savor every bite of food in a new way. And afterwards I would highly recommend to anyone who might have the chance to engage in a long fast to do it. It is good for body and soul.

Meanwhile, we returned to our daily lives, each in his or own way fighting the occupation. We hoped we could make an impact with our efforts, sometimes smaller and sometimes greater. There was so much to be done, so much to be challenged.

Travel and ease of movement continue to be a huge problem for Palestinians, no matter where they live. Whether they are Palestinian citizens of Israel, or living as residents of East Jerusalem, like me, or residents of the West Bank, like others in my family, or residents of Gaza, or refugees living outside of Palestine, or even citizens of other nations, entering and exiting Palestine and Israel can often be a challenge. Because we have no state of our own, we are at the mercy of whatever state we happen to live in, including Israel. Two-thirds of our people are refugees residing outside Palestine, and they may or may not hold the passports of the countries where they reside. Thus, when Palestinians travel internationally, they do so under a variety of documents of which the status is not always clear.

I am one of the most fortunate Palestinians because I have a U. S. passport as well as a Jerusalem ID that was issued by Israel. These two documents give me a great margin of freedom and mobility that most Palestinians are not fortunate enough to experience. Some of my family members have in fact lost their residency. Even attempting to visit Palestine can be a risky business.

Kamal Boullatah, a Palestinian artist living in Washington, DC, is one such case.

Kamal was born in Jerusalem and grew up in the Old City. To his great misfortune, he happened to be abroad studying art in Rome when the 1967 War occurred. Because he was not at home when Israel conducted its census after it began to occupy East Jerusalem and the West Bank, he was not listed as a resident and so he was never allowed to return home. He spent the rest of his life in exile.

Mubarak had become friends with him while living in Washington, DC, and he is the one who introduced me to Kamal. At that time Kamal was writing poetry, but mostly painting and studying art. He had become quite a scholar of Islamic art and particularly the unique art form known as *arabesque*. He had gained his love of this kind of art as a child. When he was only ten years old he would take his little stool and drawing equipment to the Dome of the Rock, where he spent hours copying and drawing the intricate patterns and designs of the *Al Haram Al Sharif*, the "Noble Sanctuary."

Kamal was one of the kindest, gentlest people I have ever met. We would sit and discuss Jerusalem for hours. We would talk about nonviolence, international law, and human rights, but we always somehow came back to faith and religion.

Once, during a random conversation, he remarked, "Can you imagine Christianity without wine? It flows throughout the Bible. Jesus said, 'I am the vine, and you are the branches.' The vine is a sign of God's blessing. The vine and wine are basic to Jesus's life and teachings. No wonder the Holy Communion consists of bread and wine. These are the two essentials of life, which feed the body and the spirit."

Now I had grown up in a teetotaling household, believing that drinking wine and other forms of alcohol was a serious sin—and here was my friend, a true Christian, steeped in Christian history and traditions, promoting the glories of wine—and quoting from the Bible, no less. He blew away all my previous understanding on this subject with his simple question: how could anyone imagine Christianity without wine? I was dumbfounded, and I could not think of a retort.

I would often stop at Kamal's apartment in Washington D.C., near Dupont Circle. He had two inexpensive apartments, which were "rent-controlled" and would always give me the keys to his "guest apartment," from which I could come and go as I pleased. He did not feel he had to entertain me or change his schedule when I was in town, though I always liked to at least have a meal with him and his lovely wife, Lily, and to talk about his Jerusalem.

In 1985, after he had obtained a U.S. passport, his Dutch Jewish friend, a filmmaker named Van Denberg, decided to make a film of his life and his dream of returning home. Since Kamal now had a U.S. passport, he would be able to return to Jerusalem as a tourist for the first time since 1967. Kamal was so excited and asked me to help in the project. I was glad to do so.

The film, which was called *Stranger at Home*, turned out to be poignant and emotional both for Kamal and his Jewish friend. In one touching scene, Kamal visited his old home, which was now inhabited by others. In another, he visited the *mukhtar* of the Greek Orthodox community, Mr. Tubbeh, who took out his book of gene-alogies. He traced the history of the Boullata family for the last six hundred years, ending with Kamal's very name on the last page.

The filmmaker, along with the crew, then went to the Israeli Ministry of the Interior, where Van Denberg asked if Kamal could return to Jerusalem to live.

"Oh no," he was told. "That would be impossible."

"What about me? Can I move to Jerusalem?" asked Van Denberg.

"Oh, you can come under the Law of Return. You are Jewish."

"But I have no connection to this land. I have no family or

THE TRUTH SHALL SET YOU FREE

friends here. I do not speak Hebrew and I am not religious. In fact, I do not believe in God at all. Look at me. I am blond, blue-eyed, and completely Dutch."

"You are Jewish and that is enough."

Later, in my office, I explained to him that it was indeed the law in Israel. Zionism teaches that this land belongs only to Jews, no matter what country in the world they are from. The conversation was recorded for the documentary.

"But Kamal here is steeped in Jerusalem. He was born here. He grew up here. His family, his church, his ancestors. You saw the priest's book."

"That is all irrelevant," I said. "As far as Israeli law is concerned, he has no rights in Jerusalem whatsoever."

Kamal related that when he was still a child, Jews, Christians, and Moslems who were born in the land lived together in harmony. He told a story of Palestinian inter-religious coexistence, which was beautifully enacted and captured in that documentary. It was traditional among Palestinian Moslem women that if one was barren and could not bear a child, she would be advised to go to the oak tree of our Father Abraham in Hebron, and pray the Lord's prayer in Arabic seven times. If she did this, God would answer her prayer and give her a child, just as He had done for Abraham's barren wife, Sarah. It was a beautiful story combining Islam, Judaism, and Christianity in a totally Palestinian folk tradition. Kamal cherished this recollection of ecumenism in Palestine before Zionism claimed the land only for Jews.

After this brief visit, Kamal returned to his exile and never visited Jerusalem again. In 2019, he passed away in Hamburg,

Germany. His wife, Lily, called and asked if I could do something to help fulfill his last wish, which was to be buried in Jerusalem. I told her the chances were minimal, but that I would try my very best. Perhaps if we combined legal efforts in Germany and in Jerusalem with some behind the scenes diplomacy, as well as the threat of a public relations campaign, we might be able to succeed.

What followed was a week of intense work by my law office as well as lobbying and pressure. Also, Kamal's death had come right after Israel had refused entry to Palestinian-American congress-woman Rashida Tlaib to visit her grandmother in Palestine.

By the end of his life, Kamal had become a world-renowned artist and art historian. A number of his friends, as well as the German university where he had taught art, were willing to call and write on his behalf to the Israeli authorities. The combination of threatened legal action and an embarrassing public relations campaign paid off. After overcoming a number of crazy obsta-cles and conditions, we finally got the needed permit. An Israeli Jewish religious company that handles issues of bringing Jewish bodies for burial in Israel handled the logistics locally, and Ka-mal's body was flown in and buried in the Boullata family plot at the cemetery on Mount Zion in Jerusalem. I was glad to repay a small part of the debt of friendship I owed to Kamal, though the injustice of barring him from his beloved city during his life still stung.

Sometimes though, these stories hit even closer to home.

In 2006, my sister Grace was denied entry into Israel and Pal-estine at the Allenby Bridge crossing. She was traveling to Israel for a wedding in which she was to be the bridesmaid for one of her husband's relatives. The officer at the bridge simply told her that she could not enter. Even though she was born in Jerusalem and was included in the census Israel took in 1967, it was claimed that she had "ceased to be a resident." Her U.S. passport did not help her. The fact that she had been born in Palestine prior to 1967, and had once been a resident of the West Bank, with an ID card and number, was apparently a reason to deny her entry. Perhaps they were afraid that she would claim some sort of residency and refuse to leave when her visitor's visa expired. Therefore, it was simply easier to deny her—and many others like her—entry altogether. Today, she is living in Florida with her husband, a Lutheran minister who is also from Palestine. If she ever decides to visit the West Bank again, she has no assurance of being admitted. To the Israeli government she is now a stranger, with no right even to visit her homeland. No security reason is given or needed. The imperative of needing to make Israel Jewish, and to keep it for Jews and Jews only was the only explanation for this injustice.

People in the West Bank are somewhat fortunate in that they can have Jordanian passports. Though visiting Jerusalem or travelling anywhere on the Israeli side of the border is difficult, at least they have ease of international travel. When Jordan annexed the West Bank, including East Jerusalem, after 1948, it issued Jordanian passports to its inhabitants and continued to do so even after 1967, when the West Bank began to be occupied by Israel.

People in the Gaza Strip were not as fortunate, since Egypt did not annex Gaza and therefore did not issue its population with Egyptian passports. Israel at first issued special permits for people who wanted to travel. The permit looked like a *laissez passer* document, which some countries recognized for travel purposes, but it was very precarious.

Mona Rishmawi, my colleague at Al Haq, comes from a Christian family from Gaza, but she has lived in Ramallah all her life. Through a difficult and lengthy process, and with much intervention by Fouad Shehadeh, the lawyer in whose office we both started, she and her family managed to acquire Jordanian passports, like other West Bankers, which they used for international travel. One day, Al Haq received an invitation to attend the Arab Lawyers' Conference in Kuwait. We decided that Mona and I would go to represent Palestine and to speak about our human rights situation. While people assume that the Arab world is automatically supportive of Palestinian rights, the daily experience of Palestinians in many Arab countries is sometimes a very painful one, as we were about to find out.

Mona and I travelled to Kuwait through Amman, Jordan. The plane that took us from Amman to Kuwait also carried a large delegation from the Jordanian Bar Association who were travelling to attend the same conference. Somehow, on the plane, some of the lawyers discovered that the two of us were working lawyers, who appeared regularly in Israeli military courts to defend Palestinian prisoners.

The Jordanian Bar Association had declared a strike in 1967 and refused to allow its members to appear before Israeli military courts. While there were good reasons initially for the strike, it did not make sense to continue it indefinitely. After two decades, the situation was comical, if not tragic. An entire society was left practically without lawyers. and Palestinian prisoners would have no support or representation whatsoever, and they would have to rely on Jewish or Israeli-Arab lawyers to defend them. An Israeli military order, which I had taken advantage of, allowed Israeli lawyers to appear before military courts as well as practice in West Bank courts.

In contrast, Jordan supported the striking lawyers by giving them a monthly stipend. They officially treated working lawyers as somewhat unpatriotic for violating the strike—even though by this time there were as many working lawyers as there were striking lawyers. The strike had lost all its meaning and logic and would instantly collapse if Jordan were to stop paying the striking lawyers a monthly salary.

When the plane arrived in Kuwait, we were met by Kuwaiti officials, who were there to meet the different lawyers' delegations from all over the Arab world. They welcomed us to the VIP lounge and took our passports to be processed. We were taken to the hotel and treated like visiting dignitaries. In a few hours, the passports were returned to the head of the Jordanian lawyers' delegation, duly stamped.

As the passports were distributed to the lawyers, there was no sign of my or Mona's passport. We asked our Kuwaiti hosts, who told us that they had returned all the passports in one stack to a representative of the Jordanian Bar Association, and we should ask them for our passports. The head of the delegation denied that he received them. He said he had nothing to do with us, as we were not members of his Bar Association at all.

For me, it was not that big of a deal. I could go to the U.S. embassy and be issued a replacement passport on the spot, which I did. For Mona, however, it was a major catastrophe. She had no embassy to turn to, and the Jordanian Government—judging by the head of the Bar Association—was totally hostile to her. She was in fact totally stranded. She could be arrested, imprisoned, and later deported to Jordan, where she might or might not be allowed in. She could even be left in prison until her situation was clarified. When the Jordanian authorities discovered that she was originally from Gaza, they might even refuse to reissue a replacement Jordanian passport. The Israelis would also refuse to allow her back into Palestine without documents. She would be truly stateless. At the very least, she would suffer weeks or months of hassle, worry, and uncertainty. Meanwhile, some Jordanian lawyer would be laughing his head off for having "showed her" the error of her ways for not abiding by the strike.

I tried to talk to the head of the Jordanian delegation about the matter, but he refused to talk to me. He said it was not his concern. Other lawyers at the conference were not even aware of the problem. Perhaps some of them had heard about us from the Jordanian delegation: that two lawyers—perhaps Zionists, traitors, or people of questionable character—had somehow tried to infiltrate the conference, and the official delegation of the Jordanian Bar Association, which also included West Bank striking lawyers, would have nothing to do with them.

So for us, the eagerly anticipated conference had suddenly turned into a nightmare. I felt that I needed to do something, but I had no idea what to do.

On the last day of the conference, we were supposed to attend a banquet given in our honor by a Kuwaiti princess. I made up my mind that I would make a scene at the dinner. I planned to march up to the princess and loudly ask in front of everyone if this is how Kuwaitis treat their guests. I would explain that our passports had been stolen by her passport control people. As the evening approached, I told anybody who would listen what I was going to do if Mona did not get her passport by that evening.

Nothing happened.

All the lawyers from different countries were ushered into a large hall, through portable metal detectors that were hastily installed. We stood there until the princess and her entourage entered. I was standing halfway through the throng when she took the podium. I said a quick prayer under my breath and began to make my way to the front. I was concentrating on formulating my words and preparing myself for the scene which was sure to follow. I also eyed the burly guards standing menacingly around the princess, who was seated on the dais.

As I got closer to the front, someone tapped me on the shoulder and quietly handed me a passport. It was Mona's, duly stamped. After the man handed me the passport, he left. I never saw him again.

I was able to get my own American passport replacement in one day, and Mona and I travelled back to the West Bank without further incident. But that was a harsh reminder of the troubles that arise from not having a state of our own and living under occupation.

I have another advantage that other Palestinians do not, and that is my knowledge of Israel's legal system.

One day Beth, my American wife, told me that she needed to get her Jerusalem ID card renewed and documented into her U.S. passport so that she could maintain her residency status. The same operation had to be carried out for me and for our two children, as well. Without our *hawiyyeh* status, our entry into Israel could be denied at any time. We could be permanently thrown out of the country like Mubarak and many others. Since I travel a lot and my wife and children were in Amman for her United Nations job, it was essential that I go to the Ministry of the Interior to get our *hawiyyehs* renewed.

The problem is that there was only one office of the Israeli Ministry of Interior in East Jerusalem, which serves a population of three hundred thousand people. Every new birth, marriage, change of address, and every single renewal of identity cards or travel documents had to be done at that location. There was nowhere else to do it.

The building which housed the Ministry of Interior on Nablus Road was a sad-looking structure, and totally inadequate for the task. Crowds of people waited outside the building in the sun or rain hoping to enter the building, where additional long lines awaited them. The building was guarded by a private security company who hired formidable looking newly arrived immigrants from Russia to keep the crowds in check.

It was doubly ironic that Palestinians would jostle each other and sometimes fight to get in before others in the crowd. Others would try to bribe Israeli employees to carry out these functions on their behalf. Once inside the building, they all understood the nature of the game. They knew that Israel would rather not have any of them in the country at all. Under the ruling established in the Mubarak Awad case, they needed to prove that they resided in Jerusalem, and that it continued to be "the center of their life and activity." The burden was on them to produce sufficient documentary evidence that they paid their municipal taxes, and had their children enrolled in schools there, paid utility bills for a residence within the municipal boundaries, and provide other sorts of documentation. If they became too fatigued to continue the process and gave up, or if their paperwork was not in order, or if they could not prove continued residency in Jerusalem itself—for example, if they resided in Bethlehem or Ramallah, or elsewhere in the West Bank—they could lose their status forever. The Jewish State would be rid of them and be a little closer to its proclaimed goal of being a truly Jewish state.

Beth had tried twice to stand in line to renew her *hawiyyeh*. She had heard that if one arrived in the early morning hours, at four or five a.m., and managed to keep their place in line, it was possible to get in, but she could not afford to do that. The process was so laborious that I tried to pay one of my colleagues to do the function on our behalf, but he said he no longer took on those kinds of tasks.

I decided that I would flex my legal muscles and bring a petition to the Israeli Supreme Court, asking for an "Order to Show Cause" why I should not be allowed to set foot inside the building. In Hebrew it sounds even more poetic. I said that I wanted "the bottom of my foot to touch the inside floor of the Ministry of Interior building and no more".

I drafted the petition in my best Hebrew complete with attachments, showing how I was required under Israeli law to carry the *hawiyyeh* on my person at all times. But though I was required to renew the documents in question, I could not elbow and push my way into the building. Furthermore, as an officer of the court, I was not allowed to pay bribes to public officials. I therefore petitioned the Supreme Court, sitting as a High Court of Justice, to intervene and order the State of Israel to permit me to set foot inside the building—and nothing else. I paid the fees, submitted the petition with its attachments in seven copies, and served it upon the Ministry of Interior at their headquarters in West Jerusalem.

After one week, the phone in my office rang. "This is the High Court Division in the Ministry of Justice. May I speak to attorney Jonathan Kuttab?"

"This is he."

The voice at the other end was laced with irritation. "What kind of joke is this? I just saw your petition. Are you serious?"

"Before I answer you, please tell me, sir—do you live in this country? Or on Mars?"

"What do you mean?" he asked, puzzled and irritated.

"Are you aware that the only place I can file my papers as an East Jerusalemite is in the office of the Interior Ministry on Nablus Road?"

"So, what is the problem? Why are they refusing to give you your extensions?"

"Actually, there is no problem with that. They have not refused me anything. I just cannot get inside the building. I cannot shove and push and fight to get in and I refuse to pay bribes as an officer of the court. There is always a huge crowd from the early morning hours. There are also two Russian gorillas at the door who do not speak Hebrew, Arabic, English, or French, and who bar entry."

"Well, what do you want?"

"Nothing extraordinary. I simply want to set foot inside the building in order to carry out the most mundane of civil functions. I merely want to be allowed renew my *hawiyyeh* and get my residency permit into my passport before it expires."

"You will get a call within two hours," he said shortly. Then he hung up.

A half-hour later, I got another call. This time it was from the Legal Advisor to the Ministry of the Interior. I had the same conversation with him. He promised to call back in two hours—and he did.

"Are you free on Sunday at ten a.m.?"

"I will be!" Ordinarily I would be in church, but Sunday is a working day in Israel, and I was not about to enter into an argument.

"Good. You have an appointment with Ms. Idkeidik at the Ministry of Interior office in Jerusalem at ten a.m. on Sunday."

"Great. But please tell the two gorillas at the entrance to let me in."

When my friend Sari Nuseibeh heard that I had an appointment at the Ministry of Interior, he gave me his passport, along with the British passports of his wife and his two children.

And that is how I found myself at the entrance of the Ministry of Interior that Sunday, with a stack of passports. I stood at the edge of the crowd and yelled in Arabic and Hebrew, "By order of the High Court, I have an appointment here with Ms. Idkeidik."

The sea of people parted, and I entered the building. Within half an hour I was back outside . . . and with five-year, multiple re-entry permits affixed to every passport in my possession!

Several years later, I was stopped at the Allenby Bridge crossing into the West Bank and told that I could no longer enter the country without a visa from the Israeli Embassy in the United States, since according to their computer I had "ceased to be a resident." I had an argument with them, which I won only when I showed them the re-entry permit affixed in my passport. They could not argue with that. Instead, they told me to report to the office of the Ministry of Interior in East Jerusalem within two weeks.

This time, I didn't bother to go. I simply sent a letter with a copy of my still-valid re-entry permit. I also threatened to once again complain to the High Court if they did not recognize my residency. I never heard back from the ministry, but there is no doubt in my mind that if I hadn't had that re-entry permit, I might well have been barred from returning to Jerusalem . . . just like Mubarak, my sister Grace, and Kamal Boullatah.

The attempts to systematically purge Israel of Palestinian residents is an ongoing battle. The demographic make-up of the country is a nightmare for many Zionists. Even some liberal Israelis were worried that Israel might one day lose its Jewish majority.

In 2017, the Israeli Ministry of Interior proudly announced that it had managed to "revoke the residency of 14,595 East Jerusalemites" who had failed to prove that Jerusalem was the "center of their lives." If I had not fought them, I could easily have been just one more statistic.

CHAPTER 19

A FURTHER IRONY is that for most West Bankers, particularly young people, the *hawiyyeh* is not just a proof of residency: it also serves also as a powerful means of control for the Israeli army. Any Israeli soldier can order you to produce your ID card upon demand. Once you hand it over to him, you are his prisoner. You must wait until he returns it to you. He can order you to do anything, or simply keep you waiting for hours. If he takes your *hawiyyeh* with him, you will have to go to the military headquarters to retrieve it. There you might have to sit and wait for hours. There are daily incidents where Israeli soldiers harass and mock Palestinian youth. After taking their *hawiyyeh*, they might make them sing or eat grass like animals or simply wait in the heat of the sun for hours. All of this is just for the "fun" of harassing them.

One member of the Hakawati theatre was stopped at a checkpoint late at night and ordered to hand over his ID while they inspected his car. When they found his violin, they ordered him to play it and entertain them for about an hour before they allowed him to go. Sometimes you have to laugh so you don't cry.

A South African lawyer was shocked when I told him about the *hawiyyeh* problem. I thought it would remind him of the passcard system used in South Africa, but he said no. "Your passcard in South Africa is your possession," he told me, "And the police cannot take it from you."

It was a surprise to learn that in some ways, things were even more difficult for Palestinians living under occupation than it was for black people in South Africa under apartheid.

The restrictions on movement and travel were only some of the myriad methods of controls, humiliations, restrictions, and harassments that governed the life of Palestinians in the occupied territories. The incarcerations and threat of imprisonment, as well as other restrictions, were a part of the daily lives of all of us. It was therefore no wonder that the entire population spontaneously and enthusiastically joined in the Intifada. We felt that we could not give up and must continue to use different methods of nonviolent resistance, attempt to make ourselves ungovernable, and trust that time was on our side and that eventually at least some measure of justice would be achieved.

At the Nonviolence Center we continued to argue that the occupation was in many ways successful because we were too willing to abide by its rules, even when there were no soldiers around to enforce them. If rules were broken, Israeli soldiers could always come back and punish entire populations. This fear kept Palestinians in their place and made the occupation less costly and cumbersome to Israel than it otherwise would have been.

Israeli forces would often punish a whole town, village, or a refugee camp for actions of a few of its inhabitants. One of the punishments they used—especially after actions of resistance such as stone throwing—was to deny access to the village or camp. They did this by placing cement blocks or large mounds of dirt at the entrances. After the soldiers left, the Palestinians would have to suffer by climbing over the barriers in order to enter or exit their community. They were afraid to remove them for fear of greater collective punishment.

This happened once at the Qalandia refugee camp, which was located near my home at the northern area of East Jerusalem. Some kids had thrown stones at passing Israeli jeeps or settler cars, so as punishment, the Israeli army closed off the entrances of the camp with mounds of dirt. But these mounds stayed in place for months after the stone throwing incident had been forgotten. No one could drive in and out of the camp and all who lived in it had to climb over the mound of dirt, carrying their groceries, tools, or other possessions with them. It was especially difficult for the sick and elderly, since no vehicle could enter the camp.

I raised the subject with the legal advisor to the military government, whose headquarters were located in the settlement of Beit El. I told him that such actions were a form of collective punishment, and this is specifically prohibited by the Geneva Conventions. I reminded him that they were punishing the entire refugee camp, where thousands of people lived, for the alleged actions of a few youths.

"In any case," I said, "the area has been quiet for several months and there is no reason to continue to punish the whole camp."

The legal advisor sort of agreed with me and told me that he would not object too much if the people removed the dirt barrier.

The very next day, however, there was another incident—maybe stone throwing or a molotov cocktail—I don't remember, and the entire camp was placed under a twenty-four-hour curfew. When the curfew was lifted, I knew better than to try to get written permission to remove the dirt barrier.

I decided however, that the time had come to utilize another method of nonviolent resistance. Taking matters into my own hands, I gathered some young people from the camp and told them that we needed to remove the barriers. I was willing to take responsibility for the action. I would even write them a letter in Hebrew, giving them permission to do so. That way, if any soldiers saw them and asked them who gave them the authority to do it, they could show the letter and refer the soldiers to me.

"Get someone with a front-end loader to push the dirt out of the way quickly," I said.

The next day, they told me they could not find anyone willing to take the risk. The owner of the small bulldozer who lived in the camp was afraid the Israelis would confiscate his equipment, which he needed for his livelihood. He was afraid even after they showed him my letter.

I decided that I would go and help them remove the barrier myself.

"Bring some picks and shovels," I instructed.

When they saw me carrying a shovel while wearing my suit and tie, they all joined in the effort. Working together, we managed to remove all the barriers from the entrances, so that vehicles could travel in and out of the refugee camp.

In retrospect, I do not think this action was particularly brave or revolutionary, but at the time it took a lot to convince people that they could take charge of their lives without throwing stones or resorting to violence. We just needed a determined effort to resist. I found it strange that political factions like Fatah and PFLP, who were willing to engage in armed struggle (or at least the rhetoric of armed struggle), and who were active in the refugee camp, were not willing to lead nonviolent acts like this one.

Around this same time, the *mukhtar* of a village near Herodion asked me to represent the villagers whose land was being confiscated and given to settlers. Herodion is just south of Bethlehem in the Judean desert—the site of the ruins of Herod's palace.

I explained to the *mukhtar* that Israel used at least five different methods to take Palestinian land, not only "confiscation." Confiscation for public purposes is just one. Another is expropriation for military or security purposes; a third method is declaring the land to be state land; a fourth is claim that it is "absentee property"; a fifth is a bogus claim that it has been bought by the settlers through forgeries, or other illegitimate challenges to the Palestinian ownership. My job as a lawyer was to figure out which method was being used to take the land and then make an attempt to challenge it legally, since each one of these methods required a different strategy to challenge it in court.

Realistically, however, the Palestinian owners could not assume that simply hiring a lawyer would relieve them of worrying about the confiscation of their land. I told him that the lawyer's part is only five percent of defending the land. The other ninety-five percent depends on the willingness of the people to fight to protect it.

"But we have no weapons," he said. "How can we fight?"

"No, no," I protested. "You do not fight with weapons, but with non-violence. You must plant trees across your land and you must be willing to hold your ground even when the bulldozers arrive. You must be physically there and be prepared to defend it with your body, if necessary."

The *mukhtar* looked at me skeptically but agreed to follow my advice.

About a month later he called me and said that the bulldozers were working on the land. I reminded him of what I said earlier.

"The villagers are at the site confronting the bulldozers," he replied, "but please come and join us immediately. I think the army may soon come to arrest them."

About forty minutes later I met him at the village, and we set out on foot together to the land that was being confiscated.

Upon arriving at the land, I saw a lone bulldozer working away and forming a pile of stones. No one else was in sight. I later learned that the army had already come, arrested the villagers, and left. I went straight to the bulldozer and told the driver in Hebrew that the land was private. It belonged to my client, and he could not work it. The driver did not want any trouble, so he turned off the engine, climbed down from the bulldozer, and went to the nearby settlement of Nekema.

The word *nekema* means "vengeance" in Hebrew. Apparently, the settlement had been created and so named to avenge the death of a Jewish settler by a Palestinian in that general area. (As of this writing, it is the home of one of the members of Knesset who is a radical right-wing settler.)

When the driver of the bulldozer left, however, a settler wearing a *kippah* (a religious head covering) and carrying an M-16 rifle immediately took his place. He climbed into the cockpit of the bulldozer, fired it up, and resumed working.

I stood in front of the bulldozer and told the *mukhtar* to stand behind it, so that the bulldozer could not move without running over one of us. This frustrated him, and he began to loudly rev up the engine, hoping to scare us.

The situation was indeed scary. We were alone in the wilderness, with no one to witness what would happen if he decided to run over us. There was no network coverage where we were, and I could not call any of my journalist friends; or anyone else, for that matter. I told the *mukhtar* to run to the village, find out where everybody was, and to call some people from the press. Up until that point I had thought that the whole point of nonviolence was to publicize the evil taking place. I saw cameras and members of the press as essential tools for any nonviolent action. The idea was to fight the forces of darkness by shining the light of truth and publicity on their actions. I was about to learn what happens when there is no press, no cameras, and no witnesses.

When the *mukhtar* left, the driver was able to reverse the bulldozer and move it around to continue working from the other side.

I followed his movements, placing myself again and again between the bulldozer and the pile of rubble he was accumulating as he leveled the ground. As I stood in front of that pile of rocks in the middle of nowhere, I thought of Don Quixote fighting his windmills. It did seem absurd to be standing alone in the wilderness, defending a pile of rubble from this armed settler and his bulldozer.

The driver of the bulldozer began to rapidly drive straight towards me. I knew that if I bent down to pick up a stone, that would be the trigger for the settler to shoot me (in "self-defense," of course), and I was not about to give him that excuse. Especially since there were no witnesses around!

I took a deep breath and looked at the blue sky. "Well, this is a good day to die," I thought to myself. At that moment, I realized that I was more certain of my faith than I had previously thought. I was sure that I was ready to meet my Creator. There was no doubt or sense of panic. Strangely, I did not find myself praying for protection or deliverance from the danger. Rather, I was simply unafraid, experiencing a deep sense of peace and serenity.

In that moment, I knew—I *knew*—that God was there and that He was watching everything. So, the only thing that really mattered was that He approved of what I was doing. Faith rose within me, and I knew that defending that pile of stones with my body was the right thing to do. I would die if necessary, but I would do it nonviolently—and without anger, hatred, or retaliation. I would not threaten my opponent; I would simply stand there and hold my ground.

As the bulldozer drove closer to me, I suddenly had another idea. I turned my back on the driver. I guess I did not want to see my own death, but I also wanted to make clear to the settler that I was offering him no threat and no resistance.

An amazing thing happened.

The driver stopped within a foot of reaching me and turned off the engine.

I guess it isn't so easy to kill another human being who is not threatening you.

To confront violence against yourself without giving in to hatred or fear is an awesome thing. On that day, I managed to do it.

I realized at that time that nonviolent resistance operates on the hearts and minds of both the victim and of the oppressor, even if there is no press, no cameras, and no outside intervention. What goes on in the mind of each person in the confrontation is just as important, in some cases maybe more so.

This settler was not a monster, after all, but a very human individual, whose God-given conscience would not allow him to kill an unarmed person. Especially one who was not threatening him in any way. Thank God for that!

Soon afterwards, an army jeep arrived, and I was placed under arrest. I told the soldiers, "I am an attorney."

They said, "Then you can fight this in court."

"I fully intend to do so, but in the meantime, I still refuse to leave until the bulldozer leaves."

The soldiers spoke to the settler, who finally agreed. He drove the bulldozer away to the settlement.

I was ordered to follow the jeep in my own car, to the police station in Bethlehem, where I was interrogated, fingerprinted, and released.

I did not always have the courage to put my life on the line like I did on that day, but I needed to know how nonviolence can truly work in such a dangerous situation. It was also a strong reminder that we must never demonize the other person, nor forget that there is a part of the divine in him as well, and we must never give up on appealing to that part of him. It was also good to be reminded of what I believed: that doing the will of God is the most important thing in life.

Many years later, a group of us faced a similar challenge of putting our nonviolence to the test: this time again in the face of Israeli settlers armed with weapons.

One of my clients, Daoud Nassar and his family, own a plot of about a hundred acres of land which lies in close proximity to three new settlements south of Bethlehem. The Nassar family bought the land over a hundred years ago. Despite having ownership papers dating back to the Ottoman era and the fact that they had been living on the land continuously since that time, they were facing increasing pressure from the surrounding settlers who coveted their land.

The Israeli army and the civil administration were trying different legal tricks to strip my clients' family of their land. They claimed that the land in question belonged to the state. The army was trying to benefit from the incomplete land survey operations in two-thirds of all West Bank lands. In 1967 the Israeli government halted all land survey operations, which created great confusion over the true ownership of various lands; this worked to the advantage of the army and the settlers. They suggested that the land purchase documents that the Nassar family held were deficient. The document refers to four hundred *dunams* (a hundred acres), but the army claimed that it might be referring to a different plot of land, since it only listed the neighbors on three borders of the land. Because of that, therefore, they questioned whether my client's title deed actually pertained to this particular plot or not.

The Nassars had been harassed many times during a protracted legal battle, which had already lasted over a decade at the time of this incident. Israeli settlers had blocked the road that led to their property with large boulders, that were quite difficult to move. They had killed the family mule which the Nassar family used to work the land and harassed the family in other ways. The Nassars had tried to enlist foreigners to help them defend their land, and so had started calling it the "Tent of Nations."

Daoud Nassar called me one Friday afternoon, saying that the settlers were using a bulldozer to carve out a road right in the middle of his land. It was uprooting grapevines and olive trees. Even worse, such a road through the middle of their property would make it possible for armed settlers to easily enter the Nassar land in order to harass and threaten them.

I told Daoud that since it was Friday afternoon, the courts would be closed for the Jewish sabbath, so I would be unable to obtain any injunctions from them. But I told Daoud that I would call the governor of Bethlehem and inform the Israeli police, and that I would also come out to his property myself.

I called my cousin, Rev. Alex Awad, who brought with him a visiting Dutch pastor. Together with Sani, my law partner, and Tony Nassar, then a student at Bethlehem Bible College, the five of us went out to the Nassar farm to confront the settlers.

We came across the bulldozer busily plowing a new road right through the middle of the land.

I yelled at the driver in Hebrew, "You have to stop. This is our land!"

"It is not! Where are your papers?" he shouted back at me.

I told him, "Yes, we have the papers. I am a lawyer."

"Fine," he said. "Go to court."

I said, "We are already in court. You must stop working here now. You have no right to be here at all."

He ignored me and kept working, and I told Daoud Nassar that as a lawyer, there is nothing else I could do. "However, this is where nonviolent direct action is necessary."

He was not sure what I was getting at. "What do you mean?"

"I will show you. We need to stop him with nonviolence, by physically standing in front of the bulldozer."

I asked Sani to observe and take pictures while Alex and I stood in the middle of the path which the bulldozer was widening into a road. The bucket of the bulldozer kept inching closer and closer to our feet as it dug out more and more of the land. We stood our ground. Finally, one stroke of the blade took a chunk of earth from under our feet, and I fell into the gap that was being dug. Alex quickly pulled me up and the driver of the bulldozer turned off his engine.

"You are lucky that I have a conscience!" he yelled angrily at us.

Actually, I was seriously hoping and counting on it, I thought to myself!

The driver continued shouting at us.

"If I find out this land does not belong to you, I will come into the town of Beit Jala and shoot you myself!"

"You can do that," I said, "but the land does belong to us."

After a while, an army jeep came by, and the soldiers exchanged some words with the settler. He drove off in a huff.

We were definitely relieved.

"I learned two things today," I later told my wife as I recounted the story. "First, it is still true: nonviolence does work. It worked in Herodion, and it still works today. Second, I think I am getting too old for this kind of stuff!"

I don't mean to imply that nonviolence is a foolproof tactic which will work every time, nor that it is completely cost-free. In these two cases both drivers had a conscience, so they were not willing to kill or injure me. That is not always assured, however. Sometimes this form of resistance can be costly, even unto death.

About two weeks after that incident took place, we heard that an Israeli bulldozer driver in Gaza actually ran over a young American peace activist, Rachel Corrie. While standing between a Palestinian home and the bulldozer that was being used to destroy it, Rachel bravely held her ground and refused to move. But in Rachel's case, she was not so lucky. She was bulldozed to death. The driver later claimed that he had not seen her, but many people found that hard to believe, since she was wearing a fluorescent vest and using a bullhorn to talk to the driver during the entire event.

As usual, an Israeli government investigation ruled that the driver had done nothing wrong. A bit later the organization Rachel was with—International Solidarity Movement (ISM)—was declared by Israel to be illegal, and anyone associated with it would henceforth be barred from entry into Israel. Israeli propaganda tried to smear this young woman as a radical, Israel-hating, terrorist sympathizer who had no business being in Gaza at all.

Rachel Corrie was a true martyr for justice and nonviolence. She has become a symbol of non-violent martyrdom on behalf of the Palestinian people, and she is beloved across the land for her uncommon courage in refusing to move, even when it cost her her life.

Eventually the prolonged non-violent activism of the First Intifada opened up the anticipated conversations between Israel and individuals from the occupied territories known to be affiliated with the PLO. One of the first of such major meetings was the Madrid Conference, which in turn led to a series of long and protracted negotiations. Unfortunately, the most qualified leaders from West Bank/Gaza (many of whom I knew well) who were conducting the negotiations, were totally blindsided by secret negotiations which were taking place in Oslo. These secret meetings between Israel and Arafat and the outside leadership of the PLO resulted in a document called Declaration of Principles (DOP) that was signed by Arafat and Israel's prime minister, Yitzhak Rabin.

It was exactly as Jad Ishaq and I had suspected: the PLO leaders had managed to take control of the negotiating process and were directly overseeing the negotiations from abroad.

Regardless, there was a very hopeful atmosphere and the sense that peace was close at hand. The hope was tangible that, after over twenty-five years of occupation, Israel would withdraw from the West Bank and Gaza and allow the creation of a Palestinian State. There were still some tough issues to negotiate, including the status of Jerusalem, the fate of the settlements, and the Palestinian refugees, but there seemed to be general agreement on ending the occupation and pursuing a two-state solution. While the West Bank negotiators were insisting on addressing these issues first, Arafat was perfectly willing to make an interim agreement, and leave these thorny "final status" issues to be resolved later.

I was in Cairo with my wife, Beth, attending a conference on management by TEAM International, a management firm run by my friend Nabeel Shaa'th. He and I went back years, having worked together about a decade earlier to help get summer computer camps set up for Arab children.

Nabeel was also in Cairo at the time, not only as host of the TEAM conference, but also as a member of the Executive Committee of the PLO, which was just beginning initial meetings with the Israelis. At that time he was the chief Palestinian negotiator. At the opening session for the TEAM international conference, Nabeel announced that he had great hopes for the upcoming new Palestinian state. He pointed out that unlike most developing countries (Uganda had only eight university graduates when it obtained its independence, for example), Palestine could boast eighty thousand university graduates. Since our future state was likely to be demilitarized, he said we would not have to worry about crippling defense expenses, that typically eat up a huge chunk from the budgets of most third-world countries.

A young man passed an invitation to me and about thirty others who had come from the Occupied Territories, saying that Dr. Sha'ath would like to meet us that evening to brief us in person on the progress of the negotiations.

I attended the meeting. After Nabeel gave us a briefing on the ongoing negotiations, he asked if any of us had any questions.

I could not keep my mouth shut. I had to ask him, in light of his comments that morning, to explain why the experts, scholars, and well-educated Palestinians he boasted about were kept out of the negotiations. Why was there not a staff of experts from all different fields guiding and advising the Palestinian negotiators?

He replied that it is true that the Palestinian leadership had trouble dealing with intellectuals and experts. But there was also another reason, he said: some of those people preferred to criticize from afar and sit on the fence. "If you want a state, you have to step up, be criticized, and risk getting your feet dirty," he said. "For example, I am in desperate need of an expert in international law. What are you doing tomorrow?"

"Me? I'm here attending a conference on management by your firm TEAM International."

"This is more important. Can you be at the Semiramis Hotel tomorrow at 9:00 AM?"

What could I say? I had trapped myself.

I asked Beth to take good notes at the conference while I went to Semiramis the next morning. At 9:15, Nabeel showed up with an entourage of television cameras and reporters. When he spotted me in the lobby, he signaled for me to join him at the elevators. As we rode up to the top floor, he calmly informed me that I was now the head of the PLO's Legal Committee, and I would be negotiating the Interim Agreement between Israel and the PLO!

The other members of the committee were a Gaza lawyer, who by his own admission could not speak English unless he got very angry and then he would be able to curse in English. Another lawyer was over eighty years old and remained quiet most of the time. The third, Taher Shalash, was not even a lawyer. He was an Egyptian diplomat whose sole qualification was that he had been involved in the Camp David negotiations with Israel, years before. That was our whole team!

Talk about flying by the seat of your pants! We had no documents, no instructions, no directives, no summaries of previous sessions—nothing. Nabil introduced me to the others and left. He was the overall head of the negotiating team, so he had other committees to attend to.

The Israeli team, by contrast, consisted of several native-English-speaking attorneys and law professors; they were backed by research teams and assistants from the Israeli Justice Ministry.

At first, I listened patiently, while trying to understand what was being discussed. I said nothing until the head of the Israeli team, Ahaz Ben Ari, a former legal advisor to the military government, and Governor of Gaza, began discussing legal cooperation between Israel and the Palestinian courts. He wanted Palestinian courts to enforce Israeli judgments and provide other forms of assistance. He did not mention any obligations by Israeli courts to Palestine. When I pointed this out, he said, "Oh, but your courts will have no authority over Israelis at all!"

"What?" I said. "What about settlers?"

"None whatsoever."

"Look, Mr. Ari. I am aware this is just an interim agreement, but I have struggled all my life for human rights. I cannot be party to an arrangement that formally provides a different set of laws: one for Jewish settlers and the other for Arab citizens. That sounds like apartheid to me."

"I understand your reluctance," he said, "but this is what our leaders and your leaders have already agreed to. We are just lowly lawyers filling in the blanks and working out the technical implementation of an interim arrangement."

He then pushed a copy of the Declaration of Principles (DOP) towards me—the document that had already been signed by Yasser Arafat and Yitzhak Rabin. It was a neatly published booklet with the seal of the Israeli Government on the cover.

Mr. Ari continued. "It clearly says that once it is established, the Palestinian Authority and its courts will have no jurisdiction over settlers or any other Israelis."

Like many in the Occupied Territories, we felt that the PLO leadership abroad was a bit too eager for the chance to return and exercise control in Palestine. We could hardly blame them but felt that they were a bit out of touch and had been tricked by Israel into accepting a deal at almost any price, while we on the inside were more willing to hold out for better terms.

Until then, I had not carefully read the document. I was aware that there were criticisms of the DOP, but I was sure that the momentum towards statehood was powerful. I truly believed that negotiations were essential, and I was willing to participate in the process of bringing about the new Palestinian state. I did not agree with the critics, some of whom I considered a bit extreme. After all, this was just an interim agreement. A full peace treaty would follow, in which final status issues such as settlements, Jerusalem, refugees, borders, and security arrangements would be properly negotiated. The full peace treaty was to be concluded no later than five years from the interim agreement. Maybe small steps were necessary, as we slowly begin to build trust and show that it was possible to live side by side. I assumed that logic and facts on the ground would overcome whatever deficiencies existed in the Interim Agreement.

The negotiations settled down to a process of trying to work within the parameters already set by the DOP. There were still a lot of details to be worked out. During these negotiations the pattern became clear: Israel was only willing to cede enough authority and power to enable the Palestinian Authority (PA) to control its people, while the PA remained under Israel's control and beholden to it.

While Palestinians looked at this as an interim arrangement during which we could build trust and work slowly towards full sovereignty and statehood, we never knew if Israelis truly shared this vision or if they were simply trying to get the PLO to act as their long-term servant and sub-agent charged with the responsibility of controlling the Palestinian people. Under the terms of the agreement, anything of real value or power or interest to the Israelis was kept totally under their control but matters of interest to Palestinians were neatly delegated to "joint committees" where both parties supposedly had veto power.

What this meant was that the Israelis could always veto anything relating to us, but all matters of interest to them were within their exclusive jurisdiction.

While we were supposedly negotiating as equals, the truth is that Israel held all the cards and could dictate whatever terms it chose. In negotiations, the power of each side is determined by their ability to walk away from an agreement. Israel was in no hurry to arrive at any agreement and could always walk away. The

PLO leadership, however, was desperate; they absolutely needed an agreement. When I would refuse to budge on some point in my committee, the Israelis would simply raise the issue to a higher level (Nabeel Sha'ath and his counterpart, Amnon Lipton Shahhaq). If Nabeel became obstinate, they would raise the issue to be decided by Arafat and Rabin. Arafat would always concede.

It was therefore imperative for us to try, as much as possible, to arrive at our own solutions rather than enter into an impasse which would be raised to a higher level where our leaders could not say no.

I sometimes tried to gain an advantage by my knowledge of Hebrew and Israeli laws and procedures. I insisted that logic and morality should dictate certain outcomes. One example of this was the issue of defining (for the purposes of the legal cooperation by Palestinian courts) who an Israeli is. The DOP already stated that the Palestinian courts would have no jurisdiction over Israelis or settlers. Ahaz Ben Ari suggested a draft definition of "Israeli" which included: a) All natural persons who held Israeli citizenship or residency, and b) Corporations and other entities which are registered and incorporated in Israel.

I jumped out of my seat, shouting in Hebrew, "What is this?! I have heard of a Chosen People (I used the Biblical phrase, *Am Sgula*), but never have I heard of Chosen Corporations! (*Hivra Sgula*)."

Ben Ari had the grace to blush, as he saw clearly the racism and unfairness implicit in his position.

I said, "I fully understand why you don't want our courts to have criminal jurisdiction over settlers and Israeli Jews. You fear that we would treat you the way you treat Arabs in your courts.

But we are talking here of *civil* jurisdiction. If an Israeli person or corporation carries out business in the future Palestinian state, why should they be exempt from the jurisdiction of its courts?"

He had no answer. In the end, he conceded that Palestinian courts should be granted jurisdiction in civil matters over both Israeli corporations and individuals who "do business" in the Palestinian territories. We then worked up a complex formula to determine what "doing business" meant. But at least I felt I was getting somewhere.

One day, during an intermission, I told Ben Ari, "You know that we are doing this all wrong. We should not be in a zero-sum situation, where you begrudgingly dole out small portions of authority and sovereignty to us, and where every gain we make is a loss for you and vice-versa.

"We should instead recognize that we are on the same side—the side of peace, coexistence, reconciliation, and a joint future. We should define what the desired outcome should be and then work backwards to figure out how to achieve it with a minimum of pain.

"After that, we can strategize on how to sell it to our respective peoples and how to jointly work against those who are trying to subvert the possibility of peace."

I truly felt that he and most of his team genuinely wanted to arrive at a peace agreement. They were Israeli patriots, of course, but they recognized that peace required concessions by both sides. They were willing to be flexible as long as it did not affect their security. But I also knew that there were others in the government, including the Likud Party (who later came into power after Rabin was assassinated), who abhorred the whole process.

As far as Likud were concerned, the peace process was merely a method that they could use to legitimize their permanent colonization of all the land. They wanted to undermine a two-state solution in any way possible. They did not believe that the Palestinians should be given a state, and they had a hard time even accepting Palestinians as a legitimate people. As much as possible, they wanted to keep all the land and to settle anywhere they wished. They were reluctant to give Palestinians any rights, much less sovereignty and independence.

Even at that time, I could see that the agreement we were negotiating could go in one of two ways: Despite the many drawbacks, it could develop into genuine sovereignty and statehood, along the lines of a two-state solution. On the other hand, it could also be seen as Palestinians agreeing to give legitimacy to the occupation, which would end up consolidating and solidifying it. It could end up just becoming a process to turn the PA into no more than a "subcontractor" of the Israeli government whose job was to keep its people under Israel's control and to serve the interests of the settlers. I desperately hoped that the liberal group would have ascendancy in Israel.

But even the liberal and progressive Israelis had their own limitations as well. At one session in the negotiations, the issue of "incitement" in Palestinian schools and curriculum came up. Israelis often claim that Palestinian schools indoctrinate children to hate Israelis and that their textbooks do not educate for peace, tolerance, and coexistence. This is not true. The Israeli military Officer in Charge of Education (who acts as the Minister of Education for the West Bank and Gaza), was the sole authority who determined the Palestinian curriculum for all schools—and not just public schools.

Ben Ari said, "We are embarking upon a journey of peace. It is important that your schools stop teaching hatred and violence and instead educate and prepare people for peace."

I said, "This is a wonderful idea. I wholeheartedly agree. I would love for us to jointly review the textbooks taught both to Palestinian and Israeli children and remove any materials that promote violence or hatred. Instead, both of our curricula should concentrate on issues of coexistence. I do not want our schools nor yours to teach our children war or violence. In the new era of peace, I would also like your high schools to stop the pre-army courses and indoctrination and instead teach peace."

"No, no," he said. "Forget it. You teach what you want, and we will do whatever we choose in our schools."

The idea of stopping the equivalent of ROTC programs in Israeli high schools was not what he had in mind. He also correctly guessed that teaching our children about the *Nakba* (Catastrophe) and the occupation would not make them happy with Israel and what it did to us. He did not want us to teach our own Palestinian history and nationalism, but he wanted Israeli schools to continue to teach Zionist doctrines in schools and prepare Israeli students for war as a proper national duty.

But I was just warming up.

"You know what? I am willing to give you a *carte blanche* on this as well as any other issue we are negotiating. You set the terms and write the wording that is acceptable to you, as well as the provisions for its enforcement, and I will approve it in advance—without discussion—as long as the provisions you propose apply equally to both sides on the basis of reciprocity. We have an Arabic proverb which says: 'Equality never leads to injustice.' Whatever you think is needed, desirable, or acceptable, when applied to you as well as to me is totally fine by me."

My offer was not accepted, and the issue of incitement and textbooks never came up again during the negotiations.

Another issue that came up on the margins of the negotiations was the issue of "house sealing."

One of the methods that Israel uses for punishing Palestinians accused of security offenses is ordering the demolition of their homes. The action is administrative and does not require any court decision or proof of guilt. Furthermore, it is intended to impact the whole family and community. As a young man, one of my first memories of Israeli occupation came with the destruction of a neighbor's house in Jerusalem.

For Arabs, a house is a basic element of stability for one's life and that of the entire family. Building a house is a lifetime project, and its destruction is far more than a setback. One of the vulgar curses in Arabic is *"Yikhrib baytak"* (May God destroy your home!").

As I mentioned earlier, a lesser form of punishment often used by Israel is sealing a home. This is done when the alleged offense is smaller or when houses are so close together that blowing up a house would cause great damage to surrounding units or other apartments in a large building. (If the offense is great, the Israelis do not care about this precaution. The Emergency Defense Regulations authorize a commander to destroy any structures in the vicinity of a "terror attack," regardless of the guilt of the inhabitants).

When the soldiers seal a house, they weld its door and all accessible windows shut. The house sits there as a reminder to one and all of the power of the occupier to punish. I often thought that Palestinians should not accept this.

In open defiance of the occupation, the Palestinian Center for the Study of Nonviolence had decided to start a campaign to open the sealed homes. We organized volunteers, who were always people other than the actual owners of the home, to use pickaxes and power tools to break off the seals which welded the doors shut.

After the house was opened, the owners could then proceed to reoccupy their home at their leisure. It was a bold initiative of civil disobedience, but in the atmosphere of the First Intifada it seemed like a perfect nonviolent action for people to participate in. This action did not hurt Israelis nor affect their security. The only thing it did was to blunt one of their methods for punishing Palestinians. Israelis could, of course, come back and reseal or even destroy the houses in question, but that was the nature of the struggle.

We had already begun doing this when the negotiations started between the Israelis and the PLO in Cairo. It seemed like a good opportunity to take up the matter with Gadi Zohar, the head of the Israeli Civil Administration, who was part of the Israeli negotiating team. I caught him between negotiating sessions.

"I have a suggestion to give you," I said.

"Not as a member of the negotiating team, but as Jonathan Kuttab, of the Palestinian Center for the Study of Nonviolence. You have tens of sealed homes throughout the West Bank, and you know for a fact that you will soon be withdrawing from these towns and cities. Why don't you create some goodwill by ordering the reopening of all sealed homes?"

He said, "That sounds reasonable. Put it up on the negotiating table."

"Oh no," I said. "This is not open for negotiations. I do not want to have to give up something in return for this 'gesture.'"

"Then let Jameel Tarrifi ask me. He is the head of the Civil Committee."

He knew that I did not like Mr. Tarrifi, who did not have the best reputation among Palestinian nationalists because he had made a lot of money as a contractor building Israeli settlements. When questioned why he used Tarrifi in his negotiations with Israel, Arafat once said, "He is like the dirty boots I need to use to get through this mud."

"I have nothing to do with Jameel Tarrifi," I replied.

"Whether you like him or not, these are the people Arafat chose to lead you."

"Never mind," I said. "I am just letting you know that we will be opening up sealed houses all over the West Bank. I wanted you to take credit for it, but if you do not wish to do so, we will do it anyway."

Upon returning to Jerusalem, I told the staff of the Center that we should proceed with a campaign to open any and all sealed houses in the West Bank. We had prepared a list of over ninety houses, though no one knew the actual number.

One of the first houses we opened was in Ramallah. It went fine and nothing happened. The Israelis ignored us and did not retaliate.

So we opened another house, and then another. Soon we started getting calls at our office from Nablus and Hebron. We always gave the same answer: "Yes, you can do it. You can use our name as the authority who allowed you to open houses."

There was an almost jovial atmosphere in the air. The arrangements we were negotiating seemed to be reasonable interim steps towards statehood. Little could I have suspected then that the arrangements we were working out then would continue to exist in a much worse form over twenty-five years later. Instead of being interim steps, they were the foundation for a permanent occupation.

The truth is that unbeknownst to us, we were setting the stage for the arrival of an outside leadership that would henceforth be operating as a quasi-government. Relationships with the Israeli occupation were about to become far more complex. The reality of life in the Occupied Territories was changing rapidly. On the one hand, the occupation still continued to weigh heavily on us. On the other, we now had a Palestinian Authority that was asserting its influence over our lives and pretending very hard to be the nucleus of a new Palestinian state being formed. We could not very well oppose its development and authority, yet still, it clearly was not a state, and its presence was not in any way liberating us from the burden of occupation. If anything, it seemed to stifle the spontaneous resistance of our people, as it demanded that we leave the job of liberation, and the confrontation of the occupation to it. For Raja and the rest of us at Al Haq, our new *quasi* "state" was a good opportunity to show that we were a genuine human rights organization that was willing to apply the same rules and principles to our own government as we did to Israel. The now-disgraced Israeli apologist, Alan Dershowitz, had written a book, *Chutzpah*, in which he had mocked Al Haq as a propaganda mouthpiece for the PLO that only cared to ruin Israel's reputation. According to him, we were not a true human rights organization. He boldly asserted that we would not make an issue of the human rights violations of the Arab World or a future Palestinian state.

We got our chance to prove him wrong very quickly. A rumor was circulating that a Palestinian man had died in Palestinian Authority detention under suspicious circumstances. He had been suspected of being an Israeli collaborator and so had been arrested by the Palestinian Preventive Security Forces, under the authority of General Jibreel Rajoob. We did not have credible information of whether he was in fact tortured, but we knew that we had to establish our position quickly. If torture is wrong, and it is, we could not be silent if it was committed by the Palestinians, even against a traitor or a collaborator.

I personally knew Jibreel Rajoob, who had himself been arrested for his political activity some years ago by the Israelis. I had visited him in prison, before he was deported and joined the leadership of the PLO in exile. He proudly told me of his own involvement in nonviolence by leading a hunger strike while in prison. I had also met him later during the negotiations, after he had been released and became quite prominent in the PLO. So I went to visit him with some people from Al Haq.

Rajoob met us with great respect and friendliness. He said that he did in fact arrest the person in question, but had turned him over to another security agency, Naval Intelligence, within days of his arrest. He had no idea what happened to him after that.

To his credit, he told me that he fully understood our position. He agreed with us that he and the Palestinian Authority must be held to the same standards as Israel. He firmly asserted that he would not approve of torture or allow any of his forces to engage in the same. He said that Al Haq would have access to all the prisons under his command, at any time we chose.

Furthermore, he agreed to our proposal that his officers undertake a course by Al Haq in human rights and the rule of law. This was quite an accomplishment. We now had access to the highest levels of security services in the Palestinian Authority, along with a chance to influence their thinking and behavior.

It was important, however, that we maintain our integrity and independence. We made it clear to him we would not spare him our criticism.

"Fair enough," he said. "All I ask is that you contact me first with any problems, and we shall see if we cannot work them out."

So, we undertook a series of training workshops and lectures.

At one lecture on the rule of law, I asked the officers, "Where does your primary loyalty as law enforcement officials lie? Is it with the Palestinian Authority? Or with their party, Fatah?"

I explained to them, "Your duty is to the law itself—not to Fatah, nor Rajoob, nor Yaser Arafat, nor even to the cultural norms of Palestinian society. You are responsible for the law itself."

To illustrate this point, I gave an extreme example.

Even though Arab society, which sometimes tends to be homophobic, may mock or frown on any male who is wearing earrings, there is no law prohibiting it. And while I myself would not be caught dead wearing earrings, I cannot stop any man from doing so if he chooses.

"It is your role as police officers to uphold the law, regardless of your feelings. It is your duty to defend any male wearing earrings from being harassed or assaulted by others. The law prohibits assault and harassment, after all, but does *not* prohibit males from wearing earrings."

Our chief researcher, Rizeq Shuqair, gave a lecture to a group of about two hundred officers. Rizeq explained that torture was illegal, and a violation of both international law and Palestinian law. "If any of you were to receive a direct order to torture a prisoner or suspect, you have the moral and legal duty to refuse such an order. If you do not, you could be held accountable. Once the facts were known, even your own superiors would disown you and your actions. "Isn't that so, Mr. Rajoob?" said Rizek, turning to Rajoob, who was sitting with us on the dais and he nodded his head.

"This is very true!" Rizeq continued, "Do not expect your superiors to defend you or to agree to pay the price, if you are involved in torturing a prisoner. You will likely be left holding the bag. As you know from history, and with the example of the Nazis in the Nuremberg tribunals, it is not a defense to say that you were only obeying orders."

As far as the stalled "peace process" went, it seemed that for the incoming Palestinian leadership, the abandonment of the armed struggle meant the abandonment of all struggle. They still maintained nationalist rhetoric and talked as if Palestine were a state in the making. But aside from that, they were utterly dependent on the Israelis. They seemed to be so desperate to keep their positions that they were slowly losing their nationalist ardor. Even worse, the local people who always were in tension with the Israeli occupation were now sidelined.

Our leadership was operating in the land now, and desperately pretending to be a real state, even while the occupation was still in full force. Settlements were expanding, and more land was being confiscated, and the dream of a Palestinian state seemed further and further away. Israelis had no problem violating the Oslo agreement or limiting the powers of the PA or even publicly humiliating them, while demanding they carry out all their duties and "do more to fight terrorism" and control their own people.

Our methods of nonviolent resistance were now almost frowned upon, as the PA kept the hope that an independent state of Palestine was just around the corner. After all, the agreements we had signed were interim agreements, which we had expected to lead to a full state within five years at the most.

After the first five years passed, Israel started to firm up its control over the West Bank and Gaza, and the hopes and euphoria of the peace process began to fade. Meanwhile, the settlements only continued to grow and expand. With neither an armed struggle nor a popular nonviolent uprising, the Palestinian cause was losing steam. Life in general was becoming more miserable. I was still called upon from time to time to participate in additional negotiations over the mechanics of transfer of certain authorities, but the feeling was no longer the same. Among Palestinians, the disappointment was bitter, and the PA began to lose its glamour.

I was very deliberate about not seeking or accepting any role in the PA, which many West Bank activist did.

Pretty soon, Nabeel Sha'ath himself was also sidelined, and a Second Intifada, violent and bloody, exploded upon the scene with suicide bombings and violent repression. The dream of peace had evaporated, but the reality of the occupation continued. It was clear by now that the PA was playing a negative role within it.

I began to feel that one needed to fight both the occupation and the Palestinian Authority itself in order to achieve true freedom and independence. It would take a different set of muscles to fight the PA, though, and frankly I did not feel that I had what it would take.

Slowly, I began to withdraw from the political realm of public life. Yet I could not do so entirely. I remained passionately committed to peace and to justice. I felt that somehow, we needed to break through to the other side and to come up with a vision and a plan to achieve peace. As crazy as it might sound, we needed to find a way to live together in this place called the Holy Land, and to bring an end to the suffering of my people. I did sometimes have experiences that gave me hope.

CHAPTER 20

I RECEIVED A PHONE CALL from a worker who told me that he had a labor law problem with a settler from the settlement of Efrat, five miles south of Bethlehem. He wanted me to come to Efrat and meet with the boss there.

I knew that many Palestinians work in the Israeli settlements either as builders or laborers, even though Arabs are not even allowed to enter a settlement without a permit, and for sure they cannot live there as the settlements were for Jews only. I agreed to come and meet with his boss. Frankly, I went there to do battle, and was prepared for a harsh confrontation with the settler. I must admit that I was prepared to be neither compromising nor moderate. There's a saying in Arabic: " Do you want grapes, or just a fight with the vineyard keeper?" In this case I came for the fight; I did not particularly care to collect grapes on behalf of my client.

When I parked my car and entered the bakery, my nostrils were assaulted by the most delicious smells of baked goods. The bakery had a really nice pleasant ambience, which in another time and place I would have loved to visit and patronize. Tastefully placed tables, all painted in vibrant colors, were available where a couple or some friends could sit, enjoy pastries, and drink coffee.

Yet this was in an illegal settlement, placed on stolen Arab lands, an obstacle to peace and a two-state solution. I was totally opposed to settlements and settlers, and I hated myself for liking this place. I also hated myself for the impulse to hate it and reject it, when on a human and non-political level it was such a wonderful place, that should have brought joy to me.

The feeling was further compounded when I met the owner. He was not a fanatical, gun-wielding zealot, like my stereotyped image of Jewish settlers in the West Bank. He was a very likable fellow who treated me with dignity, humanity, and respect. If he were in Israel, I guessed, he would be a member of Peace Now, and be the kind of moderate, humane Israeli I would like to call a friend. He said that he had just bought the bakery, with money he inherited from his father in New York, and wanted to run it in a proper and humane way. He would start with new workers; he might hire some or all the workers who had already been working there, but he wanted to settle, justly and fairly, the labor rights of the four Palestinian workers who were then working there.

"I know these workers are entitled to one month's severance pay for each year of service based on their last salary," he told me. "I know Jordanian law applies in the West Bank, but from what I hear, that law is not as favorable to workers as Israeli law. I want to treat these workers fairly, and if Israeli law provides them with better protection and labor rights, I want you to calculate their rights on the basis of Israeli law. Or Jordanian law, if that is more favorable to them. Tell me what I owe them to settle their entitlements, and after that, if they wish to continue working, I can start them with a new contract, with proper fringe benefits. Of course, I will also pay your fees, but you are their lawyer, so you should look out for their interests, not mine."

His more-than-fair offer and benevolent attitude blindsided me. I had come ready to do legal battle with this Israeli settler on behalf of my fellow Palestinians, and here he was asking me to tell him what their fair rights were! Plus, he would pay my legal fees! I was astonished.

I had to remind myself that settlers were probably a cross-section of Israeli society itself, and that while some of them were clearly fanatical racists, others were decent, humane and open to coexistence. If I had decided, despite the historic injustice inflicted upon us, that we Palestinians needed to accept and live with Israeli Jews, in Israel itself, why did I persist in demonizing Jewish settlers? Zionism had done a great injustice to all of us, yet among its members were the Eddy Kaufmans and David Kretchmers and many others whom I called friends. Could I also one day have some settlers as friends? Was that truly possible? If peace and reconciliation were possible between Israel and Palestinians, could that peace also somehow include the Jewish settlers?

I know that the majority of the settlers continue to hate and oppress Palestinians, and I know that they are living illegally on our stolen property, and that they benefit from privileges and a separate system of laws that was even worse than apartheid. Is there truly a possible future of peace and justice and reconciliation for us that would include settlers as well?!

There was no doubt in my mind that a Christian should oppose structural evil, racism, and discrimination, but had I become so committed to the two-state solution that I needed to demonize even decent settlers like this one and insist that he leave the West Bank altogether and go to Israel? Was the property he would live in Israel not also property and land and houses stolen from my people in 1948? The two-state solution required that all or most settlers leave the West Bank to make way for a Palestinian state there, yet as their numbers increased, that was becoming harder and harder to envisage, much less implement.

That trip to Efrat left me more confused than ever. The issue of the four laborers was easily resolved, and they were paid according to Israeli labor laws and were pleased, but the issue of what to do about Israeli settlements remained a difficult one for me to think through.

As the situation in the West Bank continued to deteriorate and the number of settlers increased to over 700,000, it was becoming increasingly clear that the two-state solution—a Palestinian State in the West Bank/Gaza side by side with Israel—was becoming impossible. The egg was scrambled too much to unscramble it anymore. Even at the theoretical level, it was becoming impossible to contemplate a situation where Israel would return to its 1967 borders and allow a Palestinian state in the territories it occupied "temporarily" in 1967.

What was needed now was dramatic new thinking, and a reevaluation of the entire situation. Somehow, I had to acknowledge that the narratives of the two groups, Israeli Jewish Zionists and Palestinian Arab nationalists, could not be reconciled. The Israelis believed that God, history, the United Nations, the British, or necessity gave them this land, and they were entitled to take it and make it a Jewish state, while we believed it was an Arab land being overrun and colonized by outside foreigners. Somehow, we were locked into a zero-sum situation, where every advantage by one side was a loss to the other. Dividing the land along the 1967 border, which made a lot of sense at the time, seemed no longer feasible.

I had to ask myself: What is it that each ideology was promising its people? Can we think of a solution that provides each side with their minimum requirements, thereby satisfying them as much or even better than these two competing ideologies could? What did each side really need? I was not sure that Palestinians wanted a state as much as they wanted freedom and self-determination, equality and dignity, which they hoped a Palestinian state could give them. And what did the Zionists really want?

I once asked a rabbi who is a Zionist: "Why do you want a Jewish state? What is a Jewish state for you? While there are different types of Zionism, they all require a Jewish state. What makes a state Jewish, anyway, and why do you need one?"

He thought for a moment and then said: "After what happened to us, in the Holocaust, I want a state, where any Jew, any time, no questions asked, can go and live and be able to defend himself."

I said, "Maybe I can offer you something better. How about a state where any Jew, any time, no questions asked, can go and live where he does not *need* to defend himself, because no one is out to get him?"

"Is that possible?" he asked, surprised.

"Yes," I told him. "Palestinians do not hate you because you are Jewish but because you are trying to take their land and make it exclusively Jewish. For the vision I suggested to happen, for you to be truly accepted and not merely reluctantly tolerated because of your superior power, you will have to give up exclusivity. I too, as a Palestinian, will have to give up exclusivity and find a way to share, not dominate or exclusively possess this land. As long as I say *Falastin Arabiyyeh!* ("Palestine is Arab!"), I have no room or legitimacy for you, your people, or their connection to the land. You will be outsiders and intruders like all colonial settlers, who need to leave. I must alter and tweak my Palestinian nationalism to make room within it for Jewish people and their aspirations. But you, by wanting the state to be an exclusively Jewish state, will always view me and my people as dangerous outsiders, and will work tirelessly to remove, dominate, or eliminate us. If you cannot deport or kill us, you will disenfranchise us, and dominate us, and keep us under oppression, regardless of how "benevolent" you may feel. We will be forever opposing each other, where we fight over every inch of land and every additional soul born or brought into the country. This is inevitable. However, maybe we can think outside the box and come up with a different outcome. Can we have a state which is both Jewish and Arab, but not exclusively belonging to either party?"

I had personally been thinking along those lines for a long time. When I was invited by a Jewish American civil rights lawyer to speak at his synagogue in New York, I used the opportunity to flesh out my new ideas. I told my audience:

"Two groups live in this land between the Jordan River and the Mediterranean Sea. We have been fighting for over a century. Each side claims the land as its own and views the other side as an existential threat. After all the fighting and bloodletting, neither side has been able to get rid of the other. Your side might be immeasurably more powerful and win every fight, yet you have failed. Your state today is nothing but an apartheid regime of one group ruling over another by sheer military might. We have not disappeared, nor ceased to believe in our cause. Today the numbers of people living in the land are almost equal (7 million each), but power lies totally with one side. The Palestinians are either occupied (in the West Bank), besieged into a small enclave (Gaza), banished and exiled (refugees), or made into second-class, mistrusted, marginalized citizens (inside Israel proper).

"Each side has its own narrative, its own grievances, its own dreams, and desires, yet they are both going nowhere. Each side also has strong outside supporters who will keep the pot boiling and the enmity going for many generations to come. Can we learn to live together? Can we create a structure that satisfies and addresses the deepest fears and desires of both sides, and which will remain in place regardless of demographic shifts?

Being a lawyer, I thought of the problem in legal terms. Can I address the fears and desires of both sides and create a constitutional scheme that enshrines the rights and protections of both parties, and make them impervious to political or even demographic shifts? It seemed like a tall order, but I set to write it up, at least as a theoretical exercise. The result was a book I called Beyond the Two-State Solution. Since both groups wanted democracy and human rights and dignity, it was necessary to articulate a vision that provided all that, yet which would be sustainable. I tried to address Jewish security fears as well as the demographic demon: the fear that the more populous group in a democracy would oppress and delegitimize the minority group. I also tried, without pretending there is symmetry between the two sides and without seeking to place blame on either side, to look to the future. I sought to map out a just solution that would allow both sides to live in a hybrid democratic state that is both Jewish and Arab.

I firmly believe that nothing can be accomplished by violence and hatred; we must find a way to live together that provides both justice and security on a bedrock of equality and democracy.

Of course, I knew that there is a huge gap between laying out a reasonable vision and arriving there. We would need to address the power imbalance, since the privileged do not easily give up their power and privilege. We also have to contend with what I called the "holocaust syndrome": namely, that a population which has suffered so much trauma will not easily give up reliance on power nor trust its security to anyone else.

I remember when Yasser Arafat was inching towards peace with Israel. He once publicly stated that we need to talk to Israelis and the time has come to maybe even recognize them. Israeli Prime Minister Shamir reacted to this by saying "This is a declaration of war!! It shows that Arabs are getting smart, and we must therefore be doubly vigilant". Arafat's gestures towards peace were viewed as evidence of devious intent to work for the elimination of the Jewish people in Palestine. How can one work for peace if even movement towards peace is viewed with such deep suspicion. A people so traumatized by the holocaust will never feel confident enough to make peace no matter how much overwhelming power they accumulate until they are cured of that trauma. But the effort needs to be made, and at least I could show that such a future is possible, and that it can indeed be an improvement over anything else. Somehow, Palestinian liberation is tied up with Jewish liberation from that trauma. It seems unfair but somehow, we are required not only to pay the price of Western anti semitism, and of the holocaust, but must wait for the healing of Jews to gain our own liberation.

Even though the effort I described is a secular one, which is intensely political, and which espouses a solution that is meaningful to people of all religions and of no religion as well, I am fully aware that my own involvement in it, just as my own involvement in human rights advocacy, was deeply rooted in my Christian faith and in my belief in pacifism and nonviolence. Christ said blessed are the peacemakers, and he set up an example for us in his life and ministry and in his attitude towards the political structures of his time. I was trying in my humble way to follow his teachings.

Recently, I accepted a position as Executive Director of Friends of Sabeel, North America (FOSNA). This was the organization that was created to support the Sabeel movement for Palestinian liberation theology in Jerusalem. This position allowed me to work on the issue of peace and justice in the United States from a Christian perspective. In a way, it was a most appropriate assignment. The United States has been the most influential supporter of the State of Israel, and much of that support was based on the influence of

Christian Zionists in the United States. Those individuals and their organization successfully weaponized their millions of followers and translated their influence into massive support for Israel, often against the interest of the United States itself.

Not only has this influence been used to guarantee billions in aid, and military assistance, but more importantly, as far as I was concerned, it led to using the weight and influence of the United States to shield Israel from international accountability. Through the use of the veto at the United Nations, Israel is spared the prospect of any international repercussions for its policies, including policies that ran against the values and principles or even interests of the United States itself. Furthermore, the United States used its influence to bribe and cajole some of the tyrants and leaders of the Arab world to normalize their relationships with Israel without requiring a peaceful resolution of the Palestinian question first. Under the Trump administration, both Vice president Michael Pence, and Secretary of State George Pompeo, avowed evangelicals and Christian Zionists, specifically directed US foreign policy away from Palestinians and their rights, and towards unquestioning support of the most right-wing Israeli positions. The US Embassy was moved from Tel Aviv to Jerusalem signaling a new US position that supported exclusive control by Israel of all of Jerusalem. Morocco was bribed by accepting its illegal occupation of Western Sahara in return for normalizing relations with Israel under the "Abrahamic Accords". It seemed my initial concerns about the nefarious impact of Christian Zionism among evangelicals and its influence against the interest of Justice for my people were being confirmed in a massive way. Yet I was convinced that the support many evangelicals had for Christian Zionism was the result of ignorance and failure to know, much less understand and appreciate the perspective of Palestinian Christians.

Two years ago, I was on a speaking tour with my cousin Alex Awad, the minister of the Baptist church in East Jerusalem. It was part of an effort by Mennonites to educate their constituents on issues relating to Israel/Palestine in preparation for a vote at their upcoming Convention on the issue of BDS (Boycotts, Divestment and Sanctions). The Mennonite church arranged for me and Alex to visit churches, always together with a Jewish speaker from Jewish Voice for Peace. The trip was quite successful and very educational, as we visited not only Mennonite churches, but other churches and groups who were interested in this topic. I said I was not interested to preach to the choir but was particularly interested in speaking to evangelicals, including Christian Zionists as I felt this group was most in need of hearing what I had to say.

At one location, a minister asked if we would speak to the Board of CUFI (Christians United for Israel) in his state. They were willing to meet us for coffee at a local restaurant, where they had reserved a closed room for discussion.

We arrived there to see eight people, four of them wearing MAGA hats, one with a little Israeli flag stuck in it. This certainly was not the "choir". But that is what I had asked for. They did seem to be polite and attentive. We were introduced by the friend who had arranged the meeting, and we started the discussion with a word of prayer. Alex spoke briefly about the Bethlehem Bible College, and the situation of Palestinian Christians in Bethlehem, and then the questions came fast and heavy:

THE TRUTH SHALL SET YOU FREE

"Look. Our position is based on the Bible. In Genesis God said to Abraham: "I will bless those who bless thee and curse those who curse thee. Through your seed shall all the nations of the world be blessed". So, if we want God's blessing, we must support Israel."

Alex calmly answered, "It is true, but who is the Seed of Abraham"? According to Paul, "seed of Abraham is used in the singular, which is Christ" Galatians 3:28. It is through Christ, not the state of Israel, nor Benjamin Netanyahu that the nations of the world are blessed.

"But God gave this land to the Jews".

"It is true the Bible says that God promised the Land to Abraham and his seed, forever, but throughout the Old Testament, God treated this as a conditional promise. Conditioned on the obedience of the Jewish people, and when they were disobedient, whether by worshiping other Gods or failing to do justice, he banished them from the land."

"But Jesus himself was a Jew."

"That is correct. He and his early disciples were all Jews, but his message was for all people who believed in him, not just for Jews. "For God so loved the world that he gave his only begotten son so that whoever shall believe in him shall not perish but have everlasting life (John 3:16). In Hebrews, Paul addresses gentiles saying, "You were not a people before, but now are God's people, and inheritors of the promises". This applies to all of us, Jews and gentiles who have accepted Christ.

And so it went for over an hour. Every question or objection addressed with bible verses and scripture, as Alex and I thumbed through our bibles and read directly each verse of scripture we quoted.

At the end, one person said: "I have changed my mind 180 degrees."

Another said "There is not a single thing you said that I disagree with. We just never heard it before."

A couple said: "We are going to see John Hagee, the head of CUFI, in Texas after 2 weeks. Would you be willing to talk to him?"

"well, I said. John Hagee is the President of a huge organization. He may not be willing to talk to us, but if he would allow us to speak to him or any of his staff, we would be glad to do so. We would even fly down at our own expense to meet with them.

(Unfortunately, This was in February of 2020, and the pandemic soon set in and the visit never took place.)

With my new position in FOSNA, I am able to take this message not only to evangelicals, but to all Christians who had a vague affinity with Israel and who speak automatically about Judeo-Christian traditions and values, but who know little about Arabs, Moslems, and the Palestinian point of view. I also have an opportunity to further work out and articulate my own beliefs along the lines of Palestinian Liberation Theology. I could develop those ideas not only for Christians but for all who care about justice and peace.

As I write these lines, new changes appear on the horizon. A number of international bodies have published detailed reports describing the situation in Israel/Palestine as apartheid providing a system of domination by one group (Jews) over others (Palestinian Arabs) in all of the Land. Amnesty International issued a 200+ page report detailing Israeli laws and practices and showing that it amounted to apartheid under the legal definition of the term. It was a bombshell. This was swiftly followed by a report of the Israeli human Rights Organization, B'Tselem, that also stated that Israel had crossed the line and its practices both in the Occupied Territories and Israel itself constituted a deliberate policy of Jewish privilege and supremacy that amounted to Apartheid. Human Rights Watch followed with a report of its own that it had been preparing for years again meticulously analyzing and documenting Israeli practices and declaring that they amount to the crime of Apartheid under international law. The United Nations, Harvard Law Review and other international organizations followed suit with the same conclusion and with voluminous detailed documentation. All of them supported the contention Al haq had been making for years that Israeli practices amounted to Apartheid under international law. Israelis and their apologists labelled all such reports as antisemitic, but not once did they challenge the actual facts and substance of these reports.

The truth embodied in these reports was reinforced by the recent Israeli elections that brought into power not only Benjamin Netanyahu but some of the most extreme right wing elements. The policy guidelines announced by the new government boldly stated that only Jews have an exclusive and unquestionable right to settle in all of the Land of Israel including the Negev, the Galilee and Judea and Samaria. They explicitly erased the "Green Line", outlawed the Palestinian Flag, and made clear they were opposed to the two-state solution.

In a paradoxical way, that might be good news. The Truth is finally out, and the path to Freedom may well be paved now. Freedom for both Palestinian Arabs, and Israeli Jews requires them to live together in a unified state serving both populations on the basis of equality, dignity and human rights. The utopian ideas I explored in *Beyond the Two State Solution* may now be seriously considered and form a vision we can all strive towards fulfilling.

As a Christian Palestinian, I can only say that the path is now clear. I can pursue it in good conscience, for the benefit of all God's children in the Holy Land.

ACKNOWLEDGEMENTS

I WANT TO THANK all the friends and family who encouraged me to tell my story, and those who have read the manuscript and offered valuable advice and comments. I especially want to thank Mercy Aiken, who provided valuable advice, assistance and edits to the manuscript since its early stages.

I want to especially thank my editor, David Hazard, who helped me turn a jumble of stories and vignettes into a more or less coherent story, that you dear reader may find interesting and enjoyable, as well as informative.

JONATHAN KUTTAB is a Christian Palestinian attorney and human rights activist. He Cofounded Al Haq, the award winning Palestinian Human Rights organization, and Nonviolence International. He was the recipient of the Carter-DeMenill Award for Commitment to Truth and Freedom. Past Chairman of Bethlehem Bible College, and Chairman of the Holy Land Trust. He is a member of the Bar Associations in Palestine, Israel and New York. He recently wrote *Beyond the Two State Solution*, a vision for the future of Palestine/Israel that accommodates Israeli Jews and Palestinian Arabs in an inclusive democratic state. He is a Nonresident Fellow at the Arab Center of Washington DC, and frequently writes and speaks about legal issues in Israel/ Palestine. He practices law in Jerusalem and the United States. He is currently the Executive Director of Friends of Sabeel, North America (FOSNA.org).

FREE DOWNLOAD OFFER

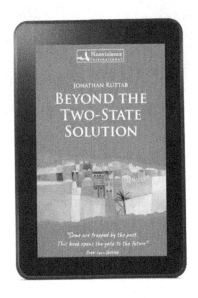

WE ARE PLEASED TO OFFER you a free download of the electronic version of the author's previous work, *Beyond the Two States Solution*, mentioned in this book.

You can download it in English, Arabic, or Hebrew from the website of Nonviolence International by using the following link in your browser:

www.nonviolenceinternational.net/beyond2states

Made in the USA
Middletown, DE
12 September 2023

38219318R00183